W9-CFQ-124

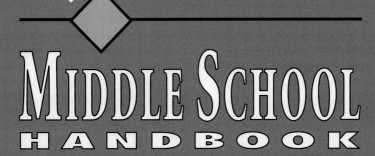

HOLT
MIDDLE SCHOOL
HANDBOOK

John E. Warriner

HOLT, RINEHART AND WINSTON
Harcourt Brace & Company

Austin • New York • Orlando • Chicago • Atlanta
San Francisco • Boston • Dallas • Toronto • London

Author

John E. Warriner developed the organizational structure upon which *Holt Middle School Handbook* is based. He was the author of *English Composition and Grammar* and coauthor of *Elements of Writing*. He coauthored the *English Workshop* series, was general editor of the *Composition: Models and Exercises* series, and was editor of *Short Stories: Characters in Conflict*. He taught English for thirty-two years in junior and senior high school and college.

Critical Readers

Grateful acknowledgment is made to the following critical readers, who reviewed pre-publication materials for this book:

Charlotte H. Geyer
Former Language Arts Director
Seminole County, Florida

Faye Nelson
Northeast High School
Greensboro, North Carolina

Richard Kidwell
Crenshaw Middle School
Canton, Ohio

Mark Sweeney
Marblehead High School
Marblehead, Massachusetts

Nancy Light
Clarence High School
Clarence, New York

Acknowledgments: See pages 470–471, which are an extension of the copyright page.

Printed in the United States of America

ISBN 0-03-094637-9

3 4 5 6 7 8 9   039   98 97 96

Contents in Brief

Table of Contents

▶ CHAPTER 2   **AGREEMENT**   75

Subject and Verb, Pronoun and Antecedent

▶ CHAPTER 3   **USING VERBS**   96

Principal Parts, Regular and Irregular Verbs, Verb Tense

▶ CHAPTER **4** **USING PRONOUNS**   115

Nominative and Objective Case Forms

▶ CHAPTER **5** **USING MODIFIERS**   129

Comparison and Placement

■■■ *Part Three*

PHRASES, CLAUSES, SENTENCES

▶ CHAPTER 6 **PHRASES**

Prepositional, Verbal, and Appositive Phrases

► CHAPTER 9 COMPLEMENTS 190

Direct and Indirect Objects, Subject Complements

► CHAPTER 10 KINDS OF SENTENCES 201

Sentence Structure and Purpose

▶ CHAPTER **11** WRITING EFFECTIVE SENTENCES   216

Revising for Completeness and Style

► CHAPTER 16 **SPELLING AND VOCABULARY**   306

Improving Your Spelling and Vocabulary; Choosing the Right Word

■■■■■ *Part Five*

COMPOSITION   328

► CHAPTER 17 **THE WRITING PROCESS**   330

▶ CHAPTER 18 PARAGRAPH AND COMPOSITION STRUCTURE 351

▶ CHAPTER 19 THE RESEARCH PAPER 376

PART ONE

WRITER'S QUICK REFERENCE

The **Writer's Quick Reference** is an alphabetical list of special terms and expressions with definitions, explanations, and examples. When you run into a grammar or usage problem in the process of writing, turn to this handy section for a brief explanation. Each entry in this section will tell you where to turn for more information. If you don't find what you are looking for in the **Writer's Quick Reference,** turn to the index on page 449.

As you'll notice, some examples in this section have the following labels:

Standard or *Formal.* These labels identify language that is appropriate in serious writing or speaking, such as compositions or speeches.

Informal. Words and expressions with this label are standard English usages that are acceptable in conversation and in everyday writing such as personal letters. Language labeled *informal* is not generally appropriate in serious writing or speaking, however.

Nonstandard. These usages do not follow the guidelines of standard English.

A

---

a, an Use *a* before words or expressions beginning with consonant sounds. Use *an* before words or expressions beginning with vowel sounds. See page 54.

EXAMPLES
- He did not consider himself **a** hero.
- Market Avenue is **a** one-way street.
- I made **a** B on my report.
- **An** oryx is **a** large antelope.
- We waited in line for **an** hour.
- Jorge's aunt is **an** FBI agent.
- The store gave **an** $800 sofa to the shelter.

abstract noun An abstract noun names an idea, a feeling, a quality, or a characteristic. See pages 48–49.

EXAMPLE
- Confucius asked his students to develop **unselfishness, courage,** and **honor** inside themselves.

accept, except *Accept* is a verb that means "to receive." *Except* may be either a verb or a preposition. As a verb, *except* means "to leave out" or "to exclude"; as a preposition, *except* means "other than" or "excluding."

EXAMPLES
- I **accept** your apology.
- Some students will be **excepted** from this assignment.
- Mark has told all his friends **except** Diego.

action verb An action verb is a verb that expresses physical or mental action. See pages 57–59.

EXAMPLE ▪ Briana **stepped** back from the blank canvas and **imagined** what she **might paint.**

adjective An adjective is a word used to modify a noun or a pronoun. See pages 53–56.

EXAMPLE ▪ **These** puppies are **cute,** but my favorite is **the small black** one there. [*These* and *cute* modify the noun *puppies. The, small,* and *black* modify the pronoun *one.*]

adjective clause An adjective clause is a subordinate clause that modifies a noun or a pronoun. See pages 166–169.

EXAMPLE ▪ The limerick **that Josh wrote** won first prize in the comic verse competition. [The adjective clause modifies the noun *limerick.*]

adjective phrase An adjective phrase is a prepositional phrase that modifies a noun or a pronoun. See pages 149–150.

EXAMPLE ▪ All **of the class** are trying out for parts **in the Spring Music Fling.** [*Of the class* modifies the pronoun *all. In the Spring Music Fling* modifies the noun *parts.*]

adverb An adverb is a word used to modify a verb, an adjective, or another adverb. See pages 62–64.

EXAMPLE ▪ There **really** is **too** much pepper in this soup! [*Really* modifies the verb *is. Too* modifies the adjective *much.*]

adverb clause An adverb clause is a subordinate clause that modifies a verb, an adjective, or an adverb. See pages 169–172.

EXAMPLE ▪ I never knew what the term *musical poetry* meant **until I read "The Raven."** [The adverb clause modifies the verb *knew.*]

adverb phrase   An adverb phrase is a prepositional phrase that modifies a verb, an adjective, or an adverb. See pages 150–151.

EXAMPLE   ▪ Would you please help me **with this box;** it's full **of heavy books.** [*With this box* modifies the verb *help. Of heavy books* modifies the adjective *full.*]

advice, advise   The noun *advice* means "a recommendation about a course of action." The verb *advise* means "to recommend a course of action" or "to give advice."

EXAMPLES   ▪ Good **advice** may be easy to give but hard to follow.
▪ I **advise** you to go on with your music lessons if you can.

affect, effect   *Affect* is a verb meaning "to influence." As a noun, *effect* means "the result of some action."

EXAMPLES   ▪ His score on this test is sure to **affect** his final grade.
▪ The **effects** of the powerful new medicine were immediate.

agreement   Agreement refers to the correspondence, or match, between grammatical forms. For example, the number and person of a subject and verb should always agree, or match. The number and gender of a pronoun and its antecedent should match also. See **Chapter 2: Agreement.**

EXAMPLES   ▪ **Many** of Anne McCaffrey's short stories **take** place on a make-believe planet called Pern. [The plural verb *take* agrees with the plural subject *many.*]
▪ Each **person** in the class read aloud the haiku that **he** or **she** had written. [The singular pronouns *he* and *she* agree with the singular antecedent *person.*]

"Beats me why I ain't gettin' no better marks
in English."

ain't Avoid this word in speaking and writing; it is non-standard English.

all ready, already *All ready* means "completely prepared." *Already* means "before a certain point in time."

EXAMPLES ▪ The mechanic checked the engine parts to make sure they were **all ready** for assembly.
▪ We have **already** served the refreshments.

all right Used as an adjective, *all right* means "unhurt" or "satisfactory." Used as an adverb, *all right* means "well enough." *All right* should always be written as two words. The spelling *alright* is nonstandard.

EXAMPLES ▪ Linda fell off the horse, but she is **all right** [*not* alright]. [adjective]
▪ Your work is **all right** [*not* alright]. [adjective]
▪ You did **all right** [*not* alright] at the track meet. [adverb]

all together, altogether The expression *all together* means "everyone or everything in the same place." The adverb *altogether* means "entirely."

EXAMPLES ▪ The director called us **all together** for rehearsal.
          ▪ He is **altogether** pleased with his victory.

a lot *A lot* should always be written as two words.

EXAMPLE   ▪ Her family donated **a lot** of money to the Red Cross.

STYLE NOTE   Many writers overuse *a lot*. Whenever you run across *a lot* as you revise your own writing, try to replace it with a more exact word or phrase.

EXAMPLES ▪ The Spaniards explored a lot of North and South America.
          ▪ The Spaniards explored **vast areas** [*or* millions of square miles] of North and South America.

altar, alter The noun *altar* means "a table for a religious ceremony." The verb *alter* means "to change."

EXAMPLES ▪ The **altar** was covered with lilies.
          ▪ The election results may **alter** the mayor's plan.

among See **between, among.**

antecedent An antecedent is a noun to which a pronoun refers. See pages 49–50.

EXAMPLE   ▪ **Alonzo** and **Denise** spend **their** Saturdays working at the local animal shelter. [The pronoun *their* refers to the nouns *Alonzo* and *Denise*.]

anywheres, everywheres, nowheres, somewheres Use these words without the final *s*.

EXAMPLE   ▪ I didn't go **anywhere** [*not* anywheres] yesterday.

appositive An appositive is a noun or a pronoun placed beside another noun or pronoun to identify or explain it. See page 158.

EXAMPLE   ▪ The Colombian writer **Gabriel García Márquez** won the Nobel Prize in literature in 1982. [The compound noun *Gabriel García Márquez* identifies the noun *writer.*]

appositive phrase An appositive phrase is made up of the appositive and its modifiers. See page 158.

EXAMPLE ▪ The Ziadehs, **our new neighbors,** moved here from Jordan. [*Our* and *new* modify the appositive *neighbors.*]

article *A, an,* and *the* are the most frequently used adjectives and are called articles. *A* and *an* are **indefinite articles.** They indicate that the noun refers to one of a general group. See **a, an** on page 2. *The* is a **definite article.** It indicates that a noun refers to someone or something in particular. See page 54.

as See **like, as.**

as if See **like, as if, as though.**

at Do not use *at* after *where.*

NONSTANDARD Where is it at?
   STANDARD Where is it?

WRITER'S QUICK REFERENCE

B

---

bad, badly *Bad* is an adjective. *Badly* is an adverb.

EXAMPLES ▪ The fish tastes **bad.** [*Bad* modifies the noun *fish.*]

    ▪ The boy's wrist was sprained **badly.** [*Badly* modifies the verb *was sprained.*]

NOTE In informal usage the expression "feel badly" has become acceptable, though ungrammatical, English.

INFORMAL Marcia felt badly about the lost cat.
  FORMAL Marcia felt bad about the lost cat.

because See **reason . . . because.**

between, among Use *between* when referring to two things at a time, even though they may be part of a group containing more than two.

EXAMPLES ▪ In homeroom, Carlos sits **between** Bob and me.
▪ Some players practice **between** innings.
[Although a game has more than two innings, the practice occurs only *between* any two of them.]

Use *among* when referring to a group rather than to separate items or individuals.

EXAMPLES ▪ We saved ten dollars **among** the three of us. [As a group, the three saved ten dollars.]
▪ There was disagreement **among** the fans about the coach's decision. [The fans are thought of as a group.]

brake, break The noun *brake* means "a stopping device." Used as a verb, *break* means "to fracture" or "to shatter." As a noun, *break* means "a fracture" or "a period of rest."

EXAMPLES ▪ Can you fix the **brake** on my bicycle?
▪ A high-pitched noise can **break** glass. [verb]
▪ The doctor says that it's not a bad **break**. [noun]
▪ Between shows, the band took a **break**. [noun]

bring, take *Bring* means "to come carrying something." *Take* means "to go carrying something." Think of *bring* as related to *come* and of *take* as related to *go*.

EXAMPLES ▪ **Bring** your skateboard when you come to my house this weekend.
▪ Please **take** these letters to the post office when you go.

bust, busted Avoid using these words as verbs. Use a form of either *burst* or *break*.

EXAMPLES ▪ The balloon **burst** [*not* busted] when it touched the ceiling.
▪ The vase **broke** [*not* busted] when I dropped it.

C

capital, capitol The noun *capital* refers to a city and means "the seat of a government." The noun *capitol* refers to a building and means "the statehouse."

EXAMPLES ▪ Olympia is the **capital** of Washington.
▪ The **capitol** of New York State is in Albany.

case Case is the form of a noun or pronoun that shows how it is used. See pages 116–121.

EXAMPLE ▪ **I** can't find **my** hat that Aunt Trish gave **me.** [*I* is in the nominative case. *My* is in the possessive case. *Me* is in the objective case.]

choose, chose *Choose* is the present tense form of the verb *choose.* It rhymes with *whose* and means "to select." *Chose* is the past tense form of *choose.* It rhymes with *grows* and means "selected."

EXAMPLES ▪ Will you **choose** speech or art as your elective next year?
▪ Sara **chose** a red pen, not a blue one.

clause A clause is a group of words that contains a verb and its subject and is used as part of a sentence. See **independent clause, subordinate clause,** and **Chapter 7: Clauses.**

EXAMPLE ▪ **What I want** is a new bike. [The noun clause *what I want* is the subject of the sentence.]

clothes, cloths The noun *clothes* means "wearing apparel." The noun *cloths* means "pieces of fabric."

EXAMPLES ▪ One can learn much about a historical period by studying its styles of **clothes.**

- You'll find some cleaning **cloths** in the drawer.

coarse, course   The adjective *coarse* means "rough." The noun *course* means "a path of action," "a unit of study," or "a route." *Course* is also used in the expression *of course.*

EXAMPLES ■ The beach is covered with **coarse** brown sand.
- If you follow that **course,** you'll succeed.
- My mother is taking a **course** in accounting.
- The wind blew the ship slightly off its **course.**
- You know, **of course,** that I'm right.

collective noun   A collective noun is a word that names a group. See page 47.

EXAMPLE ■ The **choir** sang a number of show tunes, folk songs, and spirituals.

common noun   A common noun is a general name for a person, a group of persons, a place, or a thing; it is not capitalized unless it begins a sentence or is used in a title. See pages 47–48.

EXAMPLE ■ **Fighter planes** and **battleships** are Luke's favorite modeling **subjects.**

comparative degree   Comparative degree is the form a modifier takes when comparing two things. See pages 131–135.

EXAMPLE ■ Not only is this jacket **less expensive** than that one, but it also fits **better.**

complement   A complement is a word that completes the meaning of a verb. See **Chapter 9: Complements.**

EXAMPLE ■ Did hailstones make these **dents** in your car?
[The complement *dents* completes the meaning of the verb phrase *did make.*]

complement, compliment   The noun *complement* means "something that completes." As a verb, *compliment* means "to praise someone." As a noun, it means "praise."

EXAMPLES ▪ The serious tone of the poem is a **complement** to its serious message.
          ▪ The director **complimented** Tony on his near-perfect performance.
          ▪ Thanks for the **compliment,** Diane!

complex sentence   A complex sentence has one independent clause and at least one subordinate clause. See pages 206–207.

EXAMPLE ▪ I can see that you enjoyed reading "The Tell-Tale Heart." [The sentence contains one independent clause and one subordinate clause. The subordinate clause *that you enjoyed reading "The Tell-Tale Heart"* serves as the direct object of the verb *can see*.]

compound-complex sentence   A compound-complex sentence contains two or more independent clauses and at least one subordinate clause. See pages 208–209.

EXAMPLE ▪ While we were on vacation, our water pipes burst, and the water ruined our carpeting. [one subordinate clause followed by two independent clauses]

compound noun   A compound noun is two or more words used together as a single noun. See page 47.

EXAMPLE ▪ My **grandparents** play **table tennis** every Wednesday at the **Senior Citizens' Center.**

compound sentence   A compound sentence has two or more independent clauses but no subordinate clauses. See pages 204–205.

EXAMPLE ▪ **Sharks are fish,** but **dolphins are mammals.** [two independent clauses]

compound subject   A compound subject consists of two or more subjects that are joined by a conjunction and have the same verb. See page 185.

EXAMPLE ▪ **"Belling the Cat"** and **"The Ant and the Grasshopper"** are two of Aesop's best-known fables.

compound verb A compound verb consists of two or more verbs that are joined by a conjunction and have the same subject. See pages 185–186.

EXAMPLE ▪ A woman of many gifts, Maya Angelou **writes, teaches, dances,** and **acts.**

concrete noun A concrete noun names an object that can be perceived by one or more of the senses. See pages 48–49.

EXAMPLE ▪ After **Chen** washes the **dishes,** she plays the **piano** for an hour.

conjunction A conjunction is a word used to join words or groups of words. *Coordinating conjunctions* connect words or groups of words used in the same way. *Correlative conjunctions* also connect words used in the same way and are always used in pairs. See pages 67–69.

EXAMPLES ▪ Edith Hamilton **and** Olivia Coolidge have each written books on Greek **and** Roman myths. [coordinating conjunctions]
▪ **Either** Thor **or** Balder is the Norse god of thunder. [correlative conjunction]

consul, council, counsel The noun *consul* refers to a representative of a government in a foreign country. *Council* refers to a group of people who meet together. Used as a noun, *counsel* means "advice." Used as a verb, *counsel* means "to give advice."

EXAMPLES ▪ Who is the American **consul** in Cairo?
▪ The mayor called a meeting of the city **council.**
▪ When choosing a career, seek **counsel** from your teachers.
▪ Ms. Jiménez **counseled** me to pursue a career in teaching.

could of Do not write *of* with the helping verb *could*. Write *could have*. Also avoid *ought to of, should of, would of, might of*, and *must of.*

EXAMPLE ▪ Reva **could have** [*not* could of] played the piano.

Of is also unnecessary with *had.*

EXAMPLE ▪ If I **had** [*not* had of] seen her, I would have said hello.

councilor, counselor The noun *councilor* refers to a member of a council. The noun *counselor* means "one who advises."

EXAMPLES ▪ The **councilors** discussed several issues.
▪ Shandra's guidance **counselor** helped her complete the application.

D

---

declarative sentence A declarative sentence makes a statement and is followed by a period. See page 210.

EXAMPLE ▪ Dr. Seuss's real name was Theodore Geisel.

demonstrative adjective A demonstrative adjective points out a person, a place, a thing, or an idea. See page 55.

EXAMPLE ▪ **These** old gold coins may sell for as much as $75,000.

demonstrative pronoun A demonstrative pronoun points out a person, a place, a thing, or an idea. See page 51.

EXAMPLE ▪ **That** is my favorite painting by Diego Rivera.

de'sert, desert', dessert' The noun *desert* means "a dry, sandy region." The verb *desert'* means "to abandon," "to leave." The noun *dessert'* means "the last course of a meal."

EXAMPLES
- Irrigation has brought new life to the **desert.** [noun]
- Most dogs will not **desert** a friend in trouble. [verb]
- Fruit salad is my favorite **dessert.** [noun]

direct object A direct object is a noun or a pronoun that receives the action of the verb or that shows the result of the action. It tells *what* or *whom* after an action verb. See pages 193–194.

EXAMPLE
- Stanislaw Lem's works of science fiction have won worldwide **praise** for their author. [Have won *what*? Praise.]

direct quotation A direct quotation is a person's exact words and is enclosed in quotation marks. See pages 285–288.

EXAMPLE
- "Who is ready to read these lines from *The Song of Hiawatha*?" asked Mrs. Thompson.

doesn't, don't *Doesn't* is the contraction of *does not. Don't* is the contraction of *do not.* Use *doesn't* [not *don't*] with *he, she, it, this, that,* and singular nouns.

EXAMPLES
- He **doesn't** [*not* don't] know how to swim.
- The price **doesn't** [*not* don't] include tax.

double negative A *double negative* is the use of two negative words to express one negative idea. Avoid using double negatives.

Common Negative Words			
barely	never	none	nothing
hardly	no	no one	nowhere
neither	nobody	not (-n't)	scarcely

NONSTANDARD We don't have no extra chairs.
STANDARD We have **no** extra chairs.
STANDARD We don't have **any** extra chairs.

NONSTANDARD He couldn't hardly talk.

STANDARD He **could hardly** talk.

 REFERENCE NOTE: For more on the double negative, see pages 136–137.

"CONFOUNDED DOUBLE NEGATIVES."

©1993 by Sidney Harris

E

effect See **affect, effect.**

end marks An end mark is a punctuation mark that is placed at the end of a sentence to indicate the purpose of the sentence. See **declarative sentence, exclamatory sentence, imperative sentence,** and **interrogative sentence.** See also pages 257–260.

essential clause/essential phrase An essential (or restrictive) clause or phrase is necessary to the meaning of a sentence. See page 266.

EXAMPLES ▪ The jeans **that are on sale** are over there. [essential clause]

▪ The report **about endangered species** is Darnell's. [essential phrase]

WRITER'S QUICK REFERENCE

everywheres See **anywheres,** etc.

except See **accept, except.**

exclamatory sentence An exclamatory sentence shows excitement or expresses strong feeling and is followed by an exclamation point. See page 211.

EXAMPLE   ▪ What a brave and creative person Anne Frank was!

F

---

fewer, less *Fewer* is used with plural words. *Less* is used with singular words. *Fewer* tells "how many"; *less* tells "how much."

EXAMPLES   ▪ We have **fewer** [*not* less] tickets to sell than we thought.
▪ These plants require **less** water.

formally, formerly *Formally* means "with dignity" or "according to strict rules or procedures." *Formerly* means "previously" or "in the past."

EXAMPLES   ▪ The mayor delivered the speech **formally.**
▪ Adele Zubalsky was **formerly** the principal of the school.

G

---

gerund A gerund is a verb form ending in *-ing* that is used as a noun. See page 154.

EXAMPLE   ▪ **Gardening** was a favorite hobby of the French painter Claude Monet.

gerund phrase A gerund phrase contains a gerund and all the words related to the gerund. See page 155.

EXAMPLE   ▪ Luther thought he'd save time in the morning by **showering at night.** [The gerund *showering* is modified by the prepositional phrase *at night.*]

good, well *Good* is always an adjective. Never use *good* as an adverb. Instead, use *well.*

NONSTANDARD   Nancy sang good at the audition.
STANDARD   Nancy sang **well** at the audition.

Although *well* is usually an adverb, *well* may also be used as an adjective to mean "healthy."

EXAMPLE   ▪ He didn't look **well** after eating the entire pizza all by himself.

NOTE *Feel good* and *feel well* mean different things. *Feel good* means "to feel happy or pleased." *Feel well* means "to feel healthy."

EXAMPLES   ▪ I felt **good** [*happy*] when I got an A on my report.
▪ He did not feel **well** [*healthy*] after a heavy lunch followed by an hour of racquetball.

H

---

had of See **could of.**

had ought, hadn't ought Unlike other verbs, *ought* is not used with *had.*

NONSTANDARD   Eric had ought to help us; he hadn't ought to have missed our meeting yesterday.
STANDARD   Eric **ought to** help us; he **oughtn't to have** missed our meeting yesterday.

or

Eric **should** help us; he **shouldn't have** missed our meeting yesterday.

hardly, scarcely   The words *hardly* and *scarcely* convey negative meanings. They should never be used with another negative word. See **double negative**.

EXAMPLES   ▪ I **can** [*not* can't] **hardly** read your handwriting.
           ▪ We **had** [*not* hadn't] **scarcely** enough food for everyone.

hear, here   The verb *hear* means "to perceive sounds by ear." The adverb *here* means "in this place."

EXAMPLES   ▪ Dogs can **hear** sounds that people can't **hear**.
           ▪ The treasure is buried **here**.

he, she, they   Avoid using a pronoun along with its antecedent as the subject of a verb. This error is called the *double subject*.

NONSTANDARD   Nancy Lopez she is a famous professional golfer.
   STANDARD   Nancy Lopez is a famous professional golfer.

hisself   *Hisself* is nonstandard English. Use *himself*.

EXAMPLE   ▪ Ira bought **himself** [*not* hisself] a lavender polka-dot tie.

how come   In informal situations, *how come* is often used instead of *why*. In formal situations, *why* should always be used.

INFORMAL   I don't know how come she's not here.
  FORMAL   I don't know **why** she is not here.

I

---

imperative sentence   An imperative sentence gives a command or makes a request and is followed by either a period or an exclamation point. See page 211.

EXAMPLES   ▪ Please have a seat**.** [request]

▪ Do sit down. [mild command]
▪ Sit down! [strong command]

indefinite pronoun   An indefinite pronoun refers to a person, a place, or a thing that is not specifically named. See pages 52–53.

EXAMPLE   ▪ Has **anyone** in our class read about the adventures of Gilgamesh, a king of ancient Sumer?

independent clause   An independent (or **main**) clause expresses a complete thought and can stand by itself as a sentence. See page 164.

EXAMPLE   ▪ Before we read "The Wooden People," **Mr. Ramírez told us a little about this Quiché Mayan creation myth.**

indirect object   An indirect object is a noun or pronoun that comes between the action verb and the direct object and tells *to whom* or *to what* or *for whom* or *for what* the action of the verb is done. See also pages 195–196.

EXAMPLE   ▪ We gave the **wagon** a coat of paint, and now it looks brand new. [We gave a coat of paint *to what*? The wagon.]

indirect quotation   An indirect quotation is a rewording or paraphrasing of something a person has said. Compare to **direct quotation.** See also page 285.

EXAMPLE   ▪ Mrs. Thompson asked if anyone was ready to recite a passage from *The Song of Hiawatha.*

infinitive   An infinitive is a verb form, usually preceded by *to,* that can be used as a noun, an adjective, or an adverb. See page 156.

EXAMPLE   ▪ Josephine really wants **to win.** [The infinitive *to win* is used as a noun and functions as the direct object of *wants.*]

WRITER'S QUICK REFERENCE

infinitive phrase An infinitive phrase consists of an infinitive and its modifiers and complements. See page 157.

EXAMPLE   ▪ Our assignment is **to write a parody of a famous poem.** [The infinitive *to write* has a direct object—*parody.*]

intensive pronoun An intensive pronoun emphasizes a noun or another pronoun. See pages 50–51.

EXAMPLE   ▪ Leon carved these bookends **himself.**

interjection An interjection is a word used to express emotion. It has no grammatical relation to other words in the sentence. See page 69.

EXAMPLE   ▪ **Well,** I for one enjoy Lewis Carroll's "nonsense" poems.

interrogative pronoun An interrogative pronoun introduces a question. See page 52.

EXAMPLE   ▪ **What** did you think of the movie?

interrogative sentence An interrogative sentence asks a question and is followed by a question mark. See page 211.

EXAMPLE   ▪ How old is the Indian epic poem the *Mahabharata*?

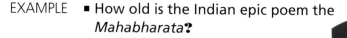

Peanuts reprinted by permission of UFS, Inc.

intransitive verb An intransitive verb expresses action or tells something about the subject without passing the action from a doer to a receiver. Compare with **transitive verb**. See also pages 58–59.

EXAMPLE ▪ The baby **has been napping** since two o'clock.
[The action of *has been napping* is not passed to a receiver.]

irregular verb An irregular verb is a verb that forms its past and past participle in some other way than by adding *-d* or *-ed* to the base form. Compare with **regular verb**. See pages 100–105.

EXAMPLE ▪ The Koran, the holy book of Muslims, was **written** in the seventh century A.D.

its, it's *Its* is a personal pronoun in the possessive form. *It's* is a contraction of *it is* or *it has*.

EXAMPLES ▪ **Its** handle is broken. [possessive pronoun]
▪ **It's** a hot day. [contraction of *it is*]
▪ **It's** been a good trip. [contraction of *it has*]

K

kind of, sort of In informal situations, *kind of* and *sort of* are often used to mean "somewhat" or "rather." In formal English, *somewhat* or *rather* is preferred.

INFORMAL He seemed kind of embarrassed by our compliments.

FORMAL He seemed **somewhat** embarrassed by our compliments.

kind, sort, type The words *this, that, these,* and *those* should agree in number with the words *kind, sort,* and *type*.

EXAMPLES ▪ Whitney likes **this kind** of music.
▪ **Those kinds** of math problems are easy.

L

lead, led *Lead* is the present tense form of the verb *lead*. It rhymes with *feed* and means "to go first" or "to be a leader." *Led* is the past tense form of the verb *lead*. The noun *lead* rhymes with *red*. It means "a heavy metal" or "graphite used in pencils."

EXAMPLES
- A small town in New Hampshire often **leads** the nation in filing its election returns.
- Mr. Tanaka **led** the scout troop back to camp.
- Many fishing nets are weighted with **lead** to hold them on the sea bottom.
- Darn! I just broke my pencil **lead**.

learn, teach *Learn* means "to gain knowledge." *Teach* means "to instruct" or "to show how."

EXAMPLES
- I am **learning** how to use this computer.
- My father is **teaching** me how to use this computer.

less See **fewer, less.**

lie, lay The verb *lie* means "to rest," "to recline," or "to be in a place." *Lie* never takes an object. The verb *lay* means "to put (something) in a place." *Lay* usually takes an object. See page 111 for the principal parts of *lie* and *lay*.

EXAMPLES
- The cows **are lying** in the shade of the oak trees. [no object]
- The servers **are laying** extra napkins beside every plate for the barbecue. [The servers are laying what? *Napkins* is the object.]
- The deer **lay** very still while the hunters passed by. [no object]
- The soldiers **laid** a trap for the enemy. [The soldiers laid what? *Trap* is the object.]
- Rip Van Winkle **had lain** asleep for twenty years. [no object]

- The lawyer **had laid** the report next to her briefcase. [The lawyer had laid what? *Report* is the object.]

Rivets reprinted with special permission of King Features Syndicate, Inc.

like, as In informal situations, the preposition *like* is often used instead of the conjunction *as* to introduce a clause. In formal situations, *as* is preferred.

EXAMPLE   ■ I looked up several words in my dictionary, **as** [*not* like] the teacher had suggested.

 REFERENCE NOTE: For more information on clauses, see **Chapter 7: Clauses.**

like, as if, as though In informal situations, the preposition *like* is often used for the compound conjunctions *as if* or *as though*. In formal situations, *as if* or *as though* is preferred.

EXAMPLES   ■ They acted **as if** [*not* like] they hadn't heard him.
              ■ You looked **as though** [*not* like] you knew the answer.

WRITER'S QUICK REFERENCE

linking verb A linking verb links, or connects, the subject with a noun, a pronoun, or an adjective in the predicate. See pages 59–60.

EXAMPLE   ■ Emily Dickinson's poetry **became** popular long after the poet's death. [*Became* links the subject *poetry* with the predicate adjective *popular.*]

loose, lose The adjective *loose* rhymes with *moose.* It means "not securely attached" or "not fitting tightly." As an adverb, *loose* means "in a loose manner." *Lose* is the present tense form of the verb *lose.* It rhymes with *whose* and means "to suffer a loss."

EXAMPLES   ■ If the knot is too **loose,** the piñata will fall. [adjective]

           ■ At one time, huge herds of mustangs ran **loose** on this land. [adverb]

           ■ Vegetables **lose** some of their vitamins when they are cooked.

M
---

might of, must of See **could of.**

N
---

nonessential clause/nonessential phrase A nonessential (or nonrestrictive) clause or phrase adds information that is not needed to understand the meaning of the sentence. It is set off by commas. Compare with **essential clause/essential phrase.** See pages 265–266.

EXAMPLES   ■ The Lowells, **who were a gifted family of writers,** lived in Massachusetts. [clause]

- The twins, **shouting and laughing,** squirted each other with water pistols. [phrase]

noun A noun is a word used to name a person, a place, a thing, or an idea. See pages 46–49.

EXAMPLE
- The **book** *Nisei Daughter* is the **story** of a Japanese American **woman.**

noun clause A noun clause is a subordinate clause used as a noun. See pages 172–173.

EXAMPLE
- I forget **what we are supposed to read for tomorrow.** [The noun clause is used as the direct object of the sentence.]

nowheres See **anywheres,** etc.

number Number is the form of a word that indicates whether the word is singular or plural. See page 77.

EXAMPLES
- **That poem is** a sonnet. [singular]
- **These poems are** ballads. [plural]

O

object An object completes the meaning of a transitive verb. See page 58. See also **direct object** and **indirect object.**

EXAMPLE
- For the Spring Talent Show, our class performed *The Toad of Toad Hall* by A. A. Milne.

object of a preposition The noun or pronoun that follows the preposition in a prepositional phrase is the object of the preposition that begins the phrase. See page 66.

EXAMPLE
- O. Henry, the famous short story writer, once jumped bail and escaped to **Honduras.** [*Honduras* is the object of the preposition *to.*]

WRITER'S QUICK REFERENCE

of Do not use *of* with other prepositions such as *inside, off,* and *outside.*

EXAMPLES ▪ He quickly walked **off** [*not* off of] the stage.
  ▪ She waited **outside** [*not* outside of] the school.
  ▪ What is **inside** [*not* inside of] this large box?

ought to of See **could of.**

P

---

parenthetical expression A parenthetical expression is a side remark that adds information or relates ideas. See page 267.

EXAMPLES ▪ You will, **of course,** be sure to indent the first line of each paragraph.
  ▪ Going to school, **according to my math teacher,** is like having a job.

participial phrase A participial phrase contains a participle and all of the words related to the participle. See page 153.

EXAMPLE   ▪ **Remembered for her best-selling children's books,** Louisa May Alcott also worked to gain women's right to vote. [The participle is *remembered.* The entire phrase acts as an adjective and modifies *Louisa May Alcott.*]

participle A participle is a verb form that can be used as an adjective. See pages 152–153.

EXAMPLE   ▪ **Whispering,** Jason told me the plans for Rachel's surprise party.

passed, past *Passed* is the past tense form of the verb *pass.* It means "went by." Used as a noun, *past* means "that which has gone by." Used as a preposition, *past* means "beyond."

EXAMPLES ▪ The people in the car waved as they **passed** us.

▪ Some people long to live in the **past**. [noun]

▪ They walked right **past** the entrance. [preposition]

peace, piece   The noun *peace* means "security, quiet, and order." The noun *piece* means "a part of something."

EXAMPLES ▪ We are striving for **peace** and prosperity.

▪ Some people can catch fish with a pole, a **piece** of string, and a bent pin.

personal pronoun   A personal pronoun refers to the one speaking (*first person*), the one spoken to (*second person*), or the one spoken about (*third person*). See page 50.

EXAMPLE ▪ I don't think **you** should have given **her** Dad's copy of *The Hobbit*.

phrase   A phrase is a group of related words that is used as a single part of speech and does not contain a verb and its subject. See **Chapter 6: Phrases.** See also **appositive phrase, gerund phrase, infinitive phrase, participial phrase, prepositional phrase,** and **verb phrase.**

EXAMPLE ▪ Both **of us had been hoping to catch a glimpse of Garth Brooks.** [*Of us* is a prepositional phrase that modifies the pronoun *both. Had been hoping* is a verb phrase. *To catch a glimpse of Garth Brooks* is an infinitive phrase acting as a noun. *Of Garth Brooks* is a prepositional phrase modifying the noun *glimpse.*]

plain, plane   Used as an adjective, *plain* means "simple, common, without decoration." Used as a noun, *plain* means "a flat area of land." The noun *plane* means "a tool," "an airplane," or "a flat surface."

EXAMPLES ▪ The actors wore **plain** costumes. [adjective]

▪ What is the difference between a prairie and a **plain**? [noun]

- The **plane** is useful in the carpenter's trade.
- Four single-engine **planes** are in the hangar.
- In geometry class we learned how to measure the angles of **planes** such as squares.

positive degree   Positive degree is the form a modifier takes when no comparison is being made. See page 131. See also **comparative degree, superlative degree.**

EXAMPLE   - There is a **little** house across the creek.

predicate   The predicate is the part of a sentence that says something about the subject. The *simple predicate,* or verb, is the main word or group of words within the complete predicate. The *complete predicate* is composed of the main verb, its helping verbs, and any complements and modifiers of the main verb. See pages 183–184.

EXAMPLE   - Alice Walker **has written poems, short stories, essays, and novels.** [The simple predicate is *has written.* The complete predicate is *has written poems, short stories, essays, and novels.*]

predicate adjective   A predicate adjective is an adjective that follows a linking verb and describes the subject. See pages 198–199.

EXAMPLE   - This review of the musical play *Sweeney Todd* is **positive.** [The adjective *positive* describes the subject *review.*]

predicate nominative   A predicate nominative is a noun that follows a linking verb and identifies the subject or refers to it. See page 197.

EXAMPLE   - Keeping track of all the names in Elaine's latest short story is a real **chore.** [The noun *chore* refers to the subject *keeping track of all the characters in Elaine's latest short story.*]

prefix   A prefix is a letter or group of letters added to the beginning of a word to change its meaning. See pages 309–310.

EXAMPLES ▪ **re** + view = **rev**iew
▪ **un** + harmed = **un**harmed
▪ **semi** + sweet = **semi**sweet

preposition A preposition is a word used to show the relationship of a noun or a pronoun to some other word or words. See pages 65–67.

EXAMPLE ▪ One **of** us should go **with** Lee. [*Of* shows the relationship between the pronoun *us* and the pronoun *one. With* shows the relationship between the noun *Lee* and the verb *should go.*]

prepositional phrase A prepositional phrase is a group of words that includes a preposition, a noun or a pronoun called the object of the preposition, and any modifiers of that object. See pages 65–67.

EXAMPLE ▪ **In his music,** Sting makes many references **to literature.**

principal parts of a verb The principal parts of a verb are a verb's forms: the *base form,* the *present participle,* the *past,* and the *past participle.* The principal parts are used to form the verb tenses. See pages 97–98.

BASE FORM	PRESENT PARTICIPLE	PAST	PAST PARTICIPLE
raise	(is) raising	raised	(have) raised
go	(is) going	went	(have) gone

principal, principle As a noun, *principal* means "the head of a school." As an adjective, it means "main or most important." The noun *principle* means "a rule of conduct" or "a main fact or law."

EXAMPLES ▪ The **principal** of the school is Mr. Arimoto.
[noun]
▪ What are the **principal** exports of Brazil?
[adjective]

- Judge Rios is a woman of high **principles**.
- We discussed some of the basic **principles** of democracy.

pronoun A pronoun is a word used in place of a noun or more than one noun. See pages 49–53 and **Chapter 4: Using Pronouns.**

EXAMPLE ▪ **Everyone** is invited to the party at **our** house.

proper adjective A proper adjective is formed from a proper noun and begins with a capital letter. See page 55.

EXAMPLE ▪ In high school, we'll study **American** and **British** literature.

proper noun A proper noun names a particular person, place, or thing and is always capitalized. See pages 47–48.

EXAMPLE ▪ The **Globe Theatre** in **London** was where the plays of **Shakespeare** were first performed.

Q

quiet, quite The adjective *quiet* means "still and peaceful" or "without noise." The adverb *quite* means "wholly or entirely" or "to a great extent."

EXAMPLES ▪ A **quiet** room is needed for concentrated study.
▪ Winters in New England can be **quite** severe.

R

real In informal situations, *real* is often used as an adverb meaning "very" or "extremely." In formal situations, *very* or *extremely* is preferred.

INFORMAL My mother is expecting a real important telephone call.

FORMAL   My mother is expecting an **extremely** important telephone call.

reason . . . because   In informal situations, *reason . . . because* is often used instead of *reason . . . that.* In formal situations, use *reason . . . that,* or revise your sentence.

INFORMAL   The reason I did well on the test was because I had studied hard.

FORMAL   The **reason** I did well on the test was **that** I had studied hard.

or

I did well on the test **because** I had studied hard.

reflexive pronoun   A reflexive pronoun refers to the subject and directs the action of the verb back to the subject. See pages 50–51.

EXAMPLE   ▪ In one Arthurian legend, the boy Percival makes **himself** armor from willow twigs.

regular verb   A regular verb is a verb that forms its past and past participle by adding *-d* or *-ed* to the base form. See page 99.

EXAMPLE   ▪ For many years, Richard Kiley **played** Don Quixote in the musical *The Man of La Mancha.*

relative pronoun   A relative pronoun introduces a noun clause or an adjective clause. See pages 52 and 167–168.

EXAMPLES   ▪ **What we should do** is have a car wash. [The relative pronoun *what* introduces the noun clause *what we should do.*]

▪ The man **who spoke to our class** writes computer manuals. [The relative pronoun *who* introduces the adjective clause *who spoke to our class.*]

rise, raise   The most common definitions of the verb *rise* are "to go up" and "to get up." With these meanings, *rise* never takes an object. The verb *raise* means "to lift up" or "to cause (something) to rise." *Raise* usually takes an object. See page 112 for the principal parts of *rise* and *raise*.

EXAMPLES ■ My neighbors **rise** very early in the morning. [no object]

■ Every morning they **raise** their shades to let the sunlight in. [They raise what? *Shades* is the object.]

■ The full moon **rose** slowly through the clouds last night. [no object]

■ The cheering crowd **raised** banners and signs over their heads, welcoming the troops home. [The crowd raised what? *Banners* and *signs* are the objects.]

■ The senators **have risen** from their seats to show respect for the Chief Justice. [no object]

■ The wind **has raised** a great, swirling cloud of dust. [The wind has raised what? *Cloud* is the object.]

run-on sentence A run-on sentence is two or more complete sentences run together as one. See pages 220–222.

RUN-ON   There are three poetic devices that Ms. Eisner wants us to identify, they are imagery, rhyme, and rhythm.

REVISED   There are three poetic devices that Ms. Eisner wants us to identify. They are imagery, rhyme, and rhythm.

or

The three poetic devices that Ms. Eisner wants us to identify are imagery, rhyme, and rhythm.

or

Ms. Eisner wants us to identify three poetic devices: imagery, rhyme, and rhythm.

S

scarcely, hardly See **hardly, scarcely.**

sentence A sentence is a group of words that contains a subject and a verb and expresses a complete thought. See **Chapter 8: Sentences.**

EXAMPLE   ▪ Charles Dickens wrote *David Copperfield.*

sentence fragment A sentence fragment is a part of a sentence that does not express a complete thought. See pages 179 and 219–220.

FRAGMENT Her homework done.
     REVISED Her homework done, Kara decided to go jogging.

shone, shown *Shone* is a past tense form of the verb *shine.* It means "gleamed" or "glowed." *Shown* is the past participle form of the verb *show.* It means "revealed."

EXAMPLES ▪ The Navajo jeweler polished the silver-and-turquoise ring until it **shone.**
     ▪ A model of the new school will be **shown** to the public next week.

NOTE   *Shine* may also mean "to direct the light of" or "to polish," but the preferred past tense form for these meanings is *shined,* not *shone.*

EXAMPLES ▪ Jackie **shined** her good shoes every Sunday.
     ▪ Grandpa **shined** a light outside.

should of See **could of.**

simple sentence A simple sentence has one independent clause and no subordinate clauses. See page 203.

EXAMPLE   ▪ Atticus Finch is one of the memorable characters in Harper Lee's *To Kill a Mockingbird.*

sit, set The verb *sit* means "to rest in an upright, seated position." *Sit* seldom takes an object. The verb *set* means "to put (something) in a place." *Set* usually takes an object.

Notice that *set* has the same form for the base form, past, and past participle. For the principal parts of *sit* and *set,* see page 110.

EXAMPLES
- Let's **sit** under the tree. [no object]
- Let's **set** the bookcase here. [Let's set what? *Bookcase* is the object.]
- The tourists **sat** on benches. [no object]
- The children **set** the dishes on the table. [The children set what? *Dishes* is the object.]
- We **had sat** down to eat when the telephone rang. [no object]
- We **have set** the reading lamp beside the couch. [We have set what? *Lamp* is the object.]

some, somewhat Do not use *some* for *somewhat* as an adverb.

NONSTANDARD My math has improved some.

STANDARD My math has improved **somewhat.**

somewheres See **anywheres,** etc.

sort See **kind, sort, type.**

sort of See **kind of, sort of.**

stationary, stationery The adjective *stationary* means "in a fixed position." The noun *stationery* means "writing paper."

EXAMPLES
- Most of the furnishings of a space capsule must be **stationary.**
- I need a new box of **stationery.**

NOTE Here's an easy way to remember the difference between *stationary* and *stationery.* You write a letter on stationery.

stringy sentence A stringy sentence is a sentence that has too many independent clauses, often strung together with words like *and* or *but.* See pages 229–230.

STRINGY I took notes, and Sheila scoured the library for more information about our research topic, but

Antony just whined about how much homework he had.

REVISED   While I took notes, Sheila scoured the library for more information on our topic. Antony just whined about how much homework he had.

subject   The subject is the part of a sentence that tells whom or what the sentence is about. The *simple subject* is the main word or group of words within the *complete subject.* The complete subject consists of the simple subject and any words, phrases, or clauses that modify the simple subject. See pages 181–182.

EXAMPLE   ■ **The winner of the 1988 Nobel Prize in literature** was Naguib Mahfouz. [The simple subject is *winner*. The complete subject is *the winner of the 1988 Nobel Prize in literature*.]

subject complement   A subject complement completes the meaning of a linking verb and identifies or describes the subject. See pages 196–199.

EXAMPLES   ■ Mark Twain's real name was **Samuel Clemens.** [*Samuel Clemens* identifies the subject *name*.]

■ Twain became **bitter** after the deaths of his wife and daughters. [*Bitter* describes the subject *Twain*.]

subordinate clause   A subordinate (or **dependent**) clause does not express a complete thought and cannot stand alone as a sentence. See pages 165–173.

EXAMPLE   ■ **If you like Sherlock Holmes stories,** you'll enjoy the film versions on public television.

subordinating conjunction   A subordinating conjunction is a word that shows the relationship between an adverb clause and the word or words that the clause modifies. See page 171.

EXAMPLE   ■ Keep stirring **until** the mixture is smooth and creamy. [*Until* introduces the adverb clause *until the mixture is smooth and creamy.* It tells *how long* to keep stirring.]

suffix A suffix is a letter or group of letters added to the end of a word to change its meaning. See pages 310–311.

EXAMPLES ▪ dirt + **y** = dirt**y**
           ▪ agree + **able** = agree**able**

superlative degree Superlative degree is the form a modifier takes when comparing more than two things. See pages 131–135.

EXAMPLE ▪ Jerome is not only the **tallest** player on the team, but he's also the **most modest.**

Frank & Ernest reprinted by permission of NEA, Inc.

syllable A syllable is a word part that can be pronounced by itself. See pages 306–307.

EXAMPLES ▪ hot   ▪ av•er•age
           ▪ ear•ly   ▪ dis•ap•point•ed

T

take See **bring, take.**

teach See **learn, teach.**

tense The tense of a verb indicates the time of the action or state of being expressed by the verb. See pages 106–109.

EXAMPLE　■ After we **had finished** painting the garage, Dad and I **rested** in the shade.

than, then *Than* is a conjunction used in making comparisons. *Then* is an adverb that means "at that time."

EXAMPLES　■ Margo is a faster runner **than** I am.
　　　　　　■ First we went to the bookstore. **Then** we went to the library.

that See **who, which, that.**

that there See **this here, that there.**

theirself, theirselves *Theirself* and *theirselves* are nonstandard English. Use *themselves*.

EXAMPLE　■ They bought **themselves** [*not* theirself *or* theirselves] a telescope.

their, there, they're *Their* is the possessive form of the pronoun *they*. *There* is used to mean "at that place" or to begin a sentence. *They're* is a contraction of *they are*.

EXAMPLES　■ **Their** team won the game.
　　　　　　■ We are planning to go **there** during spring vacation.
　　　　　　■ **There** were twenty people at the party.
　　　　　　■ **They're** the best players on the team.

them *Them* should not be used as an adjective. Use *those*.

EXAMPLE　■ Karen gave you **those** [*not* them] cassettes yesterday.

this here, that there The words *here* and *there* are unnecessary after *this* and *that*.

EXAMPLE　■ Do you like **this** [*not* this here] shirt or **that** [*not* that there] one?

this kind, sort, type See **kind,** etc.

threw, through   *Threw* is the past tense form of the verb *throw. Through* is a preposition.

EXAMPLES ▪ Our relief pitcher **threw** nine strikes in
             succession.
         ▪ The ship went **through** the series of locks
             in the Panama Canal.

to, too, two   *To* is a preposition. It is also part of the infinitive form of a verb. *Too* is an adverb that means "also" or "overly." *Two* is the number equal to one plus one.

EXAMPLES ▪ A visit **to** Chinatown is an exciting treat.
             [preposition]
         ▪ Do you know how **to** make tortillas? [sign of
             the infinitive]
         ▪ We have lived in Iowa and in Alaska, **too.**
         ▪ It is **too** cold for rain today.
         ▪ She borrowed **two** dollars from me.

transitive verb   A transitive verb is an action verb that expresses an action directed toward a person or thing. Compare with **intransitive verb.** See pages 58–59.

EXAMPLE   ▪ The baby **is taking** a nap. [The action of *is taking* is directed toward *nap.*]

try and   In informal situations, *try and* is often used instead of *try to.* In formal situations, *try to* should be used.

INFORMAL   Try and be on time for the party.
 FORMAL   **Try to** be on time for the party.

U

use to, used to   Be sure to add the *-d* to *use. Used to* is the past form.

EXAMPLE   ▪ We **used to** [*not* use to] live in Phoenix, Arizona.

V

verb A verb is a word used to express an action or a state of being. See pages 57–61 and **Chapter 3: Using Verbs.**

EXAMPLES ■ In "Rip Van Winkle," Rip **sleeps** for twenty years. [*Sleeps* expresses an action.]
  ■ The weather **has turned** colder. [*Has turned* expresses a state of being.]

verbal A verbal is a form of a verb used as a noun, an adjective, or an adverb. See pages 152–157. See also **gerund, infinitive,** and **participle.**

EXAMPLE ■ In "A **Retrieved** Reformation," Jimmy Valentine gives up **cracking** safes and turns to **making** shoes for a living. [*Retrieved* is a verbal used as an adjective. *Cracking* and *making* are verbals used as nouns.]

verb phrase A verb phrase consists of a main verb preceded by at least one *helping* (or *auxiliary*) *verb.* See page 60.

EXAMPLE ■ If I **had had** time, I **would have** read more of Ogden Nash's humorous poems.

W

way, ways Use *way,* not *ways,* in referring to a distance.

EXAMPLE ■ They still had a long **way** [*not* ways] to go.

weak, week *Weak* is an adjective that means "not strong" or "feeble." *Week* is a noun that means "seven days."

EXAMPLES ■ The patient is too **weak** to have visitors.
  ■ Your pictures of Josh's bar mitzvah will be ready in about a **week.**

weather, whether *Weather* is a noun that means "the condition of the air or atmosphere." *Whether* is a conjunction that means "if."

EXAMPLES   ■ The **weather** is hot and humid.
            ■ Jessica wondered **whether** or not she should go hiking.

well See **good, well.**

when, where Do not use *when* or *where* incorrectly in writing a definition.

NONSTANDARD   In bowling, a "turkey" is when a person rolls three strikes in a row.
STANDARD   In bowling, a "turkey" is rolling three strikes in a row.

where Do not use *where* for *that.*

NONSTANDARD   I read in our newspaper where Monica Seles won the tennis tournament.
STANDARD   I read in our newspaper **that** Monica Seles won the tennis tournament.

who's, whose *Who's* is the contraction of *who is* or *who has.* *Whose* is the possessive form of *who.* See page 297.

EXAMPLES   ■ **Who's** [Who is] keeping score?
            ■ **Who's** [Who has] been using my typewriter?
            ■ **Whose** baseball glove is this?

who, which, that The relative pronoun *who* refers to people only; *which* refers to things only; *that* refers to either people or things.

EXAMPLES   ■ Kim is the only one **who** got the right answer. [person]
            ■ My bike, **which** has ten speeds, is for sale. [thing]
            ■ He is the one person **that** can help you. [person]
            ■ This is the ring **that** I want to buy. [thing]

without, unless Do not use the preposition *without* in place of the conjunction *unless.*

EXAMPLE   ▪ My mother said that I can't go to the game **unless** [*not* without] I finish my homework first.

would of See **could of.**

Y

---

your, you're *Your* is the possessive form of the pronoun *you. You're* is the contraction of *you are.* See page 297.

EXAMPLES ▪ **Your** dinner is on the table.
▪ **You're** one of my closest friends.

WRITER'S QUICK REFERENCE

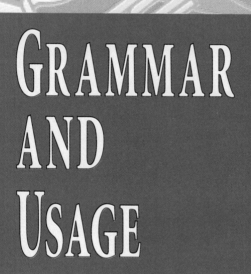

GRAMMAR AND USAGE

1 PARTS OF SPEECH

The Work That Words Do

 **Checking What You Know**

A. Identifying Nouns, Pronouns, and Adjectives

Identify each italicized word in the following sentences as a *noun,* a *pronoun,* or an *adjective.*

EXAMPLE   **1.** The biplane had two *wings* and a *wooden* propeller.
     1. *wings—noun; wooden—adjective*

1. Inger's mother gave *each* of us a glass of *cold* milk.
2. One by one, *each* Siberian husky trotted out into the *cold.*
3. *Who* went to the movie *Saturday* night?
4. When the *Neville Brothers* came to town, we went to *their* concert.
5. The house across the street has been up for *sale* since *Tuesday.*
6. *That* rifle doesn't belong to *anyone.*

7. *Somebody* said that there would be no more *discount* movie tickets.

8. I got a *discount* on *our* tickets, though.

9. Hobbies take up so *much* time that they often become *work*.

10. My aunt's *work* schedule often takes *her* out of town.

B. Identifying Verbs, Adverbs, Prepositions, Conjunctions, and Interjections

Write the italicized word or word group in each of the following sentences. Label each as an *action verb*, a *linking verb*, a *helping verb*, an *adverb*, a *preposition*, a *conjunction*, or an *interjection*.

EXAMPLE   **1.** That girl has *traveled* widely with her family.
          1. *traveled*—action verb

11. *Wow,* that's the best meal I've eaten in a long time!

12. That dog looks mean *in spite of* his wagging tail.

13. *Have* you ever celebrated Cinco de Mayo?

14. If Ken will *not* help us, then he cannot share in the rewards.

15. The road that runs *close* to the railroad tracks is usually crowded.

16. Several of my friends *enjoy* the music of Quincy Jones.

17. No one could do much to help, *for* the damage had already been done.

18. May I have a glass of milk and a combination sandwich *without* onions?

19. James *became* impatient, but he waited quietly.

20. My uncle visits during Hanukkah, *and* he always brings us presents.

✓

The Eight Parts of Speech			
noun	pronoun	verb	conjunction
adverb	adjective	preposition	interjection

The Noun

1a. A *noun* is a word used to name a person, a place, a thing, or an idea.

PERSONS	PLACES	THINGS	IDEAS
Alice Walker	desert	money	courage
Dr. Lacy	neighborhood	wind	love
children	outer space	animals	freedom
architect	New York City	*Voyager 2*	luck
team	Grand Canyon	Statue of Liberty	equality
baby sitter	Nigeria	Newbery Medal	self-control
gymnast	Golden Gate	orange juice	democracy
waiter	Park	perfume	anger

"Now!—That should clear up a few things around here!"

Compound Nouns

A *compound noun* is two or more words used together as a single noun. The parts of a compound noun may be written as one word, as separate words, or as a hyphenated word.

ONE WORD	seafood, filmmaker, videocassette, footsteps, grasshopper, daydream, Passover, Iceland
SEPARATE WORDS	compact disc, House of Representatives, police officer, John F. Kennedy, *The Call of the Wild*
HYPHENATED WORD	self-esteem, fund-raiser, sister-in-law, fourteen-year-old, great-grandparents

 NOTE When you are not sure how to write a compound noun, look in a dictionary.

Collective Nouns

A *collective noun* is a word that names a group.

EXAMPLES faculty   family   herd   team   congress
                  audience   flock   crew   jury   committee

Common Nouns and Proper Nouns

A *common noun* is a general name for a person, place, thing, or idea. A *proper noun* names a particular person, place, thing, or idea. Proper nouns always begin with a capital letter. Common nouns begin with a capital letter only when they come at the beginning of a sentence.

COMMON NOUNS	PROPER NOUNS
poem	"The Raven," "I Am Joaquín"
nation	Mexico, United States of America
athlete	Joe Montana, Zina Garrison-Jackson
ship	*Mayflower*, U.S.S. *Constitution*

(continued)

COMMON NOUNS	PROPER NOUNS
newspaper	*The New York Times, USA Today*
river	Rio Grande, Congo River
street	Market Street, University Avenue
day	Friday, Independence Day
city	Los Angeles, New Delhi
organization	National Forensic League, Girl Scouts of the United States of America
language	English, Hebrew
holiday	Thanksgiving, Labor Day

 QUICK CHECK 1   **Classifying Nouns**

Identify the nouns in the following sentences. Classify each noun as *common* or *proper*. Also label any *compound* nouns.

1. Each day huge crowds of people visit the Lincoln Memorial in Washington, D.C.
2. The monument was designed by Henry Bacon and was dedicated on Memorial Day.
3. The Lincoln Memorial consists of a large marble hall that encloses a gigantic lifelike statue of Abraham Lincoln.
4. The figure, which was carved out of blocks of white marble, sits in a large armchair as if in deep meditation.
5. On the north wall is found a famous passage from an inaugural address by Lincoln, and the Gettysburg Address is inscribed on the south wall.

Concrete Nouns and Abstract Nouns

A *concrete noun* names a person, place, or thing that can be perceived by one or more of the senses (sight, hearing, taste, touch, or smell). An *abstract noun* names an idea, a feeling, a quality, or a characteristic.

CONCRETE NOUNS	hummingbird, telephone, teacher, popcorn, ocean, George Washington Bridge, Jesse Jackson, sneeze, stone, refrigerator, rain
ABSTRACT NOUNS	knowledge, patriotism, love, humor, beliefs, beauty, competition, Zen Buddhism, education, peace, honor, health

The Pronoun

1b. A *pronoun* is a word used in place of one noun or more than one noun.

EXAMPLES   When Kelly saw the signal, Kelly pointed the signal out to Enrique.
When Kelly saw the signal, **she** pointed **it** out to Enrique.

Lee and Pat went fishing. Lee caught three bass, and Pat caught three bass.
Lee and Pat went fishing. **Each** caught three bass.

The word that a pronoun stands for is called its *antecedent*. In the following examples, an arrow is drawn from each pronoun to its antecedent.

EXAMPLES   Elena read the **book** and returned **it** to the library.

The **photographers** bought **themselves** new lenses.

Catherine told **her** father **she** would be late.

"Do **you** know the answer?" Ms. Rios asked **Chen**.

Sometimes the antecedent of a pronoun is not stated.

EXAMPLES **Who** invented the telephone?

No one could solve the riddle.

I thought **you** said that **everybody** would help.

Personal Pronouns

A *personal pronoun* refers to the one speaking (*first person*), the one spoken to (*second person*), or the one spoken about (*third person*).

PERSONAL PRONOUNS		
	SINGULAR	**PLURAL**
First Person	I, me, my, mine	we, us, our, ours
Second Person	you, your, yours	you, your, yours
Third Person	he, him, his, she, her, hers, it, its	they, them, their, theirs

EXAMPLES During spring break, **I** visited **my** relatives. [first person]

Did **you** say this pen is **yours**? [second person]

The coach gathered the players around **her** and gave **them** a pep talk. [third person]

The seagull picked up the clam shell and dropped **it** with a crash onto the pavement. [third person]

NOTE Some authorities prefer to call possessive forms of pronouns (such as *my, his,* and *their*) adjectives. Follow your teacher's instructions regarding possessive forms.

Reflexive and Intensive Pronouns

A *reflexive pronoun* refers to the subject and directs the action of the verb back to the subject. An *intensive pronoun* emphasizes a noun or another pronoun. Notice that reflexive and intensive pronouns have the same form.

REFLEXIVE AND INTENSIVE PRONOUNS	
First Person	myself, ourselves
Second Person	yourself, yourselves
Third Person	himself, herself, itself, themselves

REFLEXIVE   Juan wrote **himself** a note as a reminder.
The rescuers did not consider **themselves** heroes.

INTENSIVE   Amelia designed the costumes **herself**.
I **myself** sold more than fifty tickets.

 NOTE   If you are not sure whether a pronoun is reflexive or intensive, use this test. Read the sentence aloud, omitting the pronoun. If the meaning of the sentence stays the same, the pronoun is intensive. If the meaning changes, the pronoun is reflexive.

EXAMPLES   Rachel painted the fence **herself**.
Rachel painted the fence. [Without *herself*, the meaning stays the same. The pronoun is intensive.]
They treated **themselves** to a picnic.
They treated to a picnic. [Without *themselves*, the sentence doesn't make sense. The pronoun is reflexive.]

Demonstrative Pronouns

A *demonstrative pronoun* points out a person, a place, a thing, or an idea.

Demonstrative Pronouns			
this	that	these	those

EXAMPLES   **This** is the most valuable baseball card I have.
These are the names of **those** who volunteered.

 REFERENCE NOTE: The words *this, that, these,* and *those* can also be used as adjectives. Used in this way, they are called *demonstrative adjectives.* See page 55.

GRAMMAR/USAGE

Interrogative Pronouns

An *interrogative pronoun* introduces a question.

		Interrogative Pronouns		
what	which	who	whom	whose

EXAMPLES   **What** is the largest planet in our solar system?
Who scored the most points in the game?

Relative Pronouns

A *relative pronoun* introduces a subordinate clause.

		Relative Pronouns			
that	what	which	who	whom	whose

EXAMPLES   The Bactrian camel, **which** has two humps, is native to central Asia.
Ray Charles is one of several blind performers **who** have had a number of hit recordings.

 REFERENCE NOTE: For more information about subordinate clauses, see pages 165–173.

Indefinite Pronouns

An *indefinite pronoun* refers to a person, a place, or a thing that is not specifically named.

Common Indefinite Pronouns				
all	both	few	nobody	several
another	each	many	none	some
any	either	more	no one	somebody
anybody	everybody	most	nothing	someone
anyone	everyone	much	one	something
anything	everything	neither	other	such

EXAMPLES   **Everyone** completed the test before the bell rang.
Neither of the actors knew what costume the
other was planning to wear.

Many indefinite pronouns can also serve as adjectives.

EXAMPLES   Look in **both** cabinets. [*Both* is an adjective modifying *cabinets*.]
Both contain winter clothing. [*Both* is an indefinite pronoun.]
Each player took **one** cap. [*Each* is an adjective modifying *player*; *one* is an adjective modifying *cap*.]
Each of the players took **one** of the caps. [*Each* and *one* are indefinite pronouns.]

 QUICK CHECK 2 **Identifying Pronouns**

Identify each of the pronouns in the following sentences as *personal, reflexive, intensive, demonstrative, interrogative, relative,* or *indefinite.*

1. Juana went to the mall by herself.
2. That is a Gokuyu mask.
3. Sometimes I don't feel well when it gets cloudy and the dark sky threatens rain.
4. Ms. Blankenship showed us the rare book that she had found at the flea market.
5. Who can tell me whose bicycle this is?

The Adjective

1c. An *adjective* is a word used to modify a noun or a pronoun.

To *modify* a word means to describe the word or to make its meaning more definite. An adjective modifies a word by telling *what kind, which one, how much,* or *how many.*

WHAT KIND?	WHICH ONE?	HOW MUCH? or HOW MANY?
tall woman	*another* one	*less* time
steep mountain	*this* year	*more* money
long hike	*last* answer	*many* mistakes
eager clerk	*those* people	*several* others
tired dog	*that* dress	*few* marbles
exciting story	*middle* row	*larger* share
sleepy child	*next* week	*four* horses

Articles

The most frequently used adjectives are *a, an,* and *the.* These adjectives are called **articles.**

The adjectives *a* and *an* are **indefinite articles.** Each one indicates that the noun refers to someone or something in general. *A* is used before a word beginning with a consonant sound. *An* is used before a word beginning with a vowel sound.

EXAMPLES   How is **a** gerbil different from **a** hamster?
An accident stalled traffic for **an** hour.
It was **an** honor to receive the award.

The adjective *the* is a **definite article.** It indicates that the noun refers to someone or something in particular.

EXAMPLE   **The** key would not open **the** lock.

An adjective may come before or after the word it modifies.

EXAMPLES   **Each one** of the students brought **used books** for the auction. [The adjective *each* modifies *one.* The adjective *used* modifies *books.*]
The **map,** although **old** and **worn,** was **useful** to the explorer. [The adjectives *old, worn,* and *useful* modify *map.*]

Proper Adjectives

A *proper adjective* is formed from a proper noun and be-gins with a capital letter.

PROPER NOUN	PROPER ADJECTIVE
Africa	**African** nations
China	**Chinese** calendar
Shakespeare	**Shakespearean** drama
Islam	**Islamic** law
Rio Grande	**Rio Grande** valley

NOTE Some proper nouns, such as *Rio Grande*, do not change spelling when they are used as adjectives.

REFERENCE NOTE: For more information about nouns used as adjectives, see below.

Demonstrative Adjectives

This, that, these, and *those* can be used both as adjectives and as pronouns. When they modify a noun or a pronoun, these words are called *demonstrative adjectives*. When they are used alone, they are called *demonstrative pronouns*.

DEMONSTRATIVE
ADJECTIVES
Is **this** outfit less expensive than **that** one?
Those revisions really improved your essay.

DEMONSTRATIVE
PRONOUNS
That is the color I want.
Are **these** the haiku that you wrote?

REFERENCE NOTE: For more information about demonstrative pronouns, see page 51.

Nouns Used as Adjectives

When a noun modifies another noun or a pronoun, it is considered an adjective.

GRAMMAR/USAGE

NOUNS	NOUNS USED AS ADJECTIVES
tuna	**tuna** salad
concert	**concert** tickets
soccer	**soccer** uniform
cooking	**cooking** school
Memorial Day	**Memorial Day** weekend
insurance	**insurance** company
water	**water** supply
cotton	**cotton** sweater
feather	**feather** pillow

 NOTE Most compound nouns, such as *Memorial Day*, can be used as adjectives.

 REFERENCE NOTE: For more information on words used as different parts of speech, see page 70.

Shoe, by Jeff MacNelly, reprinted by permission:
Tribune Media Services.

QUICK CHECK 3 **Identifying Adjectives**

Identify each adjective in the following sentences as a *common*, *proper*, or *demonstrative* adjective. Then give the word the adjective modifies. Do not include the articles *a, an,* and *the.*

1. My little sister, afraid of thunder and lightning, hid under the bed.
2. Give me some ice water, please.
3. This parakeet screeches if he doesn't get enough seed.
4. The German shepherd puppy is a lively rascal.
5. Each club decorated a float for the Cinco de Mayo parade.

The Verb

1d. A *verb* is a word used to express action or a state of being.

EXAMPLES   James Fenimore Cooper **wrote** *The Last of the Mohicans.*
Doug **seems** awfully happy today.

Every sentence must have a verb. The verb says something about the subject.

☞ REFERENCE NOTE: For more information about subjects and verbs, see pages 181–186.

Action Verbs

1e. An *action verb* may express physical action or mental action.

PHYSICAL   *jump, shout, search, carry, run*
ACTION   Langston Hughes **wrote** volumes of poetry.
A distinguished cinematographer, James Wong Howe, **filmed** the movie.

MENTAL   *worry, think, believe, imagine, remember*
ACTION   The scientist **studied** the ant colony.
         Mario **knew** the answer to every question on
         the test.

Transitive and Intransitive Verbs

(1) A *transitive verb* is an action verb that expresses an action directed toward a person or thing.

EXAMPLES   Joel **held** the baby. [The action of *held* is directed toward *baby*.]
           Loretta **brought** flowers. [The action of *brought* is directed toward *flowers*.]

With transitive verbs, the action passes from the doer—the subject—to the receiver of the action. Words that receive the action of a transitive verb are called *objects.*

EXAMPLES   Our scout troop made a **quilt**. [*Quilt* is the object of the verb *made*.]
           The voters elected **him**. [*Him* is the object of the verb *elected*.]

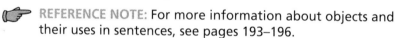 REFERENCE NOTE: For more information about objects and their uses in sentences, see pages 193–196.

(2) An *intransitive verb* expresses action (or tells something about the subject) without passing the action to a receiver.

EXAMPLES   Samuel Ramey **sang** beautifully in the opera *Don Giovanni*. [The action of *sang* is not directed toward a receiver.]
           The Evans twins **played** quietly indoors the whole afternoon. [The verb *played* does not have an object.]

A verb may be transitive in one sentence and intransitive in another.

EXAMPLES   Janet **swam** ten laps. [transitive]
           Janet **swam** well. [intransitive]

The teacher **read** a poem. [transitive]
The teacher **read** aloud. [intransitive]

Linking Verbs

1f. A *linking verb* links, or connects, the subject with a noun, a pronoun, or an adjective in the predicate.

EXAMPLES The star's name **is** Whoopi Goldberg. [name = Whoopi Goldberg]
Marie Curie **became** a famous scientist. [Marie Curie = scientist]
Tranh **is** one of the finalists. [Tranh = one]
Wild animals **remain** free on the great animal reserves in Africa. [free animals]
The watermelon **looks** ripe. [ripe watermelon]
After it rains, the earth **seems** clean and refreshed. [clean, refreshed earth]

LINKING VERBS		
Formed from the Verb *Be*		
am	be	being
are	been	is
has been	may be	was
have been	could be	were
will be	should be	should have been
was being	would be	will have been
Other Linking Verbs		
appear	look	sound
become	remain	stay
feel	seem	taste
grow	smell	turn

NOTE The verb *be* does not always link the subject with a noun, pronoun, or adjective in the predicate. *Be* can express a state of being without having a complement. In the sentences below, for example, forms of *be* are followed by words or word groups that tell *where*.

EXAMPLES   Geraldo **is** here.
Your roller skates **are** in the attic.

All the linking verbs except the forms of *be* and *seem* may also be used as action verbs. Whether a verb is used to link words or to express action depends on its meaning in a sentence.

LINKING   The tiger **looked** tame.
ACTION   The tiger **looked** for something to eat.

LINKING   The soup **tasted** good.
ACTION   I **tasted** the soup.

LINKING   She **grew** tired of playing.
ACTION   She **grew** into a fine woman.

 REFERENCE NOTE: For more information on the predicate, see pages 181–186. For more on complements used with linking verbs, or **subject complements**, see pages 196–199.

Helping Verbs

1g.   A *helping verb* (*auxiliary verb*) helps the main verb to express an action or a state of being.

EXAMPLES   **could** be
may have asked
might have been caught

A *verb phrase* consists of a main verb preceded by at least one helping verb.

The following sentences contain verb phrases.

Seiji Ozawa **will conduct** many outstanding orchestras. [The main verb is *conduct*.]
He **has been praised** for his fine conducting. [The main verb is *praised*.]
His recordings **should be heard** by anyone interested in classical music. [The main verb is *heard*.]
He **will be leading** the orchestra tonight. [The main verb is *leading*.]

COMMONLY USED HELPING VERBS				
Forms of *Be*	am are	be been	being is	was were
Forms of *Do*	do	does	did	
Forms of *Have*	have	has	had	
Other Helping Verbs	can could	may might	must shall	should will	would

Some helping verbs may also be used as main verbs.

EXAMPLES Did he **do** his homework?
She will **be** here soon.
We do not **have** enough time.

Sometimes the verb phrase is interrupted by another part of speech. In most cases, the interrupter is an adverb. In a question, however, the subject often interrupts the verb phrase.

EXAMPLES People **may** someday **communicate** freely with dolphins.
How much **do** you **know** about Lucy Stone, the suffragist?
Because of the fog, we **could** not [or couldn't] **see** the road.

Notice in the last example that the word *not* is not included in the verb phrase.

 REFERENCE NOTE: For more information about contractions, see page 297.

 QUICK CHECK 4 **Identifying Verbs**

Identify the italicized verb in each of the following sentences as an *action verb*, a *linking verb*, or a *helping verb*. Then, for each action verb, tell whether the verb is *transitive* or *intransitive*.

1. This rose *smells* lovely.
2. Pat *hit* a home run and tied the score.

3. School can *be* fun sometimes.
4. Brent *was* taking in the wash for his mother.
5. Ms. Kwan *assigned* us a fun homework project.

The Adverb

1h. An *adverb* is a word used to modify a verb, an adjective, or another adverb.

An adverb tells *where, when, how,* or *to what extent* (*how much* or *how long*).

WHERE?	WHEN?
The forest fire started **here**.	The police will arrive **soon**.
The couple was married **nearby**.	**Then** the suspects were questioned.
HOW?	**TO WHAT EXTENT?**
The accident occurred **suddenly**.	The tub is draining **rather** slowly.
The prime minister spoke **carefully**.	We need to make **extremely** careful calculations.

WORDS OFTEN USED AS ADVERBS					
Where?	here	there	away	up	outside
When?	now	then	later	soon	ago
How?	clearly	easily	quietly	slowly	
How often? *or* How long?	never frequently	always usually	often forever	seldom rarely	
To what extent? *or* How much?	very most	too nearly	almost quite	so less	really only

NOTE The word *not* is an adverb. When *not* is part of a contraction like *hadn't*, the *-n't* is an adverb.

The Position of Adverbs

Adverbs may appear at various places in a sentence. Adverbs may come before, after, or between the words they modify.

EXAMPLES   **Slowly**, the shark was circling the boat.
The shark was **slowly** circling the boat.
The shark was circling the boat **slowly**.

Adverbs Modifying Verbs

Adverbs may come before or after the verbs they modify.

EXAMPLES   **Slowly** the man crawled **down**. [The adverb *slowly* tells how the man crawled, and the adverb *down* tells where he crawled.]
I **seldom** see you **nowadays**. [The adverb *seldom* tells to what extent I see you, and the adverb *nowadays* tells when I see you.]

Adverbs may come between the parts of verb phrases.

EXAMPLES   Keisha has **already** completed her part of the project. [The adverb interrupts and modifies *has completed*.]
Many students did **not** understand all of the directions. [The adverb interrupts and modifies *did understand*.]

Adverbs are sometimes used to ask questions.

EXAMPLES   **Where** are you going?
How did you do on the test?

Adverbs Modifying Adjectives

EXAMPLES   An **unusually** fast starter, Karen won the race. [The adverb *unusually* modifies the adjective *fast*, telling *how fast* the starter was.]
Our committee is **especially** busy at this time of year. [The adverb *especially* modifies the adjective *busy*, telling *how busy* the committee is.]

Adverbs Modifying Other Adverbs

EXAMPLES   Elena finished the problem **more** quickly than I
did. [The adverb *more* modifies the adverb
quickly, telling *how quickly* Elena finished the
problem.]
Our guest left **quite** abruptly. [The adverb *quite*
modifies the adverb *abruptly*, telling *how
abruptly* our guest left.]

 NOTE   Many adverbs end in *-ly*: *quietly, briefly, calmly*. However,
some words that end in *-ly* are adjectives: *friendly, lonely,
timely*. If you're not sure whether a word is an adjective
or an adverb, ask yourself what it modifies. If a word
modifies a noun or a pronoun, it's an adjective. If a
word modifies a verb, an adjective, or an adverb, then
it's an adverb.

 REFERENCE NOTE: For more information about adjectives,
see pages 53–56. For more on modifiers in general, see
Chapter 5: Using Modifiers.

STYLE NOTE   The adverb *very* is overused. In your writing,
try to replace *very* with more descriptive ad-
verbs. Or revise the sentence so that other
words carry more of the descriptive meaning.

EXAMPLE   Vikram Seth's novel *A Suitable Boy* is very long.
REVISED   Vikram Seth's novel *A Suitable Boy* is **extremely**
long.

or

Vikram Seth's novel *A Suitable Boy* is **1,349
pages** long and **weighs four pounds.**

 QUICK CHECK 5   **Identifying Adverbs**

Identify the adverb(s) in each of the following sentences.
Then give the word or phrase each adverb modifies.

GRAMMAR/USAGE

1. Today we studied the contributions that ancient North Africans made to mathematics.
2. Neither Carlos nor Jan went very far into the water.
3. How did the other team win easily?
4. Clever replies never occur to me until the situation is long past.
5. Darlene says that these poems by Ogden Nash are quite funny.

The Preposition

1i. A *preposition* is a word used to show the relationship of a noun or a pronoun to another word.

Notice how a change in the preposition changes the relationship between *package* and *tree* in each of the following examples.

EXAMPLES   The package **under** the tree is mine.
The package **in** the tree is mine.
The package **near** the tree is mine.
The package **behind** the tree is mine.
The package **next to** the tree is mine.
The package **in front of** the tree is mine.

Prepositions that consist of more than one word, such as *in front of*, are called *compound prepositions.*

Commonly Used Prepositions			
aboard	along	at	besides
about	along with	because of	between
above	amid	before	beyond
according to	among	behind	but
across	around	below	(except)
after	aside from	beneath	by
against	as of	beside	down

(continued)

GRAMMAR/USAGE

during	instead of	out	under
except	into	out of	underneath
for	like	over	until
from	near	past	unto
in	next to	since	up
in addition to	of	through	upon
in front of	off	throughout	with
inside	on	to	within
in spite of	on account of	toward	without

The Prepositional Phrase

A preposition is always followed by a noun or a pronoun. This noun or pronoun following the preposition is called the ***object of the preposition***. All together, the preposition, its object, and the modifiers of the object are called a ***prepositional phrase***.

EXAMPLE   The wagon train slowly traveled **across the dusty prairie.** [The prepositional phrase consists of the preposition *across*, its object *prairie*, and two adjectives modifying the object—*the* and *dusty*.]

A preposition may have more than one object.

EXAMPLE   Mrs. Larson told us to look closely **at the poem's rhyme and rhythm**. [The prepositional phrase consists of the preposition *at*, its objects *rhyme* and *rhythm*, and the modifiers *the* and *poem's*.]

 REFERENCE NOTE: For more information about prepositional phrases, see pages 138–139 and 148–151.

 NOTE Be careful not to confuse a prepositional phrase that begins with *to* (*to town*, *to her club*) with a verb form that begins with *to* (*to run*, *to be seen*).

Adverb or Preposition?

Some words may be used as either prepositions or adverbs. To tell an adverb from a preposition, remember that a preposition is always followed by a noun or pronoun object.

ADVERB	The plane circled **above.**
PREPOSITION	The plane circled **above** the field. [Note the object of the preposition—*field*.]
ADVERB	Can you come **over** to my house?
PREPOSITION	We saw a bald eagle fly **over** the treetops. [Note the object of the preposition—*treetops*.]

 QUICK CHECK 6 **Identifying Prepositions**

Identify the preposition(s) in each of the following sentences. Then give the object of each preposition.

1. Lou's older sister was a cheerleader during her senior year.
2. There isn't enough granola for breakfast.
3. Ethan tried again in spite of his previous difficulty.
4. I had an argument with Tomás, and I haven't seen him since.
5. The moat in front of the castle is spanned by a drawbridge.

The Conjunction

1j. A **conjunction** is a word used to join words or groups of words.

(1) *Coordinating conjunctions* connect words or groups of words used in the same way.

Coordinating Conjunctions						
and	but	or	nor	for	so	yet

EXAMPLES Theo **or** Tyler [two nouns]
small **but** comfortable [two adjectives]

through a forest **and** across a river [two prepositional phrases]

The stars seem motionless, **but** they are actually moving rapidly through space. [two complete independent clauses]

 REFERENCE NOTE: Coordinating conjunctions that join independent clauses are almost always preceded by a comma. See page 264 for more about this use of the comma.

When *for* is used as a conjunction, it connects groups of words that are sentences, and it is always preceded by a comma. On all other occasions, *for* is used as a preposition.

CONJUNCTION We wrote to the tourist bureau, **for** we wanted information on places to visit.

PREPOSITION We waited patiently **for** a reply.

STYLE NOTE
The conjunction *so* is often overused. Whenever possible, reword a sentence to avoid using *so*.

EXAMPLE You are new, so you'll probably get lost.
REVISED **Because** you are new, you'll probably get lost.

(2) *Correlative conjunctions* are pairs of conjunctions that connect words or groups of words used in the same way.

Correlative Conjunctions		
both. . .and	neither. . .nor	whether. . .or
either. . .or	not only. . .but also	

EXAMPLES **Both** horses **and** cattle were introduced to North America by the Spanish. [two nouns]
The student council will meet **not only** on Tuesday **but also** on Thursday this week. [two prepositional phrases]

Either leave a message on my answering machine, **or** call me after 7:00 P.M. [two complete ideas]

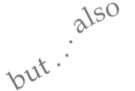

Peanuts reprinted by permission of UFS, Inc.

The Interjection

1k. An *interjection* is a word used to express emotion. It does not have a grammatical relation to other words in the sentence. Usually an interjection is followed by an exclamation point. Sometimes an interjection is set off by a comma.

EXAMPLES   **Oh!** You surprised me.
          Wow! Am I tired!
          Well, I did my best.

Common Interjections			
aha	goodness	ow	whew
alas	hey	ouch	wow
aw	hooray	shucks	yikes
golly	oops	well	yippee

 *QUICK CHECK 7*   **Identifying Conjunctions and Interjections**

Identify the *conjunctions* and *interjections* in the following sentences.

1. Oh, I didn't know he had already volunteered for the bake sale.
2. The car swerved suddenly, yet the driver remained in control.
3. Both the dog and the cat are dirty and need baths.
4. The Chinese vegetables with rice tasted especially good, for we were very hungry.
5. Whoops! I dropped my ring under the counter.

Determining Parts of Speech

The part of speech of a word is determined by the way the word is used in a sentence. Many words can be used as more than one part of speech.

EXAMPLES   **Each** cost three dollars. [pronoun]
Each student baked a cake. [adjective]

A member of the crew has spotted **land**. [noun]
The pilot can **land** here safely. [verb]

The **well** has gone dry. [noun]
Well, he seems to have recovered. [interjection]
He doesn't look **well** to me. [adjective]

These pillows are stuffed with goose **down**. [noun]
Have you ever slept under a **down** comforter? [adjective]

The tired shoppers sat **down** for a while. [adverb]
The ball rolled **down** the hill. [preposition]

 QUICK CHECK 8   **Identifying Parts of Speech**

Identify the part of speech of the italicized word in each sentence.

1a. The English test was easy *for* him.
  b. He didn't go to the movies, *for* he wanted to practice on the drums.

2a. It was a steep *climb*, but we made it to the top of the hill.

b. Kimiko and I *climb* the stairs for exercise.

3a. *Some* volunteered to sell tickets.

b. We donated *some* clothes and old furniture to the rummage sale.

4a. Looking for shells, the girl strolled *along* the shore.

b. When we went sailing, Raul and his brother Manuel came *along*.

5a. I lost *my* book report!

b. *My!* This is not a good day!

✓ *Chapter Review 1*

A. Identifying Nouns, Pronouns, and Adjectives

Identify each numbered, italicized word or word group in the following paragraph as a *noun*, a *pronoun*, or an *adjective*.

EXAMPLES   The [1] *president* has a [2] *private* airplane
known as Air Force One.
1. president—noun
2. private—adjective

[1] *American* presidents have used many different types of transportation. President Thomas Jefferson's way of getting to his first inauguration was [2] *simple*. [3] *He* walked there and then walked home after taking the [4] *oath* of office. President Zachary Taylor rode the [5] *same* horse throughout the [6] *Mexican War* and later during his term of office. James Monroe had the [7] *honor* of being the first president to ride aboard a steamship. In 1899, William McKinley became the [8] *first* president to ride in an automobile. President Theodore Roosevelt, [9] *whose* love of adventure is famous, rode in a submarine in 1905. Probably [10] *nobody* was surprised when the president himself took over the controls.

B. Identifying Different Parts of Speech

Identify each italicized word or word group in the following paragraph as a *verb*, an *adverb*, a *preposition*, or a *conjunction*. [Note: Keep in mind that correlative conjunctions and some prepositions have more than one word.]

EXAMPLE   [1] You likely know that Christopher Columbus
was a famous explorer, *but* do you know anything *about* his personal life?
   1. *but—conjunction; about—preposition*

[11] I've *learned* some interesting facts *about* Christopher Columbus. [12] He was born *into* a hard-working Italian family and *learned* how to sail as a boy. [13] He became *not only* a master sailor *but also* a mapmaker. [14] Although he had *barely* any formal education, he did *study* both Portuguese and Spanish. [15] The writings *of* ancient scholars about astronomy and geography *especially* interested him. [16] Columbus *apparently had* keen powers of observation. [17] These *served* him *well* on his expeditions. [18] On his voyages to find a sea route *to* the East Indies, Columbus *was* a determined, optimistic leader. [19] He let *neither* doubters *nor* hardships interfere *with* his plans. [20] Columbus was married *twice and* had two sons, Diego and Ferdinand.

 Chapter Review 2

Writing Sentences Using Different Parts of Speech

Write two sentences using each of the following words as the parts of speech given in parentheses. Underline the word in the sentence, and write its part of speech after the sentence.

EXAMPLE   **1.** over (adverb and preposition)
   1. *The skies began to clear when the storm was*
   <u>over</u>. (adverb)
   The horse jumped <u>over</u> the fence. (preposition)

1. but (conjunction and preposition)
2. like (verb and preposition)
3. run (noun and verb)
4. well (adverb and interjection)
5. that (pronoun and adjective)
6. more (adjective and adverb)
7. last (verb and adjective)
8. past (noun and preposition)
9. near (verb and preposition)
10. around (preposition and adverb)

SUMMARY OF PARTS OF SPEECH

Rule	Part of Speech	Use	Examples
1a	noun	names a person, a place, a thing, or an idea	Despite her **fear** of the **dark, Maya** enjoyed her **trip** through **Mammoth Cave.**
1b	pronoun	takes the place of a noun	**I myself** do not know **anyone who** saw **it.**
1c	adjective	modifies a noun or a pronoun	**The last stand-up** comedian, **talented** and **confident,** was **hilarious.**
1d	verb	shows action or a state of being	If we **had arrived** earlier, we **would have seen** many celebrities. We **were** upset. No one **was** there.
1h	adverb	modifies a verb, an adjective, or another adverb	I did **not** answer the last question **correctly.** It was **much more** difficult than the other questions.

(continued)

SUMMARY OF PARTS OF SPEECH *(continued)*

1i	preposition	relates a noun or a pronoun to another word	**Because of** the storm the bridge **across** the bay was closed.
1j	conjunction	joins words or groups of words	Teachers **and** students will perform in the talent show. **Either** the principal **or** I will emcee the show.
1k	interjection	expresses emotion	**Ouch!** That hurts! **Aw,** that's just great.

2 AGREEMENT

Subject and Verb, Pronoun and Antecedent

✓ Checking What You Know

A. Identifying Verbs That Agree with Their Subjects

In each of the following sentences, if the italicized verb agrees with its subject, write C. If the italicized verb does not agree with its subject, write the correct form of the verb.

EXAMPLES
1. The answers to that question *don't* make sense.
1. C

2. Ms. Suarez, our gym teacher, *don't* know what happened.
2. *doesn't*

1. When *is* Bill's parents coming to pick us up?
2. I can guess what <u>James and the Giant Peach</u> *are* about.
3. Neither of the bar mitzvahs *have* been scheduled for next month.

4. Twenty-five dollars *are* more than I am able to spend on concert tickets.
5. My baseball bat and my catcher's mitt *was* back in my room.
6. Neither Ésteban nor Tina *have* tried out yet for the school play.
7. All of our guests *have* been to Fort Worth's Japanese Garden.
8. *Don't* the team captain plan to put her into the game before it's over?
9. The team *are* trying on their uniforms.
10. The Bill of Rights *give* American citizens the right to worship as they please.

B. Identifying Pronouns That Agree with Their Antecedents

In each of the following sentences, if the italicized pronoun agrees with its antecedent, write C. If the italicized pronoun does not agree with its antecedent, write the correct form of the pronoun.

EXAMPLES **1.** One of the does was accompanied by *her* fawn.
1. C

2. Each of the boys brought *their* permission slip.
2. *his*

11. Have all of the winners taken *their* science fair projects home?
12. My older sister is studying physics, and I can't wait to learn about *them,* too.
13. Many of the buildings had green ribbons on *its* windows for the Saint Patrick's Day Parade.
14. Neither Stephanie nor Marilyn had worn *their* gym suit to class.
15. If you really need ten dollars, ask Mom for *them.*

16. Someone in the scout troop camped near poison ivy and has gotten it all over *themselves.*
17. Only a few of the carpenters had brought tools with *them* to the job.
18. *Their* successes in World War II allowed the United States to claim the role of world power.
19. According to the teacher, both of those titles should have lines drawn underneath *it.*
20. That Ray Charles song is familiar, but I can't remember *its* title. ✓

Number

Number is the form of a word that indicates whether the word is singular or plural.

2a. When a word refers to one person, place, thing, or idea, it is *singular* in number. When a word refers to more than one, it is *plural* in number.

SINGULAR	book	woman	fox	I	he	each
PLURAL	books	women	foxes	we	they	all

 REFERENCE NOTE: For information on forming plurals, see pages 316–319.

Agreement of Subject and Verb

2b. A verb agrees with its subject in number.

A subject and verb *agree* when they have the same number.

(1) Singular subjects take singular verbs.

EXAMPLES   The **car comes** to a sudden stop. [The singular verb *comes* agrees with the singular subject *car.*]

GRAMMAR/USAGE

On that route the **plane flies** at a low altitude. [The singular verb *flies* agrees with the singular subject *plane*.]

(2) Plural subjects take plural verbs.

EXAMPLES   Many **senators oppose** the new tax bill. [The plural verb *oppose* agrees with the plural subject *senators*.]

Again and again, the **dolphins leap** playfully. [The plural verb *leap* agrees with the plural subject *dolphins*.]

NOTE   Generally, nouns ending in *s* are plural (*candles, ideas, neighbors, horses*), and verbs ending in *s* are singular (*sees, writes, speaks, carries*). However, verbs used with the singular pronouns *I* and *you* do not end in *s*.

EXAMPLES   **Jeremy** walk**s** to school.
Do **you** walk to school?

The first auxiliary (helping) verb in a verb phrase must agree with its subject.

EXAMPLES   **He is** building a bird feeder.
They are building a bird feeder.

Does anyone know the answer?
Do any **students** know the answer?

Shoe, by Jeff MacNelly, reprinted by permission: Tribune Media Services.

GRAMMAR/USAGE

☑ *QUICK CHECK 1*   **Identifying Verbs That Agree in Number with Their Subjects**

For each of the following sentences, choose the correct form of the verb in parentheses.

1. The rapper KRS-One (*is, are*) one of my favorite performers.
2. In fact, I (*has, have*) a picture of him hanging in my room and in my locker.
3. In the picture, KRS's face (*reflects, reflect*) his positive attitude.
4. KRS (*encourages, encourage*) people to think for themselves.
5. Many performers (*believes, believe*) in using rap music to improve people's lives and to end violence.

Problems in Agreement

Prepositional Phrases Between Subjects and Verbs

2c. The number of a subject is not changed by a prepositional phrase following the subject.

NONSTANDARD	The lights on the Christmas tree creates a festive atmosphere.
STANDARD	The **lights** on the Christmas tree **create** a festive atmosphere.
NONSTANDARD	The distance between the two posts for the clothesline are eight feet.
STANDARD	The **distance** between the two posts for the clothesline **is** eight feet.
EXCEPTION	In the case of the indefinite pronouns *all, any, most, none,* and *some,* that can be either singular or plural, the number of a subject *is* decided by a prepositional phrase following the subject.

EXAMPLES   **Most** of the **students have** read *Old Yeller*. [*Most* refers to the plural word *students*. Therefore, *most* is plural and agrees with the plural helping verb *have*.]
Most of Dylan's **report is** finished. [*Most* refers to the singular word *report*. Therefore, *most* is singular and agrees with the singular verb *is*.]

 REFERENCE NOTE: For more about indefinite pronouns that may be either singular or plural, see page 81.

Indefinite Pronouns

Some pronouns do not refer to a definite person, place, thing, or idea and are therefore called *indefinite* pronouns.

2d. The following indefinite pronouns are singular: *anybody, anyone, each, either, everybody, everyone, neither, nobody, no one, one, somebody, someone.*

Pronouns like *each* and *one* are frequently followed by prepositional phrases. Remember that the verb agrees with the subject of the sentence, not with a word in a prepositional phrase.

EXAMPLES   **Everyone was invited** to the celebration.
Either of the answers **is** correct.
One of the tapes **belongs** to Sabrena.
Someone high up in the bleachers **has been waving** at us.

2e. The following indefinite pronouns are plural: *both, few, many, several.*

EXAMPLES   **Both** of the apples **are** good.
Few of the guests **know** about the surprise.
Many of the students **walk** to school.
Several of the club members **have** not **paid** their dues.

GRAMMAR/USAGE

2f. The following indefinite pronouns may be either singular or plural: *all, any, most, none, some.*

The number of the indefinite pronoun *all, any, most, none* or *some* is determined by the number of a word in the prepositional phrase that follows—the word that the pronoun refers to. Indefinite pronouns that refer to singular words take singular verbs. Indefinite pronouns that refer to plural words take plural verbs.

EXAMPLES **All** of the watermelon **has been eaten.** [*All* refers to the singular object *watermelon.*]

All of the pears **look** ripe. [*All* refers to the plural object *pears.*]

Some of the equipment **has been stored** in the garage. [*Some* refers to the singular object *equipment.*]

Some of the supplies **have been stored** in the garage. [*Some* refers to the plural object *supplies.*]

 QUICK CHECK 2   **Identifying Verbs That Agree with Their Subjects**

Identify the subject in each of the following sentences. Choose the form of the verb in parentheses that agrees with the subject.

1. Outside, the chorus of crickets (*chirps, chirp*) loudly enough to keep me awake.
2. Several of Teresa's haiku (*is, are*) being published in a magazine of student writing.
3. (*Does, Do*) either of those poems use personification?
4. Most of the contestants (*looks, look*) nervous.
5. The price of these jeans (*is, are*) too high.

COMPUTER NOTE   Using indefinite pronouns correctly can be tricky. To help yourself, you may want to create an indefinite pronoun guide. First, summarize the information in rules 2d–2f and 2p–2s. Then choose several examples to illustrate the rules. If you use a computer, you can create a "Help" file in which to store this information. Call up your "Help" file whenever you run into difficulty with indefinite pronouns in your writing. If you don't use a computer, keep a writing notebook.

Compound Subjects

2g. Subjects joined by *and* usually take a plural verb.

The following compound subjects joined by *and* name more than one person or thing and take plural verbs.

EXAMPLES   **Antonia Brico** and **Sarah Caldwell are** famous conductors. [Two persons are conductors.]
Last year a **library** and a **museum were built** in our town. [Two things were built.]

A compound subject that names only one person or thing takes a singular verb.

EXAMPLES   The **captain** and **quarterback** of the team **is** Lyle. [One person is both the captain and the quarterback.]
Chicken and dumplings is a favorite Southern dish. [Chicken and dumplings is one dish.]

2h. When subjects are joined by *or* or *nor*, the verb agrees with the subject nearer the verb.

This rule applies when both subjects are singular or plural.

EXAMPLES   Neither **Miami** nor **Jacksonville is** the capital of Florida. [The verb *is* agrees with the singular subject *Jacksonville*.]
These **pens** or those **pencils are** on sale. [The verb *are* agrees with the plural subject *pencils*.]

The rule also applies when one subject is singular and the other is plural.

GRAMMAR/USAGE

EXAMPLES   Neither the **director** nor the **players were** on time for rehearsal. [The verb agrees with the nearer subject, *players*.]
Neither the **players** nor the **director was** on time for rehearsal. [The verb agrees with the nearer subject, *director*.]

Whenever possible, avoid this kind of construction by revising the sentence. For instance, the second example above could be revised in the following way.

Both the players and the director were late for rehearsal.

QUICK CHECK 3   **Choosing Verbs That Agree in Number with Compound Subjects**

Choose the form of the verb in parentheses that agrees with the compound subject in each of the following sentences.

1. Either Sylvia or her brothers (*washes, wash*) the kitchen floor each Saturday morning.
2. This whole-wheat bread and this oat cereal (*contains, contain*) no preservatives or dyes.
3. Either the students or the teacher (*reads, read*) aloud during the last ten minutes of each class period.
4. The heavy rain clouds and the powerful winds (*indicates, indicate*) that a hurricane is approaching.
5. Neither the seal nor the clowns (*catches, catch*) the ball that the monkey throws into the circus ring.

Other Problems in Subject-Verb Agreement

2i. Collective nouns may be either singular or plural.

A *collective noun* is singular in form but names a group of persons, animals, or things.

Common Collective Nouns			
army	club	fleet	public
assembly	committee	flock	swarm
audience	crowd	group	team
class	family	herd	troop

A collective noun takes a singular verb when the noun refers to the group as a unit. A collective noun takes a plural verb when the noun refers to the individual parts or members of the group.

EXAMPLES   The science **class is taking** a field trip to the planetarium. [The class as a unit is taking a field trip.]

Today, the science **class are working** on their astronomy projects. [The members of the class are working on various projects.]

The **family has moved** to Little Rock, Arkansas. [The family as a unit has moved.]

The **family have been** unable to agree on where to spend their next vacation. [The members of the family have different opinions.]

2j.   A verb agrees with its subject, not with its predicate nominative.

              S   V   PN

EXAMPLES   The best **time** to visit **is** weekday mornings.

              S   V   PN

Weekday **mornings are** the best time to visit.

2k.   When the subject follows the verb, find the subject and make sure the verb agrees with it. The subject usually follows the verb in sentences beginning with *here* or *there* and in questions.

EXAMPLES   Here **is** my **seat.**
Here **are** our **seats.**

GRAMMAR/USAGE

There **is** an exciting **ride** at the fair.
There **are** exciting **rides** at the fair.

Where **is** the **bread?**
Where **are** the **loaves** of bread?

Does he know them?
Do they know him?

NOTE When the subject of a sentence follows the verb, the word order is said to be *inverted.* To find the subject of a sentence with inverted order, restate the sentence in normal word order.

INVERTED   There **go** our **chances** of winning the pennant.
NORMAL   Our **chances** of winning the pennant **go** there.

INVERTED   **Does P. D. James write** only detective stories?
NORMAL   **P. D. James does write** only detective stories.

INVERTED   Into the clearing **stepped** a tiny **fawn.**
NORMAL   A tiny **fawn stepped** into the clearing.

The contractions *here's, there's,* and *where's* contain the verb *is* and should be used with only singular subjects.

NONSTANDARD   There's the books.
STANDARD   There **are** the **books.**
STANDARD   There's the **book.**

REFERENCE NOTE: For more information about contractions, see page 297.

21. The contractions *don't* and *doesn't* must agree with their subjects.

Use *don't* with plural subjects and with the pronouns *I* and *you.*

EXAMPLES   These **gloves don't** fit.
          I don't like that song.
          You don't have enough money to buy that.

Use *doesn't* with other singular subjects.

EXAMPLES   The **music box doesn't** play.
          She doesn't like cold weather.
          It doesn't matter.

QUICK CHECK 4 **Choosing Verbs That Agree with Their Subjects**

Identify the subject in each of the following sentences. Choose the form of the verb in parentheses that agrees with the subject.

1. When (*was, were*) the Joneses planning on having their barbecue?
2. Our birthday present to Manuel (*is, are*) tickets to see Los Lobos in concert.
3. You (*doesn't, don't*) have to knock; just come on in.
4. Here (*comes, come*) the Astros' new power hitter.
5. Why (*is, are*) the jury taking so long to reach its decision?

2m. Words stating amounts are usually singular.

A word or phrase stating a weight, a measurement, or an amount of money or time is usually considered one item. Such a word or phrase takes a singular verb.

EXAMPLES   Three **ounces** of cooked lean meat **equals** one serving.
Three hundred **feet is** the length of a football field from goal line to goal line.
I'm afraid that two **dollars is** not enough to buy this poster.
Five **hours was** the amount of time we allowed for sanding and weatherproofing the deck.

2n. The title of a book or the name of an organization or country, even when plural in form, usually takes a singular verb.

EXAMPLES   ***Gulliver's Travels* remains** one of the greatest English-language satires. [one book]
Gamblers Anonymous is a support group for people who want to stop gambling. [one organization]

The **United States has been called** both a "melting pot" and a "tossed salad." [one country]

2o. A few nouns, though plural in form, are singular and take singular verbs.

EXAMPLES   The **news comes** on at 10:00 P.M.
Measles resembles chicken pox; both diseases cause red spots on the skin.
Mathematics is my best subject.

NOTE   Some nouns that end in *-s* and name a *pair* (such as *pants*) take a plural verb even though they refer to a singular item.

EXAMPLES   These **trousers need** to be hemmed.
The **scissors are** in that drawer.
Are the **pliers** in the garage?

✔ *QUICK CHECK 5*   **Choosing Verbs That Agree with Their Subjects**

In the following sentences, choose the form of the verb in parentheses that agrees with the subject.

1. *World Tales* (*is, are*) a collection of folk tales from around the world.
2. Dad said that shingles (*is, are*) the most painful disease he's ever had.
3. Two days (*is, are*) not enough time to rehearse for the play.
4. (*Has, Have*) these sneakers been on sale recently?
5. The National Association for Female Executives (*is, are*) meeting in Dallas.

Agreement of Pronoun and Antecedent

A pronoun usually refers to a noun or another pronoun that comes before it, called its *antecedent.* Whenever you

GRAMMAR/USAGE

use a pronoun, make sure that it agrees in number and gender with its antecedent.

 REFERENCE NOTE: For more information about antecedents, see pages 49–50.

2p. A pronoun agrees with its antecedent in number and gender.

Some singular personal pronouns have forms that indicate gender. Masculine pronouns refer to males. Feminine pronouns refer to females. Neuter pronouns refer to things (neither male nor female) and sometimes to animals.

FEMININE	she	her	hers
MASCULINE	he	him	his
NEUTER	it	it	its

EXAMPLES Bryan packed a **lunch** and put **it** in the fridge.
Dawn read the math **problem,** and then **she** answered **it.**

The antecedent of a personal pronoun can be another kind of pronoun, such as *each, neither,* or *one.* To determine the gender of a personal pronoun that refers to one of these other pronouns, look in the phrase that follows the antecedent.

EXAMPLES **Each** of the **men** put on **his** hard hat.
Neither of those **women** got what **she** ordered from the catalog.

Some antecedents may be either masculine or feminine. When referring to such antecedents, use both the masculine and the feminine forms.

EXAMPLES **No one** on the committee gave **his or her** approval.
Everybody in the class wanted to know **his or her** grade.

STYLE NOTE   Sometimes, using *his or her* to refer to an indefinite pronoun is awkward or confusing. In conversation, people often use a plural personal pronoun. This form is becoming more common in writing, too.

AWKWARD   When the singer walked out onto the stage, everyone clapped his or her hands.

CLEAR   When the singer walked out onto the stage, **everyone** clapped **their** hands.

In formal writing, however, it is always best to follow the current rules of usage. To avoid the awkward use of *his or her* in formal writing, try to rephrase the sentence by using a plural pronoun and antecedent.

EXAMPLES   **Everyone** in the club paid **his or her** dues.
All of the club members paid **their** dues.

Each of the mechanics uses **his or her** own tools.
The **mechanics** use **their** own tools.

Problems in Agreement

Indefinite Pronouns

2q.   A singular pronoun is used to refer to *anybody, anyone, each, either, everybody, everyone, neither, nobody, no one, one, someone, somebody.*

EXAMPLES   **Everybody** will have an opportunity to express **his or her** opinion.
Each of the birds built **its** own nest in the sycamore tree.
One of the girls brought **her** guitar.

2r.   A plural pronoun is used to refer to *both, few, many, several.*

EXAMPLES   **Both** of those novels by Roald Dahl are on **their** shelf in the library.

Many of the apples are bruised, but **they** will be just fine for making apple sauce.

2s. Either a singular or a plural pronoun may be used to refer to *all, any, most, none, some.*

The number of the pronoun *all, any, most,* or *some* is determined by the number of a word in the prepositional phrase that follows—the word that the pronoun refers to.

EXAMPLES   **Some** of the paint spilled on my jeans; **it** made quite a mess. [*Some* refers to the singular noun *paint.*]

Some of the children are ready for **their** naps. [*Some* refers to the plural noun *children.*]

All of Janine's older sisters work at **their** parents' grocery store. [*All* refers to the plural noun *sisters.*]

All of the produce is at **its** best early on Monday mornings. [*All* refers to the singular noun *produce.*]

Compound Antecedents

2t. A plural pronoun is used to refer to two or more antecedents joined by *and.*

EXAMPLES   My **mother and father** send **their** regards.
My **dogs and cat** never share **their** food.

2u. A singular pronoun is used to refer to two or more singular antecedents joined by *or* or *nor.*

EXAMPLES   **Julio or Van** will bring **his** football.
Neither **the mother nor the daughter** had forgotten **her** umbrella.

Sentences with singular antecedents joined by *or* or *nor* can sound awkward if the antecedents are of different genders. If the sentence sounds awkward, revise it to avoid the problem.

AWKWARD   Either Lorraine or Tony will read her or his poem.

REVISED   Either **Lorraine** will read **her** poem, or **Tony** will read **his.**

 NOTE A singular and a plural antecedent joined by *or* or *nor* can create an awkward or a confusing sentence. Revise such a sentence to avoid the problem.

AWKWARD   Either Mr. Reyes or the Wilsons promised to bring their volleyball net.

REVISED   Either **Mr. Reyes** promised to bring **his** volleyball net, or the **Wilsons** promised to bring **theirs.**

 QUICK CHECK 6   **Identifying Antecedents and Supplying Pronouns That Agree with Them**

For each blank in the following sentences, give a pronoun that will complete the meaning of the sentence. Then identify the antecedent or antecedents of that pronoun.

1. Iowa, Kansas, and Nebraska got _____ names from Native American words.
2. Two of the workers forgot to turn in _____ time card.
3. Each of the kittens played with the yarn that we gave _____.
4. The principal congratulated Lisa and Rick and gave _____ a prize for _____ science project.
5. Neither Larry nor Carlos got the grade that _____ expected.

Other Problems in Pronoun-Antecedent Agreement

2v. Either a singular or a plural pronoun may be used with a collective noun.

EXAMPLES   The **committee** has prepared **its** recommendation. [The committee as a unit has prepared the recommendation.]
The **committee** are sharing **their** ideas for the re-cycling campaign. [The members of the committee have various ideas.]

The **flock** is flying to **its** winter home in Central America. [The flock as a unit is flying to its collective home.]
The **flock** are returning to **their** nests. [The birds are returning to their individual nests.]

 REFERENCE NOTE: For a list of collective nouns, see page 84.

2w. The title of a book or the name of an organization or a country, even when plural in form, usually takes a singular pronoun.

EXAMPLES   Mrs. Chen asked whether any of us had read ***Great Expectations.*** **It** was on our summer reading list.
The **United Nations** has **its** headquarters in New York City.
When my aunt got back from the **Philippines**, I asked her what **it** was like.

2x. A few nouns, though plural in form, are singular and take singular pronouns.

EXAMPLES   **Home economics** is not only a lot of fun, but **it** is a very practical course.
Have you ever had the **mumps? Its** symptoms include fever and swelling of the glands in the neck.

2y. Words stating amounts usually take singular pronouns.

EXAMPLES   I know I had five **dollars** yesterday. Maybe I left **it** in my jeans.

GRAMMAR/USAGE

Five **feet** was the height of Brenda's last jump. **It's** her new personal best in the high jump.

 REFERENCE NOTE: For more information on the correct usage and spelling of the pronouns *its, their,* and *your,* see pages 21, 37, and 41.

 ☑ *QUICK CHECK 7* **Choosing Pronouns That Agree with Their Antecedents**

For each blank in the following sentences, give a pronoun that will complete the meaning of the sentence.

1. This litter of pups have white muzzles just like _____ father's.
2. Dana enjoyed the novel *The Outsiders* because _____ had such interesting characters.
3. Whenever Tony has an extra fifty cents, he puts _____ in a jar on his dresser.
4. Even though I've read a lot about politics, _____ still confuses me sometimes.
5. When the high school band marches, _____ looks like a long line of red ants.

✓ *Chapter Review*

A. Identifying Verbs That Agree with Their Subjects

In each of the following sentences, if the italicized verb agrees with its subject, write C. If the italicized verb does not agree with its subject, write the correct form of the verb.

EXAMPLES **1.** The people on the bus *have* all been seated.
        1. C

        2. The fish, bass mostly, *has* started feeding.
        2. *have*

1. The swarm of bees *have* deserted its hive.
2. My spelling lessons and science homework sometimes *takes* me hours to finish.
3. Somebody *don't* approve of the new rule.
4. Neither Danny Glover nor Morgan Freeman *stars* in tonight's movie.
5. The mice or the cat *have* eaten the cheese.
6. There *is* probably a few children who don't like pears.
7. Most of the guests *likes* the inn's Irish soda bread.
8. Civics *deals* with the rights and duties of citizens.
9. Evenings *is* the best time to visit her.
10. *Do* Ms. Ellis or Mrs. Riggs work for the mayor?

B. Identifying Pronouns That Agree with Their Antecedents

In each of the following sentences, if the italicized pronoun agrees with its antecedent, write *C*. If the italicized pronoun does not agree with its antecedent, write the correct form of the pronoun.

EXAMPLES **1.** Either of the men could have offered *their* help.
        1. *his*

        2. Both of the flowers had spread *their* petals.
        2. *C*

11. Why doesn't somebody raise *their* hand?
12. One of the birds lost most of *their* tail feathers.
13. The Philippines gained *its* independence from the United States in 1946.
14. Twenty-five cents doesn't buy what *they* used to.
15. The Smithsonian's National Museum of the American Indian had closed *their* doors for the day.
16. Chameleons sitting on a green leaf change *their* color.
17. Dr. Loco is a Mexican American performer and anthropologist who wants his audiences to feel proud of *its* heritage.

18. None of the children remembered to bring *his or her* permission slips.

19. Stan or Ethan will bring *their* guitar.

20. Álvar Núñez Cabeza de Vaca and Junípero Serra suffered great hardships in *his* explorations of the Americas.

3 USING VERBS

Principal Parts, Regular and Irregular Verbs, Verb Tense

 **Checking What You Know**

A. Using the Past and Past Participle Forms of Verbs

For each of the following sentences, give the correct past or past participle form of the verb in parentheses.

EXAMPLE   **1.** We didn't know why it (*take*) them so long.
          1. *took*

1. The cat (*lie*) down in front of the warm fire.
2. Since the storm began, the river has (*rise*) four feet.
3. Did you see which way they (*go*)?
4. I have (*write*) for tickets to the Alvin Ailey Dance Theater's next performance.
5. Two runners on our track team have (*break*) the school record for the mile run.
6. When the manager unlocked the door, a mob of shoppers (*burst*) into the store to take advantage of the sale.
7. Halima (*sing*) with her brother's band last night.
8. The witness said that she (*see*) the blue truck run through the red traffic light.

9. Look in the oven to see if the cake has (*rise*) yet.
10. Everyone should be in class after the bell has (*ring*).
11. Sitting Bull (*name*) his son Crowfoot.
12. Jeanette carefully (*lay*) her coat across the back of the chair.
13. By late December our pond has usually (*freeze*) hard enough to skate on.
14. Several of us (*choose*) to visit the Amish community in Pennsylvania.
15. So far, Dena has (*swim*) fifteen laps around the pool.

B. Making Tenses of Verbs Consistent

For each of the following sentences, write the italicized verb in the consistent tense.

EXAMPLE   **1.** He looked out the window and *sees* the storm approaching.
  1. *saw*

16. Jan was late, so she *decides* to run the rest of the way.
17. The man at the gate *takes* our tickets and said that we were just in time.
18. My uncle often travels in the Far East and *brought* me fascinating souvenirs.
19. After Sarah told me about the book of Yiddish folk sayings, I *buy* a copy.
20. The waitress brought my order and *asks* me if I wanted anything else.   ✓

The Principal Parts of a Verb

The four basic forms of a verb are called the *principal parts* of the verb.

3a. The principal parts of a verb are the *base form,* the *present participle,* the *past,* and the *past participle.*

Here are the principal parts of two familiar verbs.

BASE FORM	PRESENT PARTICIPLE	PAST	PAST PARTICIPLE
work	(is) working	worked	(have) worked
sing	(is) singing	sang	(have) sung

Notice that the present participle and the past participle require helping verbs (forms of *be* and *have*).

The principal parts of a verb are used to express the time that an action occurs.

PRESENT TIME	I **sing** in the school chorus.
	We **are singing** at the music festival tonight.
PAST TIME	Mahalia Jackson **sang** gospel songs at Carnegie Hall.
	We **have sung** all over the state.
FUTURE TIME	The school chorus **will sing** in the regional competition.
	By 8:00 P.M. we **will have sung** two madrigals and three spirituals.

© 1992 by Sidney Harris

☞ REFERENCE NOTE: For information about how participles are used as modifiers, see pages 152–154.

Regular Verbs

3b. A *regular* verb forms its past and past participle by adding *-d* or *-ed* to the base form.

BASE FORM	PRESENT PARTICIPLE	PAST	PAST PARTICIPLE
use	(is) using	used	(have) used
suppose	(is) supposing	supposed	(have) supposed
happen	(is) happening	happened	(have) happened
attack	(is) attacking	attacked	(have) attacked
drown	(is) drowning	drowned	(have) drowned

Avoid the following common errors when forming the past or past participle of regular verbs:

1. leaving off the *-d* or *-ed* ending

NONSTANDARD	She use to work in the library.
STANDARD	She **used** to work in the library.

NONSTANDARD	Who was suppose to bring the ball?
STANDARD	Who was **supposed** to bring the ball?

NONSTANDARD	What happen to that bike you used to ride?
STANDARD	What **happened** to that bike you used to ride?

2. adding unnecessary letters

NONSTANDARD	A swarm of bees attackted us in the orange grove.
STANDARD	A swarm of bees **attacked** us in the orange grove.

NONSTANDARD	Fortunately, no one in the boating accident drownded.
STANDARD	Fortunately, no one in the boating accident **drowned.**

QUICK CHECK 1 **Using the Past and Past Participle Forms of Regular Verbs**

For each of the following sentences, choose the correct past or past participle form of the verb given in italics.

1. *cross* Bison have _____ this plain for centuries.
2. *visit* The raccoon _____ our camp almost every morning last summer.
3. *repair* Have Ryan and Annie _____ the engine?
4. *bound* The actors _____ across the stage.
5. *use* Sylvia has _____ her computer every day.

Irregular Verbs

3c. An *irregular verb* forms its past and past participle in some other way than by adding -*d* or -*ed* to the base form.

An irregular verb forms its past and past participle by

■ changing vowels *or* consonants

BASE FORM	PAST	PAST PARTICIPLE
ring	rang	(have) rung
make	made	(have) made

■ or by changing vowels *and* consonants

BASE FORM	PAST	PAST PARTICIPLE
eat	ate	(have) eaten
go	went	(have) gone

■ or by making no changes

BASE FORM	PAST	PAST PARTICIPLE
spread	spread	(have) spread
burst	burst	(have) burst

GRAMMAR/USAGE

Avoid the following common errors when forming the past or past participle of irregular verbs:

1. using the past form with a helping verb

NONSTANDARD Carlos has went to the new shopping mall.

STANDARD Carlos **went** to the new shopping mall.

or

STANDARD Carlos **has gone** to the new shopping mall.

2. using the past participle form without a helping verb

NONSTANDARD I seen all of her movies.

STANDARD I **have seen** all of her movies.

3. adding *-d* or *-ed* to the base form

NONSTANDARD The right fielder throwed the ball to the shortstop.

STANDARD The right fielder **threw** the ball to the shortstop.

 NOTE If you are not sure about the principal parts of a verb, look in a dictionary. Entries for irregular verbs give the principal parts of the verb.

 STYLE NOTE Using the standard forms of verbs is important in almost all of the writing that you do for school. Your readers expect standard usage in essays and reports. On the other hand, readers expect the dialogue in plays and short stories to sound natural. For dialogue to sound natural, it must reflect the speech patterns of real people, and real people speak in all sorts of nonstandard ways.

NONSTANDARD "I seen it, but I don't no way believe it!"
(DIALOGUE) exclaimed Jimmy.

STANDARD Jimmy said he couldn't believe what he had seen.

You may want to discuss the use of nonstandard verb forms with your teacher. Together you can decide when and where such forms may be used appropriately in your writing.

COMMON IRREGULAR VERBS			
GROUP I: Each of these irregular verbs has the same form for its past and past participle.			
BASE FORM	PRESENT PARTICIPLE	PAST	PAST PARTICIPLE
bring	(is) bringing	brought	(have) brought
build	(is) building	built	(have) built
buy	(is) buying	bought	(have) bought
catch	(is) catching	caught	(have) caught
feel	(is) feeling	felt	(have) felt
find	(is) finding	found	(have) found
get	(is) getting	got	(have) got *or* gotten
have	(is) having	had	(have) had
hold	(is) holding	held	(have) held
keep	(is) keeping	kept	(have) kept
lay	(is) laying	laid	(have) laid
lead	(is) leading	led	(have) led
leave	(is) leaving	left	(have) left
lend	(is) lending	lent	(have) lent
lose	(is) losing	lost	(have) lost
make	(is) making	made	(have) made
meet	(is) meeting	met	(have) met
pay	(is) paying	paid	(have) paid
say	(is) saying	said	(have) said
sell	(is) selling	sold	(have) sold
send	(is) sending	sent	(have) sent
sit	(is) sitting	sat	(have) sat
spend	(is) spending	spent	(have) spent
spin	(is) spinning	spun	(have) spun
stand	(is) standing	stood	(have) stood
swing	(is) swinging	swung	(have) swung
teach	(is) teaching	taught	(have) taught
tell	(is) telling	told	(have) told
think	(is) thinking	thought	(have) thought
win	(is) winning	won	(have) won

GRAMMAR/USAGE

QUICK CHECK 2 | **Using the Past and Past Participle Forms of Verbs**

For each of the following sentences, give the correct past or past participle form of the verb in parentheses.

1. I had (*think*) that only humans use tools, but animals can use tools, too.
2. In fact, scientists have (*spend*) many hours watching wild animals make and use tools.
3. In several studies, chimpanzees using twigs (*catch*) termites.
4. I've been (*tell*) that some finches use twigs to dig insects out of cracks in tree bark.
5. Some animals, such as termites and ants, have (*build*) things by using their gluelike body fluids to hold objects together.

COMMON IRREGULAR VERBS			
GROUP II: Each of these irregular verbs has a different form for its past and past participle.			
BASE FORM	**PRESENT PARTICIPLE**	**PAST**	**PAST PARTICIPLE**
be	(is) being	was/were	(have) been
begin	(is) beginning	began	(have) begun
blow	(is) blowing	blew	(have) blown
break	(is) breaking	broke	(have) broken
choose	(is) choosing	chose	(have) chosen
come	(is) coming	came	(have) come
do	(is) doing	did	(have) done
draw	(is) drawing	drew	(have) drawn
drink	(is) drinking	drank	(have) drunk
drive	(is) driving	drove	(have) driven
eat	(is) eating	ate	(have) eaten
fall	(is) falling	fell	(have) fallen
fly	(is) flying	flew	(have) flown
freeze	(is) freezing	froze	(have) frozen
give	(is) giving	gave	(have) given

(continued)

GRAMMAR/USAGE

GRAMMAR/USAGE

COMMON IRREGULAR VERBS *(continued)*

GROUP II: Each of these irregular verbs has a different form for its past and past participle.

BASE FORM	PRESENT PARTICIPLE	PAST	PAST PARTICIPLE
go	(is) going	went	(have) gone
grow	(is) growing	grew	(have) grown
know	(is) knowing	knew	(have) known
lie	(is) lying	lay	(have) lain
ride	(is) riding	rode	(have) ridden
ring	(is) ringing	rang	(have) rung
rise	(is) rising	rose	(have) risen
run	(is) running	ran	(have) run
see	(is) seeing	saw	(have) seen
shake	(is) shaking	shook	(have) shaken
sing	(is) singing	sang	(have) sung
sink	(is) sinking	sank	(have) sunk
speak	(is) speaking	spoke	(have) spoken
steal	(is) stealing	stole	(have) stolen
swim	(is) swimming	swam	(have) swum
take	(is) taking	took	(have) taken
tear	(is) tearing	tore	(have) torn
throw	(is) throwing	threw	(have) thrown
wear	(is) wearing	wore	(have) worn
write	(is) writing	wrote	(have) written

"You don't say 'he taked my chair' . . . it's 'my chair was tooken.' "

Family Circus reprinted with special permission of King Features Syndicate, Inc.

QUICK CHECK 3

Using the Past and Past Participle Forms of Verbs

For each of the following sentences, give the correct past or past participle form of the verb in parentheses.

1. Did you say that the telephone (*ring*) while I was in the shower?
2. The outfielder (*throw*) the ball to home plate.
3. Diana Nyad (*swim*) sixty miles from the Bahamas to Florida.
4. Uncle Olaf has (*drive*) his new snowmobile up to the remote mountain cabin.
5. The librarian has (*choose*) a book by Jose Aruego.

COMMON IRREGULAR VERBS			
GROUP III: Each of these irregular verbs has the same form for its base form, past, and past participle.			
BASE FORM	**PRESENT PARTICIPLE**	**PAST**	**PAST PARTICIPLE**
burst	(is) bursting	burst	(have) burst
cost	(is) costing	cost	(have) cost
cut	(is) cutting	cut	(have) cut
hit	(is) hitting	hit	(have) hit
hurt	(is) hurting	hurt	(have) hurt
let	(is) letting	let	(have) let
put	(is) putting	put	(have) put
read	(is) reading	read	(have) read
set	(is) setting	set	(have) set
spread	(is) spreading	spread	(have) spread

QUICK CHECK 4

Using the Past and Past Participle Forms of Verbs

For each of the following sentences, give the correct past or past participle form of the verb in italics.

1. *let* Yolanda should have _____ Joshua borrow her calculator.

2. *burst*   Has the balloon _____ already?

3. *cost*   Last week these jeans were on sale and _____ only fifteen dollars.

4. *set*   Fumbling for his keys, Pablo _____ the groceries down too hard and broke a couple of eggs.

5. *spread*   Have you ever heard the legend of Johnny Appleseed, who _____ apple seeds throughout the United States?

Verb Tense

3d. The *tense* of a verb indicates the time of the action or state of being expressed by the verb.

Every verb has six tenses.

Present	Past	Future
Present Perfect	Past Perfect	Future Perfect

This time line shows how the six tenses are related to one another.

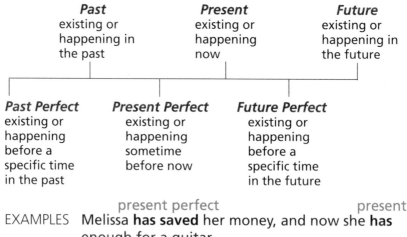

EXAMPLES   Melissa **has saved** her money, and now she **has** enough for a guitar.

             I **have lived** in the United States since November of 1990.

past perfect
The scouts **had hiked** five miles before they

past
stopped for lunch.

future perfect
The executive **will have seen** the report by next

future
week and **will make** a decision then.

Listing all the forms of a verb in the six tenses is called *conjugating* a verb.

CONJUGATION OF THE VERB *WRITE*	
PRESENT TENSE	
SINGULAR	*PLURAL*
I write	we write
you write	you write
he, she, *or* it writes	they write
PAST TENSE	
SINGULAR	*PLURAL*
I wrote	we wrote
you wrote	you wrote
he, she, *or* it wrote	they wrote
FUTURE TENSE	
SINGULAR	*PLURAL*
I will (shall) write	we will (shall) write
you will write	you will write
he, she, *or* it will write	they will write
PRESENT PERFECT TENSE	
SINGULAR	*PLURAL*
I have written	we have written
you have written	you have written
he, she, *or* it has written	they have written

(continued)

GRAMMAR/USAGE

GRAMMAR/USAGE

CONJUGATION OF THE VERB *WRITE* (continued)	
PAST PERFECT TENSE	
SINGULAR	*PLURAL*
I had written	we had written
you had written	you had written
he, she, *or* it had written	they had written
FUTURE PERFECT TENSE	
SINGULAR	*PLURAL*
I will (shall) have written	we will (shall) have written
you will have written	you will have written
he, she, *or* it will have written	they will have written

Consistency of Tense

3e. Do not change needlessly from one tense to another.

When writing about events that take place in the present, use verbs in the present tense. Similarly, when writing about events that occurred in the past, use verbs in the past tense.

INCONSISTENT	When we were comfortable, we begin to do our homework. [*Were* is past tense, and *begin* is present tense.]
CONSISTENT	When we **are** comfortable, we **begin** to do our homework. [Both *are* and *begin* are present tense.]
CONSISTENT	When we **were** comfortable, we **began** to do our homework. [Both *were* and *began* are past tense.]
INCONSISTENT	Suddenly the great door opened, and an uninvited guest bursts excitedly into the dining hall. [*Opened* is past tense, and *bursts* is present tense.]

CONSISTENT   Suddenly the great door **opens,** and an un-invited guest **bursts** excitedly into the dining hall. [Both *opens* and *bursts* are present tense.]

CONSISTENT   Suddenly the great door **opened,** and an uninvited guest **burst** excitedly into the dining hall. [Both *opened* and *burst* are past tense.]

 *QUICK CHECK 5*   **Proofreading a Paragraph to Make the Verb Tense Consistent**

Read the following paragraph and decide whether it should be rewritten in the present or past tense. Then, change the appropriate verb forms to make the verb tense consistent.

EXAMPLE   [1] At my grandparents' house, I wake up before anyone else, quietly grabbed the fishing pole, and head for the pond.

   1. *At my grandparents' house, I wake up before anyone else, quietly grab the fishing pole, and head for the pond.*

or

At my grandparents' house, I woke up before anyone else, quietly grabbed the fishing pole, and headed for the pond.

[1] Across the water, I saw the ripples. [2] "I have to catch some fish," I say to myself. [3] I threw my lure near where I see the ripples and reeled in the line. [4] The fish don't seem interested. [5] I saw more ripples and throw the line in the water again. [6] "I have a strike!" I shout to the trees around me. [7] As I reeled in the line, a beautiful trout jumps out of the water and spit out the hook. [8] Feeling down, I go back to the house. [9] Grandpa was sitting at the kitchen table with a bowl of hot oatmeal for me. [10] I say, "Oh well, maybe tomorrow we'll have fresh trout for breakfast."

COMPUTER NOTE Most word processors can help you check your writing to be sure that you've used verbs correctly. For example, a spell-checking feature will highlight misspelled verb forms such as *drownded* or *costed.* Style-checking software can point out inconsistent verb tense, and it may also highlight questionable uses of problem verb pairs such as *lie* and *lay* or *rise* and *raise.* Remember, though, that the computer is just a tool to help you improve your writing. As a writer, you are responsible for making all the style and content choices that affect your writing.

Special Problems with Verbs

Sit and *Set*

(1) The verb *sit* means "to rest in an upright, seated position." *Sit* seldom takes an object.

(2) The verb *set* means "to put (something) in a place." *Set* usually takes an object. Notice that *set* has the same form for the base, past, and past participle.

BASE FORM	PRESENT PARTICIPLE	PAST	PAST PARTICIPLE
sit (to rest)	(is) sitting	sat	(have) sat
set (to put)	(is) setting	set	(have) set

EXAMPLES Let's **sit** under the tree. [no object]
Let's **set** the bookcase here. [Let's set what? *Bookcase* is the object.]

The tourists **sat** on benches. [no object]
The children **set** the dishes on the table. [The children set what? *Dishes* is the object.]

We had **sat** down to eat when the telephone rang. [no object]

We have **set** the reading lamp beside the couch.
[We have set what? *Lamp* is the object.]

Lie and *Lay*

(1) The verb *lie* means "to rest," "to recline," or "to be in a place." *Lie* never takes an object.

(2) The verb *lay* means "to put (something) in a place." *Lay* usually takes an object.

BASE FORM	PRESENT PARTICIPLE	PAST	PAST PARTICIPLE
lie (to rest)	(is) lying	lay	(have) lain
lay (to put)	(is) laying	laid	(have) laid

EXAMPLES   The cows **are lying** in the shade. [no object]
The servers **are laying** extra napkins beside every plate for the barbecue. [The servers are laying what? *Napkins* is the object.]

The deer **lay** very still while the hunters passed by. [no object]
The soldiers **laid** a trap for the enemy. [The soldiers laid what? *Trap* is the object.]

Rip Van Winkle **had lain** asleep for twenty years. [no object]
The lawyer **had** laid the report next to her briefcase. [The lawyer had laid what? *Report* is the object.]

Rise and *Raise*

(1) The verb *rise* means "to go up" or "to get up." *Rise* rarely takes an object.

(2) The verb *raise* means "to lift up" or "to cause (something) to rise." *Raise* usually takes an object.

BASE FORM	PRESENT PARTICIPLE	PAST	PAST PARTICIPLE
rise (to go up)	(is) rising	rose	(have) risen
raise (to lift up)	(is) raising	raised	(have) raised

EXAMPLES   My neighbors **rise** very early in the morning. [no object]

Every morning they **raise** their windows to let the sunlight inside. [They raise what? *Windows* is the object.]

The full moon **rose** slowly through the clouds last night. [no object]

The cheering crowd **raised** banners and signs over their heads, welcoming the troops home. [The crowd raised what? *Banners* and *signs* are the objects.]

The senators **have risen** from their seats to show respect for the chief justice. [no object]

The wind **has raised** a cloud of dust. [The wind has raised what? *Cloud* is the object.]

 QUICK CHECK 6

Choosing the Forms of *Rise* and *Raise*, *Sit* and *Set*, and *Lie* and *Lay*

For each of the following sentences, choose the correct verb in parentheses.

1. Please (*raise, rise*) your hand when you want to speak.
2. The audience (*sat, set*) near the stage.
3. To study solar energy, our class (*sit, set*) a solar panel outside the window of our classroom.
4. The sun (*rises, raises*) later each morning.
5. He (*lay, laid*) his glasses on the table and left his collection of Isaac Bashevis Singer stories (*lying, laying*) next to them.

GRAMMAR/USAGE

✓ Chapter Review

A. Using the Past and Past Participle Forms of Verbs

For each of the following sentences, give the correct past or past participle form of the verb in parentheses.

EXAMPLES **1.** The deer (*run*) right in front of our car.
   1. *ran*

   2. Her dog has (*run*) away from home.
   2. *run*

1. She (*buy*) several boxes decorated with colorful Amish designs.

2. As soon as they had (*raise*) the drawbridge, we could sail out to the bay.

3. I don't think I should have (*eat*) that last handful of sunflower seeds.

4. Our teacher (*tell*) us that the ukulele is a musical instrument from Hawaii.

5. She is the most talented person I have ever (*know*).

6. You had just (*set*) that down on the floor, hadn't you?

7. That phone has (*ring*) every five minutes since I got home.

8. Earl thought and thought, but the answer never (*come*) to him.

9. The treasure had (*lie*) at the bottom of the sea for more than four hundred years.

10. Through the ocean depths the whales (*sing*) to one another.

11. The coach (*give*) us all a pep talk before the game.

12. While she (*sit*) on the porch, Nashota read a folk tale about Coyote, the trickster.

13. That job shouldn't have (*take*) you all day.

14. The waiter (*bring*) us couscous, a popular North African dish.

15. Though it had (*fall*) from the top of the tree, the baby squirrel was all right.

16. Have you (*write*) your history report yet?

17. When the medicine finally began to work, his fever (*break*).

18. When that happened to me, I (*freeze*) with fear.

19. We knew that it would start to rain soon because the crickets had (*begin*) chirping.

20. To avoid stepping on a snake, he looked on the other side of logs that (*lie*) in the path.

B. Making Tenses of Verbs Consistent

For each of the following sentences, write the italicized verb in the consistent tense.

EXAMPLE   **1.** My father looked at his watch and *decides* that it was time to leave.
         1. *decided*

21. Marjorie's sister refused to give us a ride in her car, and then she *asks* us to lend her some money for gas.

22. He says he's sorry, but he *didn't* mean it.

23. The pine trees grow close together and *had* straight trunks.

24. When the show ended, we *get* up to leave, but a crowd had already gathered.

25. Several mechanics worked on my aunt's car before one of them finally *finds* the problem.

4 USING PRONOUNS

Nominative and Objective Case Forms

✓ Checking What You Know

Identifying Correct Forms of Pronouns

For each of the following sentences, identify the correct pronoun in parentheses.

EXAMPLE **1.** When I got home, a package was waiting for (*I, me*).

   1. *me*

1. Just between you and (*I, me*), I think he's wrong.
2. I don't know (*who, whom*) I'll invite to the dance.
3. We saw (*they, them*) at a Mardi Gras parade in New Orleans.
4. The winners in the contest were Amelia and (*I, me*).
5. The wasp flew in the window and stung (*he, him*) on the arm.
6. Elton and (*she, her*) will give reports this morning.
7. The two scouts who have earned the most merit badges are Angelo and (*he, himself*).
8. The boys cleared the empty lot and measured out a baseball diamond by (*themselves, theirselves*).
9. Nina usually sits behind Alex and (*I, me*) on the bus every morning.

10. My father and (*he, him*) are planning to go into business together.
11. We thought that we'd be facing (*they, them*) in the finals.
12. May I sit next to Terence and (*he, him*)?
13. The tour guide showed Kimberly and (*she, her*) some Japanese *raku* pottery.
14. My aunt once gave (*me, I*) two dolls made from cornhusks.
15. Did you know that it was (*I, me*) who called?
16. Corey's mother and my father said that (*we, us*) boys could go on the field trip.
17. Our friends asked (*we, us*) if we had ever been to San Francisco's Chinatown.
18. Invite (*she, her*) and the new girl in our class to the party.
19. (*Who, Whom*) was chosen for the team?
20. The best soloists in the band are (*they, themselves*). ✓

Case

Case is the form of a noun or a pronoun that shows how it is used. There are three cases:

- nominative
- objective
- possessive

The form of a noun is the same for both the nominative and the objective cases. For example, a noun used as a subject (nominative case) will have the same form when used as an indirect object (objective case).

NOMINATIVE CASE	The **singer** received a standing ovation. [subject]
OBJECTIVE CASE	The audience gave the **singer** a standing ovation. [indirect object]

A noun changes its form for the possessive case, usually by the addition of an apostrophe and an *s*.

POSSESSIVE CASE   Many of the **singer's** fans waited outside the theater.

Unlike nouns, most personal pronouns have different forms for all three cases.

PERSONAL PRONOUNS SINGULAR		
NOMINATIVE CASE	OBJECTIVE CASE	POSSESSIVE CASE
I	me	my, mine
you	you	your, yours
he, she, it	him, her, it	his, her, hers, its
PLURAL		
NOMINATIVE CASE	OBJECTIVE CASE	POSSESSIVE CASE
we	us	our, ours
you	you	your, yours
they	them	their, theirs

NOTE Some teachers prefer to call possessive pronouns (such as *my, your,* and *our*) adjectives. Follow your teacher's directions in labeling possessive forms.

REFERENCE NOTE: For more information on possessive pronouns, see pages 37, 41, and 50.

Berry's World reprinted by permission of NEA, Inc.

GRAMMAR/USAGE

GRAMMAR/USAGE

The Nominative Case

4a. A subject of a verb is in the nominative case.

EXAMPLES   **I** like classical music. [*I* is the subject of *like*.]
He and **she** sold tickets. [*He* and *she* are the subjects of *sold*.]
They called while **we** were away. [*They* is the subject of *called*. *We* is the subject of *were*.]

To help you choose the correct pronoun in a compound subject, try each form of the pronoun separately.

EXAMPLE: Candida and (*me, I*) like to dance.
Me like to dance.
I like to dance.
ANSWER: Candida and **I** like to dance.

EXAMPLE: (*He, Him*) and (*I, me*) read "The Raven" to the class.
He read "The Raven."
Him read "The Raven."
I read "The Raven."
Me read "The Raven."
ANSWER: **He** and **I** read "The Raven" to the class.

4b. A *predicate nominative* is in the nominative case.

A ***predicate nominative*** follows a linking verb and explains or identifies the subject of the verb. A personal pronoun used as a predicate nominative follows a form of the verb *be* (*am, is, are, was, were, be,* or *been*).

EXAMPLES   The last one to leave was **he**. [*He* follows the linking verb *was* and identifies the subject *one*.]
Do you think it may have been **they**? [*They* follows the linking verb *may have been* and identifies the subject *it*.]

NOTE   To help you choose the correct form of a pronoun used as a predicate nominative, remember that the pronoun could just as well be used as the subject in the sentence.

EXAMPLE   The fastest runners are **she** and **I**. [predicate
nominatives]
She and **I** are the fastest runners. [subjects]

 REFERENCE NOTE: For more information about predicate
nominatives, see page 197.

For more information about predicate nominatives, see page 197.

**STYLE
NOTE**   Expressions such as *It's me, That's her,* and *It
was them* are accepted in everyday speaking.
In writing, however, such expressions are generally considered nonstandard and should be avoided.

✓ *QUICK CHECK 1*   **Using Pronouns as Subjects and
Predicate Nominatives**

For each of the following sentences, identify the correct
personal pronoun in parentheses.

1. My parents and (*they, them*) are good friends.
2. We hoped it was (*she, her*) at the door.
3. Were (*he, him*) and (*she, her*) on the Old Spanish Trail?
4. It may have been (*he, him*), but I'm not sure.
5. Was it Claudia or (*she, her*) who brought the Chinese
   egg rolls?

The Objective Case

4c.   A *direct object* is in the objective case.

A *direct object* follows an action verb and tells *who* or *what*
receives the action of the verb.

EXAMPLES   Evan surprised **us**. [*Us* tells *whom* Evan surprised.]
Uncle Ramón took **me** to the rodeo. [*Me* tells
whom Uncle Ramón took.]
The class read some Norse myths and enjoyed
them very much. [*Them* tells *what* the class enjoyed.]

To help you choose the correct pronoun in a compound direct object, try each form of the pronoun separately in the sentence.

EXAMPLE: We met Tara and (*she, her*) at the video arcade.
We met *she* at the video arcade.
We met *her* at the video arcade.

ANSWER: We met Tara and **her** at the video arcade.

☞ REFERENCE NOTE: For more information about direct objects, see pages 193–194.

4d. An *indirect object* is in the objective case.

An ***indirect object*** comes between an action verb and a direct object and tells *to whom* or *to what* or *for whom* or *for what*.

EXAMPLES Coach Méndez gave **them** a pep talk. [*Them* tells *to whom* Coach Méndez gave a pep talk.]
His mother bought **him** a footlocker. [*Him* tells *for whom* his mother bought a footlocker.]
The science teacher gave **us** posters of the solar system. [*Us* tells *to whom* the teacher gave posters.]
Lana takes good care of her cockatiel, Lobo, and often feeds **him** fresh spinach. [*Him* tells *to what* Lana feeds spinach.]

To help you choose the correct pronoun in a compound indirect object, try each form of the pronoun separately in the sentence.

EXAMPLE: Our neighbor gave Kristen and (*I, me*) a job for the summer.
Our neighbor gave *I* a job for the summer.
Our neighbor gave *me* a job for the summer.

ANSWER: Our neighbor gave Kristen and **me** a job for the summer.

☞ REFERENCE NOTE: For more information about indirect objects, see pages 195–196.

4e. An *object of a preposition* is in the objective case.

The *object of a preposition* is a noun or a pronoun that follows a preposition. Together with any of the object's modifiers, the preposition and its object make a *prepositional phrase.*

EXAMPLES   to **Lee**   in an **hour**   like red **clay**
            without **me**   near **her**   except **them**

👉 REFERENCE NOTE: For a list of prepositions, see pages 65–66. For more on prepositional phrases, see pages 148–151.

A pronoun used as the object of a preposition should always be in the objective case.

EXAMPLES   When did you mail the package to **them**? [*Them* is the object of the preposition *to.*]
            Are you still planning to go to the movies with **us**? [*Us* is the object of the preposition *with.*]
            The reward money was divided equally between **him** and **her.** [*Him* and *her* are the objects of the preposition *between.*]

To help you choose the correct pronoun when the object of a preposition is compound, try each form of the pronoun separately in the sentence.

EXAMPLE: Todd sat behind (*he, him*) and (*I, me*).
            Todd sat behind *he.*
            Todd sat behind *him.*
            Todd sat behind *I.*
            Todd sat behind *me.*
ANSWER: Todd sat behind **him** and **me.**

 QUICK CHECK 2   **Using Pronouns as Objects**

For each of the following sentences, choose the correct personal pronoun in parentheses.

1. Rochelle invited my sister and (*she, her*) to the Whitney Houston concert.
2. Let's keep this secret just between you and (*I, me*).

3. Do you think Coach will give (*we, us*) and (*he, him*) a break this afternoon?
4. Rita said that she can usually find Alberto and (*they, them*) at your house.
5. Everyone except Bill and (*I, me*) saw the Navajo rugs.

STYLE NOTE   Just as there are good manners in behavior, there are also good manners in language.

In English it is considered polite to put first-person pronouns (*I, me, mine, we, us, ours*) last in compound constructions.

EXAMPLE   **Dana, Juan, and I** took the old newspapers to the recycling collection center.

Special Pronoun Problems

Who and Whom

The pronoun *who* has different forms in the nominative and objective cases. *Who* is the nominative form; *whom* is the objective form.

When deciding whether to use *who* or *whom* in a question, follow these steps:

STEP 1:   Rephrase the question as a statement.
STEP 2:   Decide how the pronoun is used in the statement—as subject, predicate nominative, object of the verb, or object of a preposition.
STEP 3:   Determine the case of the pronoun according to the rules of standard English.
STEP 4:   Select the correct form of the pronoun.

EXAMPLE: (*Who, Whom*) were you talking about?
STEP 1:   The statement is *You were talking about* (*who, whom*).

STEP 2: The subject is *you*, the verb is *were talking*, and the pronoun is an object of a preposition.

STEP 3: A pronoun used as an object of a preposition should be in the objective case.

STEP 4: The objective form is *whom*.

ANSWER: **Whom** were you talking about?

 NOTE In spoken English, the use of *whom* is becoming less common. In fact, when you are speaking, you may correctly begin any question with *who* regardless of the grammar of the sentence. In written English, however, you should distinguish between *who* and *whom*.

When you are choosing between *who* or *whom* in a subordinate clause, follow these steps:

STEP 1: Find the subordinate clause.

STEP 2: Decide how the pronoun is used in the clause—as subject, predicate nominative, object of the verb, or object of a preposition.

STEP 3: Determine the case of the pronoun according to the rules of standard English.

STEP 4: Select the correct form of the pronoun.

EXAMPLE: Do you know (*who, whom*) they are?

STEP 1: The subordinate clause is (*who, whom*) *they are.*

STEP 2: In this clause, the subject is *they*, the verb is *are*, and the pronoun is the predicate nominative: *They are* (*who, whom*).

STEP 3: A pronoun used as a predicate nominative should be in the nominative case.

STEP 4: The nominative form is *who*.

ANSWER: Do you know **who** they are?

EXAMPLE: Isaac Bashevis Singer, (*who, whom*) I admire, wrote interesting books.

STEP 1: The subordinate clause is (*who, whom*) *I admire.*

STEP 2: In this clause, the subject is *I*, and the verb is *admire*. The pronoun is the direct object of the verb: *I admire* (*who, whom*).

STEP 3: A pronoun used as a direct object should be in the objective case.

STEP 4: The objective form is *whom.*

ANSWER: Isaac Bashevis Singer, **whom** I admire, wrote interesting books.

 REFERENCE NOTE: For a discussion of subordinate clauses, see pages 165–173.

✓ *QUICK CHECK 3* **Using *Who* and *Whom* Correctly**

For each of the following sentences, choose the correct pronoun in parentheses.

1. For (*who, whom*) do the gauchos in Argentina work?
2. (*Who, Whom*) won the speech contest?
3. Martin Luther King, Jr., was a man (*who, whom*) we honor.
4. (*Who, Whom*) did they suggest for the job?
5. The Inupiats are the only people (*who, whom*) live in some parts of Alaska.

Peanuts reprinted by permission of UFS, Inc.

Pronouns with Appositives

Sometimes a pronoun is followed directly by a noun that identifies the pronoun. Such a noun is called an *appositive.* To help you choose which pronoun to use before an appositive, omit the appositive and try each form of the pronoun separately.

EXAMPLE: **(We, Us)** cheerleaders practice after school.
[*Cheerleaders* is the appositive.]
We practice after school.
Us practice after school.

ANSWER: **We** cheerleaders practice after school.

EXAMPLE: The coach threw a party for (*we, us*) players.
[*Players* is the appositive.]
The coach threw a party for *we.*
The coach threw a party for *us.*

ANSWER: The coach threw a party for **us** players.

 REFERENCE NOTE: For more on appositives, see page 158.

Reflexive Pronouns

Reflexive pronouns (such as *myself, himself,* and *yourselves*) can be used as objects.

EXAMPLES Janet bought **herself** a new tennis racket.
[*Herself* is an indirect object.]
Sometimes I surprise **myself.** [*Myself* is a direct object.]

Do not use the nonstandard forms *hisself* and *theirself* or *theirselves* in place of *himself* and *themselves.*

NONSTANDARD Daniel painted the garage all by hisself.
STANDARD Daniel painted the garage all by **himself.**
NONSTANDARD Each spring, robins make nests for theirselves in that tree.
STANDARD Each spring, robins make nests for **themselves** in that tree.

A reflexive pronoun *must* refer to another noun or pronoun in the sentence.

NONSTANDARD Uncle Ted brought this video game for yourself. [*Yourself* does not refer to a noun or pronoun in the sentence.]

STANDARD   Uncle Ted brought this video game for **you.**

NONSTANDARD   Leon and myself prefer hiking to rock climbing. [A reflexive pronoun should never be used as a subject.]

STANDARD   Leon and I prefer hiking to rock climbing.

 REFERENCE NOTE: For more information about reflexive pronouns, see pages 50–51.

 A computer may be able to help you find pronoun problems in your writing. For example, a spelling checker will catch nonstandard forms such as *hisself* and *theirself*. To find other problems, you may need to use the "Search" command. Let's say that you sometimes use reflexive pronouns in place of personal pronouns. Use the "Search" command to highlight all reflexive pronouns in your essay. (A complete list of these pronouns is on page 51.) Then examine how each pronoun is used. If a pronoun is used incorrectly, replace it with the correct form.

 QUICK CHECK 4   **Identifying Correct Forms of Pronouns**

For each of the following sentences, choose the correct pronoun in parentheses.

1. (*We, Us*) students are having a carnival next Saturday to raise money.
2. The team elected Josh and (*me, myself*) as co-captains.
3. The head nurse gave (*we, us*) volunteers a tour of the new hospital wing.
4. When Mr. and Mrs. Smith retired, they treated (*theirselves, themselves*) to a Caribbean cruise.
5. Did you know that (*we, us*) girls are going to the 10,000 Maniacs concert?

✓ *Chapter Review*

A. Proofreading for Correct Forms of Pronouns

Most of the following sentences contain at least one pronoun that has been used incorrectly. Identify each incorrect pronoun, and then give its correct form. If the sentence is correct, write C.

EXAMPLE   **1. The teacher told Derek and I a funny story.**
          1. *I—me*

1. That sports announcer calls hisself Jake "Locker Room" Levine.
2. The winners of the science fair were Felicia and he.
3. Who did you and Marie send flowers to?
4. Us teammates have to stick together, right?
5. Aunt Ida bought we boys some boiled peanuts.
6. Coach Johnson said he was proud of Ling and myself.
7. Is he the person who we met at Dan's party?
8. We split the pizza between he and I.
9. My grandmother and me enjoy the English custom of having afternoon tea.
10. The little boy asked Neil and him for help.

B. Identifying Correct Forms of Personal Pronouns

For each sentence in the following paragraph, choose the correct pronoun from the pair in parentheses.

EXAMPLE **[1] Mrs. Lang gave (*we, us*) third-period students a list of good books for summer reading.**
        1. *us*

[11] Beth and (*I, me*) plan to read the first five books on Mrs. Lang's list soon. [12] We asked (*she, her*) for some more information about them. [13] (*She, Her*) said that *The Man Who Was Poe* is by Avi. [14] The author of *The True Confessions of Charlotte Doyle* is also (*he, him*). [15] We probably will like Avi's books because (*they, them*) combine fic-

tion and history. **[16]** Both of (*we, us*) want to read *Where the Lilies Bloom* by Vera and Bill Cleaver, too. **[17]** Together, the two of (*they, them*) have written numerous books for young readers. **[18]** The first book (*I, me*) am going to read is *Jacob Have I Loved* by Katherine Paterson. **[19]** But Beth said that *A Gathering of Days: A New England Girl's Journal, 1830–1832* by Joan W. Blos will be the first book for (*she, her*). **[20]** Mrs. Lang told Beth and (*I, me*) that our summer reading project is a good idea.

5 USING MODIFIERS

Comparison and Placement

 Checking What You Know

A. Using the Correct Forms of Modifiers

The following sentences contain errors in the use of modifiers. Revise each sentence, using the correct form of the modifier.

EXAMPLE   **1.** Your cough sounds worser today.
             1. *Your cough sounds worse today.*

1. Of all the actors in *Robin Hood: Prince of Thieves*, Morgan Freeman is the most funniest.
2. Alan thinks that this dessert tastes gooder than the others he tried.
3. I couldn't hardly believe she said that.
4. Yoshi is the tallest of the twins.
5. The movie made me curiouser about Spanish settlements in the Philippines.
6. The movie doesn't cost much, but I don't have no money.

7. They offer so many combinations that I don't know which one I like more.
8. The house on Drury Avenue is the one we like bestest.
9. For supper, there's nothing I like more better than barbecued chicken.
10. Why doesn't the teacher give us questions that are more easier?

B. Correcting Misplaced and Dangling Modifiers

Each of the following sentences contains a dangling or a misplaced modifier in italics. Revise each sentence so that it is clear and correct.

EXAMPLE   **1.** Waiting at the curb for the bus, a car splashed water on me.

          1. *While I was waiting at the curb for the bus, a car splashed water on me.*

11. *Looking in her purse,* two French francs and one Italian lira were all she found.
12. The library has several books about dinosaurs *in our school.*
13. *Sleeping soundly,* Howard woke his father when supper was ready.
14. The book is not in the library *that I wanted to read.*
15. Aunt Lucia sent away a coupon for a free recipe book *from a magazine.*
16. My favorite bluegrass band is from Kentucky *which is performing next week.*
17. *Left alone for the first time in his life,* strange sounds in the night scared my little brother.
18. *After eating all their food,* we put the cats outside for the night.
19. *Often slaughtered for their tusks,* many African nations prohibit the hunting of elephants.
20. *Sitting in the bleachers,* the outfielder caught the ball right in front of us. ✔

Comparison of Modifiers

A *modifier* is a word, a phrase, or a clause that describes or limits the meaning of another word. Two kinds of modifiers—*adjectives* and *adverbs*—may be used to compare things. In making comparisons, adjectives and adverbs take different forms. The specific form that is used depends upon how many syllables the modifier has and how many things are being compared.

ADJECTIVES   This building is **tall**. [no comparison]
This building is **taller** than that one. [one compared with another]
This building is the **tallest** one in the world. [one compared with many others]

ADVERBS   I ski **frequently**. [no comparison]
I ski **more frequently** than she does. [one compared with another]
Of the three of us, I ski **most frequently**. [one compared with two others]

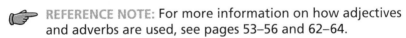 REFERENCE NOTE: For more information on how adjectives and adverbs are used, see pages 53–56 and 62–64.

5a. The three degrees of comparison of modifiers are *positive*, *comparative*, and *superlative*.

POSITIVE	COMPARATIVE	SUPERLATIVE
weak	weaker	weakest
proudly	more proudly	most proudly
likely	less likely	least likely
bad	worse	worst

Regular Comparison

(1) Most one-syllable modifiers form their comparative and superlative degrees by adding *-er* and *-est*.

GRAMMAR/USAGE

POSITIVE	COMPARATIVE	SUPERLATIVE
near	nearer	nearest
bright	brighter	brightest
brave	braver	bravest
dry	drier	driest

 REFERENCE NOTE: For guidelines on how to spell words when adding *-er* or *-est*, see pages 313–315.

(2) Some two-syllable modifiers form their comparative and superlative degrees by adding *-er* and *-est*. Other two-syllable modifiers form their comparative and superlative degrees by using *more* and *most*.

POSITIVE	COMPARATIVE	SUPERLATIVE
simple	simpler	simplest
healthy	healthier	healthiest
clearly	more clearly	most clearly
often	more often	most often

When you are not sure how a two-syllable modifier forms its degrees of comparison, look up the word in a dictionary.

(3) Modifiers that have three or more syllables form their comparative and superlative degrees by using *more* and *most*.

POSITIVE	COMPARATIVE	SUPERLATIVE
important	more important	most important
creative	more creative	most creative
happily	more happily	most happily
accurately	more accurately	most accurately

(4) To show decreasing comparisons, all modifiers form their comparative and superlative degrees with *less* and *least*.

POSITIVE	COMPARATIVE	SUPERLATIVE
safe	less safe	least safe
expensive	less expensive	least expensive
often	less often	least often
gracefully	less gracefully	least gracefully

 *QUICK CHECK 1*   **Forming the Comparative and Superlative Degrees of Modifiers**

Give the forms for the comparative and superlative degrees of the following modifiers.

1. slow

2. cautiously

3. early

4. thankful

5. possible

6. short

7. easy

8. confident

9. seriously

10. loyal

Frank & Ernest reprinted by permission of NEA, Inc.

GRAMMAR/USAGE

GRAMMAR/USAGE

Irregular Comparison

Some modifiers do not form their comparative and superlative degrees by using the regular methods.

POSITIVE	COMPARATIVE	SUPERLATIVE
bad	worse	worst
far	farther	farthest
good	better	best
well	better	best
many	more	most
much	more	most

 QUICK CHECK 2 **Forming the Comparative and Superlative Degrees of Modifiers**

Give the forms for the comparative and superlative degrees of the following modifiers.

1. much
2. easily
3. many
4. tasty
5. enthusiastic
6. generous
7. hot
8. good
9. well
10. bad

Uses of Comparative and Superlative Forms

5b. Use the comparative degree when comparing two things. Use the superlative degree when comparing more than two.

COMPARATIVE   The second problem is **harder** than the first. Luisa can perform the gymnastic routine **more gracefully** than I. Of the two tape players, this one costs **less**.

SUPERLATIVE	Mount Everest is the world's **highest** mountain peak.
	This is the **most valuable** coin in my collection.
	Of the three dogs, that one barks the **least**.

Avoid the common mistake of using the superlative degree to compare two things.

NONSTANDARD	Of the two plans, this is the best one.
STANDARD	Of the two plans, this is the **better** one.

NONSTANDARD	Felicia is the youngest of the two girls.
STANDARD	Felicia is the **younger** of the two girls.

STYLE NOTE In everyday speech, you may hear and use expressions such as *Put your best foot forward* and *May the best team win*. This use of the superlative is acceptable in spoken English. However, in your writing for school and other formal situations, you should follow rule 5b.

5c. Include the word *other* or *else* when comparing a member of a group with the rest of the group.

NONSTANDARD	Jupiter is larger than any planet in the solar system. [Jupiter is one of the planets in the solar system and cannot be larger than itself.]
STANDARD	Jupiter is larger than any **other** planet in the solar system.

NONSTANDARD	Roland can type faster than anyone in his computer class. [Roland is one of the students in his computer class and cannot type faster than himself.]
STANDARD	Roland can type faster than anyone **else** in his computer class.

5d. Avoid using double comparisons.

A *double comparison* is the use of both *-er* and *more (less)* or both *-est* and *most (least)* to form a comparison. A comparison should be formed in only one of these two ways, not both.

NONSTANDARD The Asian elephant is more smaller than the African elephant.

STANDARD The Asian elephant is **smaller** than the African elephant.

NONSTANDARD Ribbon Falls, in Yosemite National Park, is the most beautifulest waterfall I have ever seen.

STANDARD Ribbon Falls, in Yosemite National Park, is the **most beautiful** waterfall I have ever seen.

 *QUICK CHECK 3* **Using the Degrees of Comparison Correctly**

The following sentences contain incorrect forms of comparison. Revise each sentence, using the correct form of comparison.

1. Juanita, the pitcher, is worse at bat than anyone that is on the team.
2. The most largest ancient cliff dwellings in Arizona are in Navajo National Monument.
3. After watching the two kittens for a few minutes, Rudy chose the most playful one.
4. New York City has a larger population than any city in the United States.
5. Karl likes homemade sauerkraut more better than canned sauerkraut.

5e. A *double negative* is the use of two negative words to express one negative idea.

Common Negative Words			
barely	never	none	nothing
hardly	no	no one	nowhere
neither	nobody	not (-n't)	scarcely

NONSTANDARD I can't never remember what his name is.
 STANDARD I **can't** ever remember what his name is.

NONSTANDARD We couldn't barely hear.
 STANDARD We could **barely** hear.

 QUICK CHECK 4 **Correcting Double Negatives**

Revise each of the following sentences to eliminate the double negative.

1. We don't hardly have time to relax.
2. Josie hasn't never been to Tennessee.
3. He never had no problem with public speaking.
4. The athletes don't hardly have a break between events.
5. The authorities don't allow no cars on Michigan's popular Mackinac Island.

Hagar the Horrible reprinted with special permission of King Features Syndicate, Inc.

Placement of Modifiers

Notice how the meaning of the following sentence changes when the position of the phrase *from Canada* changes.

The professor **from Canada** gave a televised lecture on famous writers. [The phrase modifies *professor*.]
The professor gave a televised lecture on famous writers **from Canada**. [The phrase modifies *writers*.]
The professor gave a televised lecture **from Canada** on famous writers. [The phrase modifies *gave*.]

5f. Place modifying phrases and clauses as close as possible to the words they modify.

Prepositional Phrases

A *prepositional phrase* consists of a preposition, a noun or a pronoun called the object of the preposition, and any modifiers of that object.

 REFERENCE NOTE: For more information about prepositions, see pages 65–67. For more discussion of prepositional phrases, see pages 66 and 148–151.

A prepositional phrase used as an adjective should be placed directly after the word it modifies.

MISPLACED	This book describes Nat Turner's struggle for freedom by Judith Berry Griffin.
CLEAR	This book **by Judith Berry Griffin** describes Nat Turner's struggle for freedom.

A prepositional phrase used as an adverb should be placed near the word it modifies.

MISPLACED	Spanish explorers discovered gold along the river that runs near my house during the 1500s.
CLEAR	**During the 1500s**, Spanish explorers discovered gold along the river that runs near my house.

Avoid placing a prepositional phrase in such a way that it appears to modify either of two words. Place the phrase so that it clearly modifies the word you intend it to modify.

MISPLACED   Gabriela said in the morning she was going to Chicago. [Does the phrase modify *said* or *was going*?]

CLEAR   Gabriela said she was going to Chicago **in the morning.** [The phrase modifies *was going*.]

CLEAR   **In the morning** Gabriela said she was going to Chicago. [The phrase modifies *said*.]

Participial Phrases

A *participial phrase* consists of a verb form—either a present participle or a past participle—and its related words. A participial phrase modifies a noun or a pronoun.

 REFERENCE NOTE: For more information about participial phrases, see pages 153–154. For guidelines on using commas with participial phrases, see page 269.

Like a prepositional phrase, a participial phrase should be placed as close as possible to the word it modifies.

MISPLACED   The bandits chased the stagecoach yelling wildly.

CLEAR   **Yelling wildly**, the bandits chased the stagecoach.

MISPLACED   The vase was lying on the floor broken into many pieces.

CLEAR   The vase, **broken into many pieces**, was lying on the floor.

A participial phrase that does not clearly and sensibly modify any word in the sentence is a *dangling participial phrase*. To correct a dangling phrase, supply a word that the phrase can modify, or add a subject and a verb to the dangling modifier.

DANGLING   Jogging down the sidewalk, my ankle was sprained.

CLEAR   Jogging down the sidewalk, **I** sprained my ankle.

CLEAR   I sprained my ankle **while I was** jogging down the sidewalk.

DANGLING	Dressed in warm clothing, the cold was no problem.
CLEAR	Dressed in warm clothing, **we** had no problem with the cold.
CLEAR	**Since we were** dressed in warm clothing, the cold was no problem.

Clauses

A *clause* is a group of words that contains a verb and its subject and is used as a part of a sentence. An *adjective clause* modifies a noun or a pronoun. Most adjective clauses begin with a relative pronoun, such as *that, which, who, whom,* or *whose.* An *adverb clause* modifies a verb, an adjective, or another adverb. Most adverb clauses begin with a subordinate conjunction, such as *although, while, if,* or *because.*

 REFERENCE NOTE: For more information about adjective and adverb clauses, see pages 166–172. For guidelines on using commas with adjective clauses, see pages 265–266.

Like phrases, clauses should be placed as close as possible to the words they modify.

MISPLACED	My brother saw a hawk circling as he looked up. [Who or what looked up?]
CLEAR	**As he looked up**, my brother saw a hawk circling.
MISPLACED	A little boy came up to us who was lost. [Who was lost?]
CLEAR	A little boy **who was lost** came up to us.

 A computer can help you find and correct problems with modifiers. A spell checker can easily find nonstandard forms such as *baddest, expensiver,* and *mostest.* However, you will need to examine phrase and clause modifiers yourself. If a phrase or a clause is misplaced, use the "Move" command to place the modifier closer to the word it modifies. If you discover a dangling participial phrase, use the "Insert" and "Delete" commands to revise the sentence and give the phrase a word to modify.

 QUICK CHECK 5 **Using Modifiers Correctly**

In each of the following sentences, a modifier is dangling or misplaced. Revise each sentence so that it is clear and correct.

1. The singing group was protected from being swarmed by guards while they performed.
2. Attempting to raise money for the homeless, many songs were sung by the group.
3. Hoping to please the fans, brand-new songs were performed by the group.
4. Few fans could tell the first time they played their new songs how nervous the singers were.
5. Cheering heartily, the singers' fears were relieved.

 Chapter Review

A. Using the Correct Forms of Modifiers

Most of the sentences in the following paragraphs contain errors in the use of modifiers. Identify each error. Then revise the sentence, using the correct form of the modifier. If a sentence is correct, write *C*.

EXAMPLE   [1] My family is the more important thing to me.
        1. *more important—My family is the most important thing to me.*

[1] The wonderfullest place in the whole world is my grandmother's house. [2] We used to live there before we got an apartment of our own. [3] Since her house is bigger than any house in the neighborhood, we all had plenty of room. [4] Grandma was glad to have us stay because my mom and dad can fix things so that they're gooder than

new. [5] They plastered and painted the walls in a spare room so that I wouldn't have to share a room no more with my sister. [6] I don't know which was best—having so much space of my own or having privacy from my sister.

[7] My grandmother can sew better than anybody can. [8] She taught my sister and me how to make the beautifullest clothes. [9] She has three sewing machines and my mother has one, but I like Grandma's oldest one better. [10] We started with the more simpler kinds of stitches. [11] After we could do those, Grandma showed us fancier stitches and sewing tricks. [12] For instance, she taught us to wrap thread behind buttons we sew on, so that they will be more easier to button. [13] We learned how to make dresses, skirts, blouses, and all sorts of other things, so that now there isn't hardly anything we can't make.

[14] I was sad when we left Grandma's house, but I like our new apartment more better than I thought I would. [15] Luckily, we moved to a place near my grandmother's, and after school I can go over there or go home— whichever I want to do most.

B. Correcting Misplaced and Dangling Modifiers

Each of the following sentences contains a misplaced or a dangling modifier. Revise each sentence so that it is clear and correct. You may add or change words if necessary.

EXAMPLE   **1.** Tearing away his umbrella, the storm drenched Mr. Pérez.
          1. *Tearing away his umbrella, Mr. Pérez became drenched in the storm.*

16. Our teacher told us that she had been a nurse in class today.
17. One of the performers found our cat who is starring in the musical *Purlie*.
18. Destroyed by the fire, the man looked sadly at the charred house.

19. After missing the bus, my mother gave me a ride in the car.
20. The fox escaped from the hounds pursuing it with a crafty maneuver.
21. Walking through the park, the squirrels chattered at me.
22. The cook will win a new oven that makes the best German potato salad.
23. The squid fascinated the students preserved in formaldehyde.
24. Keeping track of the race with binoculars, the blue car with a yellow roof pulled into the lead.
25. We watched the snow pile up in drifts inside our warm house.

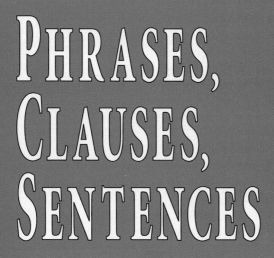

PHRASES,
CLAUSES,
SENTENCES

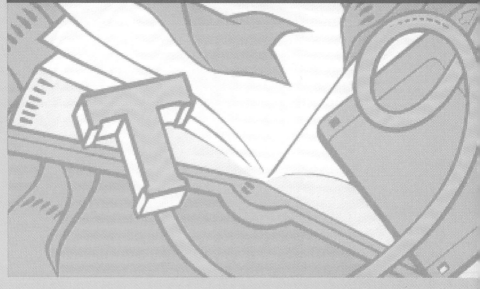

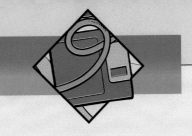

6 PHRASES

Prepositional, Verbal, and Appositive Phrases

✓ Checking What You Know

Identifying Phrases

In each of the following sentences, identify the italicized phrase as a *prepositional phrase*, a *participial phrase*, an *infinitive phrase*, a *gerund phrase*, or an *appositive phrase*. Do not separately identify a prepositional phrase that is part of a larger phrase.

EXAMPLE   **1.** My brother plans *to marry Maureen in June.*
          1. *to marry Maureen in June*—infinitive phrase

  1. *Fishing for bass* is my father's favorite pastime.
  2. The seagulls *gliding through the air* looked like pieces of paper caught in the wind.
  3. The school bus was on time *in spite of the traffic jam.*
  4. Ms. Hoban, *my science teacher,* got married last week.
  5. There is no time left *to answer your questions.*
  6. At the party, the band played songs *with a lively rock-and-roll beat.*

7. He tried *to do his best* in the race.
8. Nobody seems to be very interested in *going to the fireworks display.*
9. Have you seen my cat, *a long-haired Persian with yellow eyes?*
10. Julio said that he likes the bike *with knobby tires and the wider, softer seat.*
11. *Hoping for a new bicycle and a toy robot,* my brother couldn't sleep at all on Christmas Eve.
12. Rachel talked her friends into *watching that Mariah Carey video.*
13. In the United States, citizens have the right *to speak their minds.*
14. My aunt's car, *an old crate with a beat-up interior and a rattly engine,* used to belong to my grandfather.
15. The Mexican artist Diego Rivera enjoyed *painting pictures of children.*
16. Last Sunday, we all piled into the car and went *to the beach, the bowling alley, and the mall.*
17. The shark *chasing the school of fish* looked like a hammerhead.
18. Everyone was curious about the book, *an ancient hardback with yellowed pages.*
19. All of the invitations *sent to the club members* had the wrong date on them.
20. Both the Union and the Confederacy recruited Native Americans *to help them during the Civil War.* ✓

6a. A *phrase* is a group of related words that is used as a single part of speech and does not contain a verb and its subject.

VERB PHRASE	**should have been told** [no subject]
PREPOSITIONAL PHRASE	**from my sister and me** [no subject or verb]

NOTE A group of words that has both a subject and a verb is called a *clause*.

EXAMPLES Leta is watching television. [*Leta* is the subject of the verb *is watching.*]
before the train arrived [*Train* is the subject of the verb *arrived.*]

 REFERENCE NOTE: For more about clauses, see **Chapter 7: Clauses.**

The Prepositional Phrase

6b. A *prepositional phrase* includes a preposition, a noun or a pronoun called the *object of the preposition,* and any modifiers of that object.

EXAMPLES The Seine River flows **through Paris.** [The noun *Paris* is the object of the preposition *through.*]
The car **in front of us** slid **into a snowbank.** [The pronoun *us* is the object of the preposition *in front of.* The noun *snowbank* is the object of the preposition *into.*]

 REFERENCE NOTE: For a list of commonly used prepositions, see pages 65–66.

Any modifier that comes between the preposition and its object is part of the prepositional phrase.

EXAMPLE **During the stormy night** the horse ran off. [The adjectives *the* and *stormy* modify the object *night.*]

An object of a preposition may be compound.

EXAMPLE The dish is filled **with raw carrots and celery.** [Both *carrots* and *celery* are objects of the preposition *with.*]

Be careful not to confuse an infinitive with a prepositional phrase beginning with *to.* A prepositional phrase always has an object that is a noun or a pronoun. An infinitive is a verb form that usually begins with *to*.

PREPOSITIONAL PHRASE When we went **to Florida,** we saw the old Spanish fort in Saint Augustine.

INFINITIVE When we were in Florida, we went **to see** the old Spanish fort in Saint Augustine.

Hi & Lois reprinted with special permission of King Features Syndicate, Inc.

The Adjective Phrase

6c. An *adjective phrase* is a prepositional phrase that modifies a noun or a pronoun.

An adjective phrase tells *what kind* or *which one*.

EXAMPLES Wang Wei was a talented painter **of landscapes.**
[The phrase modifies the noun *painter,* telling what kind of painter Wang Wei was.]
Mrs. O'Meara is the one **on the left.** [The phrase modifies the pronoun *one,* telling which one Mrs. O'Meara is.]

SENTENCES

An adjective phrase always follows the word it modifies. That word may be the object of another prepositional phrase.

EXAMPLES Sicily is an island **off the coast** **of Italy.** [The phrase *off the coast* modifies the noun *island.* The phrase *of Italy* modifies the object *coast.*]

More than one adjective phrase may modify the same word.

EXAMPLE The box **of old magazines** **in the closet** is full. [The phrases *of old magazines* and *in the closet* modify the noun *box.*]

The Adverb Phrase

6d. An *adverb phrase* is a prepositional phrase that modifies a verb, an adjective, or an adverb.

An adverb phrase tells *how, when, where, why,* or *to what extent* (that is, *how long, how many,* or *how far*).

EXAMPLES The snow fell **like feathers.** [The phrase modifies the verb *fell,* telling *how* the snow fell.]
The painting looks strange **over the fireplace.** [The phrase modifies the adjective *strange,* telling *where* the painting looks strange.]
We arrived early **in the morning.** [The phrase modifies the adverb *early,* telling *when* we arrived early.]
Mr. Ortiz has taught school **for sixteen years.** [The phrase modifies the verb phrase *has taught,* telling *how long* Mr. Ortiz has taught.]

An adverb phrase may come before or after the word it modifies.

EXAMPLES The sportswriter interviewed the coach **before the game.**

Before the game the sportswriter interviewed **the coach.** [In each sentence the phrase modifies the verb *interviewed.*]

More than one adverb phrase may modify the same word or words.

EXAMPLE   **On April 24, 1990,** the Hubble Space Telescope

was launched **into space.** [Both phrases modify the verb phrase *was launched.*]

An adverb phrase may be followed by an adjective phrase modifying the object of the adverb phrase.

EXAMPLE    **In her poems** **about the Southwest,** Leslie

Marmon Silko uses word pictures that appeal to the senses. [The adverb phrase modifies the verb *uses.* The adjective phrase modifies the object *poems.*]

✔ *QUICK CHECK 1*   **Identifying Prepositional Phrases**

Identify the prepositional phrase or phrases in each numbered sentence in the following paragraph. Then label each phrase as an *adjective phrase* or an *adverb phrase.* Give the word the phrase modifies.

[1] Hubert "Geese" Ausbie was known for both his sunny smile and his athletic skill during his career. [2] For twenty-five years, Ausbie played on one of the most popular teams in basketball's history. [3] He was a star with the Harlem Globetrotters beginning in 1961. [4] The all-black team, which was started in 1927, is famous for its humorous performances. [5] The combination of skill and humor is what appeals to Globetrotter fans throughout the world.

Verbals and Verbal Phrases

A *verbal* is a form of a verb used as a noun, an adjective, or an adverb. There are three kinds of verbals: the *participle*, the *gerund*, and the *infinitive*.

The Participle

6e. A *participle* is a verb form that can be used as an adjective.

There are two kinds of participles—*present participles* and *past participles.*

(1) *Present participles* end in *-ing.*

EXAMPLES The news was **encouraging.** [*Encouraging,* a form of the verb *encourage,* acts as an adjective modifying the noun *news.*]

The horses **running** past were not frightened by the crowd. [*Running,* a form of the verb *run,* acts as an adjective modifying the noun *horses.*]

(2) Most *past participles* end in *-d* or *-ed.* Others are irregularly formed.

EXAMPLES The police officers searched the **abandoned** warehouse. [*Abandoned,* a form of the verb *abandon,* acts as an adjective modifying the noun *warehouse.*]

Charlie Parker, **known** as Bird, was a talented jazz musician. [*Known,* a form of the verb *know,* acts as an adjective modifying the noun *Charlie Parker.*]

 REFERENCE NOTE: For a list of irregular past participles, see pages 102–105.

Do not confuse a participle used as an adjective with a participle used as part of a verb phrase.

PARTICIPLE **Planning** their trip, the class learned how to read a road map.

VERB PHRASE	While they **were planning** their trip, the class learned how to read a road map.
PARTICIPLE	Most of the treasure **buried** by the pirates has never been found.
VERB PHRASE	Most of the treasure that **was buried** by the pirates has never been found.

The Participial Phrase

6f. A *participial phrase* consists of a participle and all of the words related to the participle. The entire phrase is used as an adjective.

A participle may be modified by an adverb and may also have a complement, usually a direct object. A participial phrase includes the participle, all of its modifiers, its complements, and modifiers of the complements.

EXAMPLES **Seeing itself in the mirror,** the duck seemed bewildered. [The participial phrase modifies the noun *duck*. The pronoun *itself* is the direct object of the present participle *seeing*. The adverb phrase *in the mirror* modifies the present participle *seeing*.]

After a while, we heard the curious duck **quacking noisily at its own image.** [The participial phrase modifies the noun *duck*. The adverb *noisily* and the adverb phrase *at its own image* modify the present participle *quacking*.]

Then, **disgusted with the other duck,** it pecked the mirror. [The participial phrase modifies the pronoun *it*. The adverb phrase *with the other duck* modifies the past participle *disgusted*.]

☞ REFERENCE NOTE: For more information on complements, see **Chapter 9: Complements.**

A participial phrase should be placed as close as possible to the word it modifies. Otherwise the sentence may not make sense.

SENTENCES

MISPLACED   Slithering through the grass, I saw a snake trimming the hedges this morning. [Was *I* slithering through the grass? Was *the snake* trimming the hedges?]

CORRECTED   **Trimming the hedges this morning,** I saw a snake **slithering through the grass.**

 REFERENCE NOTE: For more information about misplaced participial phrases, see pages 139–140.

 QUICK CHECK 2   **Identifying Participial Phrases**

Identify the participial phrases in the following sentences. Give the word or words that each phrase modifies.

1. Noted for her beauty, Venus was sought by all the gods.
2. Jupiter, knowing her charms, nevertheless married her to Vulcan, the ugliest of the gods.
3. Mars, known to the Greeks as Ares, was the god of war.
4. Terrified by Ares' power, many Greeks did not like to worship him.
5. They saw both land and people destroyed by him.

The Gerund

6g.   A *gerund* is a verb form ending in *-ing* that is used as a noun.

SUBJECT   **Skating** can be good exercise.
PREDICATE NOMINATIVE   My favorite hobby is **collecting baseball cards.**
OBJECT OF PREPOSITION   Lock the door before **leaving.**
DIRECT OBJECT   Did they enjoy **singing**?

NOTE   Do not confuse a gerund with a present participle used as part of a verb phrase or as an adjective.

EXAMPLE   **Pausing,** the deer **was smelling** the wind before **running** into the meadow. [*Pausing* is a participle modifying *deer,* and *smelling* is part of the verb phrase *was smelling. Running* is a gerund, serving as the object of the preposition *before.*]

The Gerund Phrase

6h. A *gerund phrase* consists of a gerund and all the words related to the gerund.

Because a gerund is a verb form, it may be modified by an adverb and have a complement, usually a direct object. Since a gerund functions as a noun, it may be modified by an adjective. A gerund phrase includes the gerund, its modifiers, its complements and their modifiers.

EXAMPLES **Having a part-time job** may interfere with your schoolwork. [The gerund phrase is the subject of the sentence. The noun *job* is the direct object of the gerund *having.* The article *a* and the adjective *part-time* modify *job.*]

The townspeople heard **the loud clanging of the fire bell.** [The gerund phrase is the direct object of the verb *heard.* The adjectives *the* and *loud* and the adjective phrase *of the fire bell* modify the gerund *clanging.*]

We crossed the stream by **stepping carefully from stone to stone.** [The gerund phrase is the object of the preposition *by.* The adverb *carefully* and the adverb phrases *from stone* and *to stone* modify the gerund *stepping.*]

 REFERENCE NOTE: For more information on complements, see **Chapter 9: Complements.**

 When a noun or a pronoun comes immediately before a gerund, use the possessive form of the noun or pronoun.

EXAMPLES **Michael's** cooking is the best I've ever tasted.
The vultures didn't let anything disturb **their** feeding.

 QUICK CHECK 3 **Identifying Gerund Phrases**

Find the gerund phrases in the following sentences. Identify each phrase as a *subject,* a *predicate nominative,* a *direct object,* or an *object of a preposition.*

1. The sound they heard was the howling of wolves.
2. We sat back and enjoyed the slow rocking of the boat.
3. People supported Cesar Chavez and the United Farm Workers by boycotting grapes.
4. The frantic darting of the fish indicated that a shark was nearby.
5. In his later years, Chief Quanah Parker was known for settling disputes fairly.

The Infinitive

6i. An *infinitive* is a verb form that can be used as a noun, an adjective, or an adverb. An infinitive usually begins with *to.*

NOUNS **To install** the ceiling fan took two hours. [*To install* is the subject of the sentence.]
Winona's ambition is **to become** a doctor. [*To become* is a predicate nominative referring to the subject *ambition.*]
Shina likes **to skate** but not **to ski.** [*To skate* and *to ski* are direct objects of the verb *likes.*]

ADJECTIVES The best time **to visit** Florida is December through April. [*To visit* modifies *time.*]
If you want information about computers, that is the magazine **to read.** [*To read* modifies *magazine.*]

ADVERBS The gymnasts were eager **to practice** their routines. [*To practice* modifies the adjective *eager.*]
The caravan stopped at the oasis **to rest.** [*To rest* modifies the verb *stopped.*]

NOTE *To* plus a noun or a pronoun (*to class, to them, to the dance*) is a prepositional phrase, not an infinitive. Be careful not to confuse infinitives with prepositional phrases beginning with *to.*

INFINITIVE I want **to go.**
PREPOSITIONAL PHRASE I want to go **to town.**

The Infinitive Phrase

6j. An *infinitive phrase* consists of an infinitive and its modifiers and complements.

An infinitive may be modified by an adjective or an adverb; it may also have a complement, which may have modifiers. The entire infinitive phrase may act as an adjective, an adverb, or a noun.

EXAMPLES The crowd grew quiet **to hear the speaker.** [The infinitive phrase is an adverb modifying the adjective *quiet.* The noun *speaker* is the direct object of the infinitive *to hear.*]

Peanuts and raisins are good snacks **to take on a camping trip.** [The infinitive phrase is an adjective modifying *snacks.* The adverb phrase *on a camping trip* modifies the infinitive *to take.*]

To lift those weights takes a lot of strength. [The infinitive phrase is a noun used as the subject of the sentence. The noun *weights* is the direct object of the infinitive *to lift.*]

 REFERENCE NOTE: For more information on complements, see **Chapter 9: Complements.**

 QUICK CHECK 4 **Identifying Infinitive Phrases**

Most of the sentences in the following paragraph contain infinitive phrases. Identify each infinitive phrase, and tell whether it is a *noun,* an *adjective,* or an *adverb.* If there is no infinitive phrase in a sentence, write *none.*

[1] My aunt Bo taught me to take care of my bicycle. [2] We used machine oil to lubricate the chain. [3] Then she showed me the valve to fill the inner tube. [4] Using a hand pump, we added air to the back tire. [5] When we finished, I thanked Aunt Bo for taking the time to give me tips about taking care of my bicycle.

S E N T E N C E S

Appositives and Appositive Phrases

6k. An *appositive* is a noun or a pronoun placed beside another noun or pronoun to identify or explain it.

Appositives are often set off by commas. But if an appositive is needed for meaning or is closely related to the word it refers to, no commas are necessary.

EXAMPLES The cosmonaut **Yuri Gagarin** was the first person in space. [The noun *Yuri Gagarin* identifies the noun *cosmonaut*.]
The explorers saw a strange animal, **something** with fur and a bill like a duck's. [The pronoun *something* refers to the noun *animal*.]
Audubon, an **artist** and **naturalist,** painted birds. [The nouns *artist* and *naturalist* explain the noun *Audubon*.]

 REFERENCE NOTE: For more information on the use of commas with appositives and appositive phrases, see page 266.

6l. An *appositive phrase* consists of an appositive and its modifiers.

EXAMPLES Officer Webb, **one of the security guards,** apprehended the burglar. [The adjective phrase *of the security guards* modifies the appositive *one*.]
Black Hawk, **a famous chief of the Sauk,** fought hard for the freedom of his people. [The article *a*, the adjective *famous,* and the adjective phrase *of the Sauk* modify the appositive *chief*.]

 QUICK CHECK 5 **Identifying Appositives and Appositive Phrases**

Identify the appositives or appositive phrases in the following sentences. Give the word or words each appositive or appositive phrase identifies or explains.

1. Some of the most popular Mexican dishes—tacos, tamales, and fajitas—are served here.
2. I'll have a sandwich, tuna salad on rye bread, please.
3. Barbara Jordan, one of my heroes, has been an important figure in both civil and human rights issues.
4. Shelley asked everyone where her friend Bianca had gone.
5. They sang the song "I've Been Working on the Railroad" over and over all the way down the path.

STYLE NOTE Knowing how to use the different kinds of phrases can help you improve your writing. For example, to revise a group of short, choppy sentences, combine them. Simply turn at least one sentence into a phrase.

CHOPPY	I missed the field trip. Jana is my best friend. Jana was worried about me.
APPOSITIVE PHRASE	Jana, **my best friend,** was worried about me when I missed the field trip.
PARTICIPIAL PHRASE	**Being my best friend,** Jana was worried when I missed the field trip.
GERUND PHRASE	Jana, who is my best friend, worried about **my missing the field trip.**

 REFERENCE NOTE: For more sentence-combining suggestions, see pages 223–229.

COMPUTER NOTE As you can see in the Style Note above, there are several ways to revise choppy sentences. It's always a good idea to create a number of different revisions. Then you can choose the one that fits best in the paragraph that you are writing. Print out a few different versions of the paragraph so that you can compare how they look and sound.

SENTENCES

✓ Chapter Review 1

Identifying Prepositional, Verbal, and Appositive Phrases

Identify each italicized phrase in the following paragraphs as *prepositional, participial, gerund, infinitive,* or *appositive.* Do not separately identify a prepositional phrase that is part of a larger phrase.

EXAMPLES   After [1] *giving me my allowance,* my father
warned me [2] *not to spend it all in one place.*
1. *giving me my allowance—gerund*
2. *not to spend it all in one place—infinitive*

Gina, [1] *my best friend since elementary school,* and I decided [2] *to go to the mall after school yesterday.* Gina suggested [3] *taking the back way* so that we could jog, but I was wearing sandals [4] *instead of my track shoes,* so we just walked. Along the way we saw Cathy [5] *sitting on her front porch* and asked her if she wanted [6] *to join us.* She was earning a little spending money by [7] *baby-sitting her neighbor's children,* though, and couldn't leave.

[8] *Walking up to the wide glass doors at the mall,* Gina and I looked in our purses. We both had a few dollars and our student passes, so we stopped [9] *to get a glass of orange juice* while we checked what movies were playing. None [10] *of the four features* looked interesting to us. However, Deven Bowers, [11] *a friend from school and an usher at the theater,* said that there would be a sneak preview [12] *of a new adventure film* later, and we told him we'd be back then.

Since stores usually do not allow customers to bring food or drinks inside, Gina and I gulped down our orange juice before [13] *going into our favorite dress shop.* We looked [14] *through most of the sale racks,* but none of the dresses, [15] *all of them formal or evening gowns,* appealed to us. A salesclerk asked us if we were shopping [16] *for something special.* After **[17]** *checking with Gina,* I told the clerk we were just looking, and we left.

We walked past a couple of shops—**[18]** *the health-food store and a toy store*—and went into Record World. **[19]** *Seeing several cassettes by my favorite group,* I picked out one. By the time we walked out of Record World, I'd spent all my money, so we never did get **[20]** *to go to the movie that day.*

✓ Chapter Review 2

Writing Sentences with Prepositional, Verbal, and Appositive Phrases

Write ten sentences, using one of the following phrases in each sentence. Follow the directions in parentheses.

EXAMPLE
    1. to write a descriptive paragraph (*use as an infinitive phrase that is the predicate nominative in the sentence*)
    1. *Our assignment for tomorrow is to write a descriptive paragraph.*

1. after the game (*use as an adverb phrase*)
2. instead of your good shoes (*use as an adverb phrase*)
3. in one of Shakespeare's plays (*use as an adjective phrase*)
4. going to school every day (*use as a gerund phrase that is the subject in the sentence*)
5. living in a small town (*use as a gerund phrase that is the object of a preposition*)
6. walking through the empty lot (*use as a participial phrase*)
7. dressed in authentic costumes (*use as a participial phrase*)
8. to drive a car for the first time (*use as an infinitive phrase that is the direct object in the sentence*)
9. the best athlete in our school (*use as an appositive phrase*)
10. my favorite pastime (*use as an appositive phrase*)

7 CLAUSES

Independent and Subordinate Clauses

✓ Checking What You Know

Identifying Independent and Subordinate Clauses

Identify each italicized clause in the following sentences as an *independent clause* or a *subordinate clause*. Indicate whether each italicized subordinate clause is used as an *adjective,* an *adverb,* or a *noun.*

EXAMPLES   **1.** The customer thumbed through the book, but *it didn't seem to interest her.*
   1. *independent clause*

   2. Anyone *who gets a high score on this test* will not have to take the final exam.
   2. *subordinate clause—adjective*

1. *After it had been snowing for several hours,* we took our sleds out to Sentry Hill.
2. The ring *that I lost at the beach last summer* had belonged to my great-grandmother.
3. If he doesn't get here soon, *I'm leaving.*
4. Do you know *who she is?*

162

5. I have not seen Shawn *since the football game ended last Saturday night.*

6. *In the morning they gathered their belongings and left* before the sun rose.

7. Nobody knew *that Derrick had worked out the solution.*

8. *The Hopi and the Zuni built their homes out of adobe,* which is sun-dried earth.

9. My dad says never to trust strangers *who seem overly friendly.*

10. *That he had been right* became obvious as the problem grew worse.

11. Julio knew the right answer *because he looked it up in a dictionary.*

12. Today's assignment is to write a three-paragraph composition on *how a bill becomes a law.*

13. On our vacation we visited my dad's old neighborhood, *which is now an industrial park.*

14. *Mr. Johnson told us* that in the late 1800s at least one fourth of all the cowboys in the West were African Americans.

15. Did you get the message *that your mother called?*

16. Tranh raked up the leaves *while his father added them to a pile for garden use.*

17. The Spanish Club sang several Mexican American *corridos,* or ballads, and *the performance was a hit.*

18. We will be over *as soon as Sandy finishes his lunch.*

19. That is the man *whose dog rescued my sister.*

20. Free samples were given to *whoever asked for them.* ✓

7a. A *clause* is a group of words that contains a verb and its subject and is used as a part of a sentence.

Every clause has a subject and a verb. However, not every clause expresses a complete thought.

SENTENCE   Writers gathered at the home of Gertrude Stein when she lived in Paris.

SENTENCES

S   V

CLAUSE   **Writers gathered at the home of Gertrude Stein.**
[complete thought]

S   V

CLAUSE   **when she lived in Paris** [incomplete thought]

There are two kinds of clauses: the *independent clause* and the *subordinate clause*.

The Independent Clause

7b. An *independent* (or *main*) *clause* expresses a complete thought and can stand by itself as a sentence.

S   V

EXAMPLES   **The sun set an hour ago.** [This entire sentence is an independent clause.]

S   V

Jean Merrill wrote *The Pushcart War,* and

S   V

Ronni Solbert illustrated the book. [This sentence contains two independent clauses.]

S   V

After I finished studying, **I went to the movies.**
[This sentence contains one independent clause and one subordinate clause.]

 QUICK CHECK 1   **Identifying Subjects and Verbs in Independent Clauses**

Identify the subject and the verb in each numbered, italicized independent clause in the following paragraph.

Before she left for college, [1] *my sister read the comics in the newspaper every day.* [2] *She told me* that Jump Start was one of her favorites. Since she liked it so much, [3] *I made a point of reading it, too.* [4] *The comic strip was created by Robb Armstrong,* who lives and works in Philadelphia. [5] *Jump Start features an African American police officer named Joe and his wife, Marcy,* who is a nurse.

The Subordinate Clause

7c. A *subordinate* (or *dependent*) *clause* does not express a complete thought and cannot stand alone as a sentence.

A word such as *that, what,* or *since* signals the beginning of a subordinate clause.

EXAMPLES
　　　　　　　S　V
　　　　　　that I wanted

　　　　　　　S　　V
　　　　what she saw

　　　　　　　　S　　V
　　　since most plants die without light

The meaning of a subordinate clause is complete only when the clause is attached to an independent clause.

EXAMPLES　The store did not have the video game **that I wanted.**
　　　　　　The witness told the police officers **what she saw.**
　　　　　　Since most plants die without light, we moved our houseplants closer to the window.

Sometimes the word that begins a subordinate clause is the subject of the clause.

EXAMPLES　　　　　　　　　　S　　V
　　　　　　The animals **that live in the game preserve** are protected from hunters.

　　　　　　　　　　　　　S　　　V
　　　　　　Can you tell me **who wrote "America the Beautiful"?**

SENTENCES

Frank & Ernest reprinted by permission of NEA, Inc.

 QUICK CHECK 2 | **Identifying Independent and Subordinate Clauses**

Identify each of the following groups of words as an *independent clause* or a *subordinate clause.*

1. we memorized the lyrics
2. as they sat on the back porch
3. if no one is coming
4. my sister was born on Valentine's Day
5. which everyone enjoyed

The Adjective Clause

7d. An *adjective clause* is a subordinate clause that modifies a noun or a pronoun.

Like an adjective or an adjective phrase, an adjective clause modifies a noun or a pronoun. But an adjective clause contains a verb and its subject. An adjective phrase does not.

ADJECTIVE	the **blond** woman
ADJECTIVE PHRASE	the woman **with blond hair**
ADJECTIVE CLAUSE	the woman **who has blond hair**
ADJECTIVE	a **steel** bridge
ADJECTIVE PHRASE	a bridge **of steel**
ADJECTIVE CLAUSE	a bridge **that is made of steel**

An adjective clause usually follows the word it modifies and tells *which one* or *what kind.*

EXAMPLES   Ms. Jackson showed slides **that she had taken in Egypt.** [The adjective clause modifies the noun *slides*, telling *which* slides.]

Helen Keller was a remarkable woman **who overcame both blindness and deafness.** [The adjective clause modifies the noun *woman*, telling *what kind* of woman.]

The ones **whose flight was delayed** spent the night in Detroit. [The adjective clause modifies the pronoun *ones*, telling *which* ones.]

Relative Pronouns

An adjective clause is usually introduced by a *relative pronoun.*

Relative Pronouns				
that	which	who	whom	whose

A ***relative pronoun*** relates an adjective clause to the word the clause modifies.

EXAMPLES   Leonardo da Vinci was the artist **who painted the *Mona Lisa*.** [The relative pronoun *who* begins the adjective clause and relates it to the noun *artist.*]

Everything **that could be done** was done. [The relative pronoun *that* begins the adjective clause and relates it to the pronoun *everything.*]

The author **whom I've chosen for my report** is Amy Tan. [The relative pronoun *whom* begins the adjective clause and relates it to the noun *author.*]

Only those **whose parents or guardians have signed a permission slip** can go on the field trip. [The relative pronoun *whose* begins the adjective clause and relates it to the pronoun *those.*]

"The Tell-Tale Heart," **which tells the story of a killer,** is great to read aloud. [The relative pronoun *which* begins the adjective clause and relates it to the compound noun *"The Tell-Tale Heart."*]

 REFERENCE NOTE: For information on when to set off adjective clauses with commas, see pages 265–266.

 NOTE The relative pronoun *that* is used to refer both to people and to things. The relative pronoun *which* is used to refer to things only.

Sometimes a relative pronoun is preceded by a preposition that is part of the adjective clause.

EXAMPLES   Have you read the book **on which the movie is based**?
The young actor **to whom I am referring** is Fred Savage.

 REFERENCE NOTE: For instructions on using *who* and *whom* correctly, see pages 122–124.

In addition to relating a subordinate clause to the rest of the sentence, a relative pronoun also has a function in the subordinate clause.

EXAMPLES   Is this the tape **that is on sale**? [*That* relates the subordinate clause to the word *tape* and also functions as the subject of the subordinate clause.]
He is a friend **on whom you can always depend.** [*Whom* relates the subordinate clause to the word *friend* and functions as the object of the preposition *on*.]

An adjective clause may be introduced by a *relative adverb* such as *when* or *where*.

EXAMPLES   This is the spot **where we caught most of the fish.**
The time period **when dinosaurs ruled** lasted millions of years.

In some cases, the relative pronoun or adverb can be omitted.

EXAMPLES   We haven't seen the silver jewelry [that *or which*] **she brought back from Mexico.**

Do you remember the time [*when or that*] **the dog caught the skunk**?

☑ *QUICK CHECK 3*   **Identifying Adjective Clauses**

Identify the adjective clause in each of the following sentences. Give the relative pronoun and the word that the relative pronoun refers to.

1. A black hole, which appears after a star has collapsed, can trap energy and matter.
2. A special award was given to the student whose work had most improved.
3. We enjoyed the poems of Gwendolyn Brooks, who for years has been poet laureate of Illinois.
4. In *Walden*, Henry David Thoreau shared ideas that have influenced many.
5. A friend is a person whom you can trust.

The Adverb Clause

7e.   An **adverb clause** is a subordinate clause that modifies a verb, an adjective, or an adverb.

Unlike an adverb or an adverb phrase, an adverb clause has a subject and a verb.

ADVERB	You may sit **anywhere.**
ADVERB PHRASE	You may sit **in any chair.**
ADVERB CLAUSE	You may sit **wherever you wish.** [*You* is the subject, and *wish* is the verb.]

An adverb clause tells *where, when, how, why, to what extent,* or *under what condition.*

EXAMPLES   You may sit **wherever you wish.** [The adverb clause modifies the verb *may sit*, telling *where* you may sit.]

When winter sets in, many animals hibernate.
[The adverb clause modifies the verb *hibernate*,
telling *when* many animals hibernate.]

My new friend and I talk **as if we've known
each other for a long time.** [The adverb clause
modifies the verb *talk*, telling *how* my new
friend and I talk.]

Because the weather was hot, the cool water
felt good. [The adverb clause modifies the adjective *good*, telling *why* the water felt good.]

Gabrielle can type faster **than I can.** [The adverb
clause modifies the adverb *faster*, telling *to what
extent* Gabrielle can type faster.]

If it does not rain tomorrow, we will go to
Crater Lake. [The adverb clause modifies the
verb *will go*, telling *under what condition* we
will go to Crater Lake.]

Notice in these examples that an adverb clause does not
always follow the word it modifies. When an adverb
clause begins a sentence, the clause is followed by a
comma.

 REFERENCE NOTE: For more information about using commas with adverb clauses, see page 269.

STYLE
NOTE

In most cases, deciding where to place an
adverb clause is a matter of style, not being
correct. Both sentences below are correct.

Though she was almost unknown during her lifetime,
Emily Dickinson is now known as a major American
poet.

Emily Dickinson is now known as a major American
poet **though she was almost unknown during her
lifetime.**

Which sentence might you use in a school paper on Emily
Dickinson? The sentence to choose would be the one that

SENTENCES

looks and sounds better in the ***context***—the rest of the paragraph to which the sentence belongs.

Subordinating Conjunctions

An adverb clause is introduced by a ***subordinating conjunction***—a word that shows the relationship between the adverb clause and the word or words that the clause modifies.

Common Subordinating Conjunctions			
after	as though	since	when
although	because	so that	whenever
as	before	than	where
as if	how	though	wherever
as long as	if	unless	whether
as soon as	in order that	until	while

NOTE The words *after, as, before, since,* and *until* are also commonly used as prepositions.

PREPOSITION	P. D. James is best known **as** a writer of fine detective novels.
SUBORDINATING CONJUNCTION	**As** the sun came up, the large birds caught the hot winds and rose into the air.
PREPOSITION	**After** lunch we'll finish making the model airplane.
SUBORDINATING CONJUNCTION	**After** you wash the dishes, I'll dry them and put them up.

COMPUTER NOTE A computer can help you proofread your writing. Use the computer's "Search" function to highlight any uses of the words *after, as, before, since,* and *until*. Look at the use of such words at the beginnings of sentences. Decide whether the word begins a prepositional phrase or a subordinate clause. In most cases an introductory prepositional phrase is not set off by a comma. An introductory adverb clause is *always* followed by a comma.

 REFERENCE NOTE: For more information about using commas with introductory phrases and clauses, see pages 268–269.

 QUICK CHECK 4 **Identifying Adverb Clauses**

Identify the adverb clause in each of the following sentences. In each clause, circle the subordinating conjunction, and underline the subject once and the verb twice.

1. Although they lived in different regions of North America, Native American children all across the continent enjoyed playing similar kinds of games.
2. These children used mainly natural objects in games since there were no toy stores.
3. Before they started playing, the children made balls out of such materials as wood and tree roots.
4. After snow had fallen, Seneca children raced small handmade "snow boats."
5. Pine cones were used in many games because the cones were so easy to find.

The Noun Clause

7f. A *noun clause* is a subordinate clause used as a noun.

A noun clause may be used as a subject, a complement (predicate nominative, direct object, indirect object), or an object of a preposition.

SUBJECT **That Felicia is angry** is obvious.

PREDICATE NOMINATIVE Three dollars was **what he offered me for this baseball card.**

DIRECT OBJECT	The judges determined **who won the piano competition.**
INDIRECT OBJECT	The sheriff gave **whoever volunteered** a flashlight.
OBJECT OF A PREPOSITION	Most of the time we agreed with **whatever he said.**

Common Introductory Words for Noun Clauses

who	whoever	which
whom	whomever	whichever
what	whatever	that

The word that introduces a noun clause often has another function within the clause.

EXAMPLES   Give a free pass to **whoever asks for one.** [The introductory word *whoever* is the subject of the verb *asks.* The entire noun clause is the object of the preposition *to.*]

Did anyone tell him **what he should do?** [The introductory word *what* is the direct object of the verb *should do—he should do what.* The entire noun clause is the direct object of the verb *did tell.*]

Their complaint was **that the milk smelled sour.** [The word *that* introduces the noun clause but has no other function in the clause. The noun clause is the predicate nominative identifying the subject *complaint.*]

 REFERENCE NOTE: For instructions on using *who* and *whom* correctly, see pages 122–124. The same instructions can be used for *whoever* and *whomever.*

 QUICK CHECK 5   **Identifying and Classifying Noun Clauses**

Identify the noun clause in each of the following sentences. Tell whether the noun clause is a *subject,* a *predicate*

SENTENCES

nominative, a *direct object*, an *indirect object*, or an *object of a preposition*.

1. Do you know what happened to the rest of my tuna sandwich?
2. The worst flaw in the story is that it doesn't have a carefully developed plot.
3. The painter gave whatever spots had dried another coat of primer.
4. At lunch, my friends and I talked about what we should do as our service project.
5. That Coretta Scott King spoke for peace surprised no one.

Chapter Review 1

Identifying Independent and Subordinate Clauses

Identify each italicized clause in the following paragraphs as an *independent clause* or a *subordinate clause*. Tell whether each italicized subordinate clause is a *noun*, an *adjective*, or an *adverb*.

EXAMPLES　When my mother got a new job, [1] *we had to move to another town.*
　　　　1. *independent clause*

　　　　[2] *When my mother got a new job,* we had to move to another town.
　　　　2. *subordinate clause—adverb*

　　　I didn't want to move [1] *because I didn't want to transfer to another school.* This is the fourth time [2] *that I have had to change schools,* and every time I've wished [3] *that I could just stay at my old school.* [4] *As soon as I make friends in a new place,* I have to move again and leave them behind. Then at the new school [5] *I am a stranger again.*

　　　We lived in our last house for three years, which is longer [6] *than I've lived in any other place* [7] *since I was little.* [8] *Living there so long, I had a chance to meet several peo-*

ple [9] *who became good friends of mine.* My best friends, Chris and Marty, said [10] *that they would write to me,* and I promised to write to them, too. However, the friends [11] *that I had had before* had promised to write, but [12] *after a letter or two we lost touch.* [13] *Why this always happens* is a mystery to me.

In my new school, I registered [14] *after the school year had already begun.* By then, everyone else would already have made friends, and [15] *I would be an outsider,* [16] *as I knew from past experience.* There are always some students who bully and tease [17] *whoever is new at school* or anyone else [18] *who is different.* Back in elementary school I would get angry and upset [19] *when people picked on me.* Since then, I've learned how to fit in and make friends in spite of [20] *whatever anyone does to hassle me or make me feel uncomfortable.*

Everywhere [21] *that I've gone to school,* some students always are friendly and offer to show me around. [22] *I used to be shy,* and I wouldn't take them up on their invitations. Since they didn't know [23] *whether I was being shy or unfriendly,* they soon left me alone. Now [24] *whenever someone is friendly to me at a new school or in a new neighborhood,* I fight down my shyness and act friendly myself. It's still hard to get used to new places and new people, but [25] *it's a lot easier with a little help from new friends.*

SENTENCES

 Chapter Review 2

Writing Sentences with Independent and Subordinate Clauses

Write your own sentences according to the following instructions. Underline the subordinate clauses.

EXAMPLE   **1.** a sentence with an independent clause and an adjective clause

       1. *I am going to the game with Guido, <u>who is my best friend</u>.*

1. a sentence with an independent clause and no subordinate clauses
2. a sentence with an independent clause and one subordinate clause
3. a sentence with an adjective clause that begins with a relative pronoun
4. a sentence with an adjective clause in which a preposition precedes the relative pronoun
5. a sentence with an introductory adverb clause
6. a sentence with an adverb clause and an adjective clause
7. a sentence with a noun clause used as a direct object
8. a sentence with a noun clause used as a subject
9. a sentence with a noun clause used as the object of a preposition
10. a sentence with a noun clause and either an adjective clause or an adverb clause

8 SENTENCES

Subject and Predicate

✓ Checking What You Know

A. Identifying Sentences and Sentence Fragments

Identify each group of words as a *sentence* or a *sentence fragment*. If the word group is a sentence fragment, correct it by adding words to make a complete sentence.

EXAMPLES   **1.** Although I know your first name.
        1. *sentence fragment—Although I know your first name, I don't know your last name.*

        2. You may call me by my given name or by my surname.
        2. *sentence*

1. While it may seem strange to go by one name.
2. People had only first names for thousands of years.
3. Calling people by one name.
4. The ancient Romans sometimes gave people second names.
5. Last names became common in the thirteenth century in Italy.

B. Identifying Subjects and Predicates

Label each italicized group of words as the *complete subject* or the *complete predicate* of the sentence.

EXAMPLES **1.** *The mean dog next door* barks fiercely.
1. *complete subject*

2. The mean dog next door *barks fiercely.*
2. *complete predicate*

6. Mr. Adams *gave me his old croquet set.*
7. Why did *that large new boat* sink on such a clear day?
8. *Trees and bushes all over the neighborhood* had been torn up by the storm.
9. Bill *was splashed by a passing car this morning.*
10. *My old bicycle with the ape-hanger handlebars* is rusting away in the garage now.
11. *The creek behind my house* rises during the summer rains.
12. Sandy's little sister *bravely dived off the high board at the community pool.*
13. *Does* Max *want another serving of pie?*
14. My cousins and I *played basketball and walked over to the mall yesterday.*
15. *Fridays and other test days* always seem longer than regular school days.

C. Identifying Simple Subjects and Verbs

Identify the simple subjects and the verbs in the following sentences.

EXAMPLE **1.** Festivals and celebrations are happy times throughout the world.
1. *subject—Festivals, celebrations; verb—are*

16. Children and nature are honored with their own festivals in Japan.
17. Among Japanese nature festivals are the Cherry Blossom Festival and the Chrysanthemum Festival.

18. Fierce dragons are paraded and huge ships fly in the sky during Singapore's Kite Festival.
19. Elaborate masks and costumes are an important part of the Carnival Lamayote in Haiti.
20. Flowers and other small gifts are presented to teachers during Teacher's Day in Czechoslovakia. ✓

The Sentence

8a. A *sentence* is a group of words that expresses a complete thought.

A sentence begins with a capital letter and ends with a period, a question mark, or an exclamation point.

EXAMPLES   Sean was chosen captain of his soccer team.
Have you read the novel *Shane*?
What a dangerous mission it must have been!

Sentence or Sentence Fragment?

When a group of words looks like a sentence but does not express a complete thought, it is a *sentence fragment.*

SENTENCE FRAGMENT   The "ragtime" music of Scott Joplin. [This is not a complete thought. What about the "ragtime" music of Scott Joplin?]

SENTENCE   The "ragtime" music of Scott Joplin has been recorded by many musicians.

SENTENCE FRAGMENT   After watching Rita Moreno. [The thought is not complete. Who watched Rita Moreno? What happened afterward?]

SENTENCE   After watching Rita Moreno, Carol decided to become an entertainer.

SENTENCE FRAGMENT   Even though she had worked a long time. [The thought is not complete. Even though she had worked a long time, what happened?]

SENTENCE   Louise Nevelson had not completed the sculpture, even though she had worked a long time.

SENTENCES

REFERENCE NOTE: For more information about sentence fragments, see pages 219–220.

 COMPUTER NOTE If sentence fragments are a problem in your writing, a computer may be able to help you. Some style-checking programs can identify and highlight sentence fragments. Such programs are useful, but they aren't perfect. The best way to eliminate fragments from your writing is still to check each sentence yourself. Be sure that each has a subject and a verb and that it expresses a complete thought.

 QUICK CHECK 1 **Identifying Sentences and Revising Sentence Fragments**

Tell whether each group of words is a *sentence* or a *sentence fragment.* If the word group is a sentence, correct it by adding a capital letter and end punctuation. If the word group is a sentence fragment, correct it by adding words to make a complete sentence.

1. catching the baseball with both hands
2. in the back of the storeroom stands a stack of boxes
3. a long, narrow passage with a hidden trapdoor at the end
4. the gymnasium is open
5. are you careful about shutting off unnecessary lights

Crock reprinted wih special permission of North America Syndicate, Inc.

The Subject and the Predicate

A sentence consists of two parts: a *subject* and a *predicate*.

8b. A *subject* tells whom or what the sentence is about. The *predicate* tells something about the subject.

EXAMPLES

         subj.   pred.
Christopher | ran the mile in record time.

         subj.   pred.
Three jars on the shelf | exploded.

         subj.   pred.
A large silver poodle | won first prize.

Finding the Subject

Usually, the subject comes before the predicate. Sometimes, however, the subject may appear elsewhere in the sentence. To find the subject of a sentence, ask *Who?* or *What?* before the predicate.

EXAMPLES At the top of the tree **a bird's nest** sat. [What sat at the top of the tree? A bird's nest sat there.]

By the way, **I** saw your friend Pilar at the fiesta. [Who saw Pilar at the fiesta? I did.]

Running down the street were **two small boys**. [Who were running down the street? Two small boys were.]

Can **horses** swim? [What can swim? Horses can swim.]

The Complete Subject and the Simple Subject

The *complete subject* consists of all the words needed to tell *whom* or *what* a sentence is about.

8c. A *simple subject* is the main word in the complete subject.

EXAMPLES   My **date** for the dance | arrived late. [The complete subject is *my date for the dance.* The simple subject is *date.*]

Finally, the difficult **trip** across the desert | was over. [The complete subject is *the difficult trip across the desert.* The simple subject is *trip.*]

Pacing back and forth in the cage was | a hungry **tiger.** [The complete subject is *a hungry tiger.* The simple subject is *tiger.*]

NOTE The simple subject of a sentence is *never* part of a prepositional phrase.

EXAMPLE   The **tips** of the rabbit's ears were sticking up behind the large cabbage. [What were sticking up? You might be tempted to say *ears,* but *ears* is part of the prepositional phrase *of the rabbit's ears. Tips* were sticking up.]

REFERENCE NOTE: For more information about prepositional phrases that come between a subject and a verb, see pages 79–80.

The simple subject may consist of more than one word. In the examples below, the simple subjects are all compound nouns.

EXAMPLES   **Stamp collecting** | is my father's hobby.
The Wonder Years | is my favorite television program.
Ann Richards | was elected governor of Texas in 1990.

REFERENCE NOTE: For more information on compound nouns, see page 47.

NOTE In other chapters of this book, the term *subject* refers to the simple subject unless otherwise indicated.

✓ *QUICK CHECK 2* **Identifying Complete Subjects and Simple Subjects**

Identify the *complete subject* and the *simple subject* in each sentence of the following paragraph.

[1] People throughout Latin America enjoy going out to a ballgame. [2] The all-American sport of baseball has been very popular there for a long time. [3] In fact, fans in countries such as Cuba, Panama, and Venezuela go wild over the game. [4] As a result, the Caribbean Baseball Leagues were formed more than fifty years ago. [5] Each year the teams in Latin America play toward a season championship known as the Caribbean World Series.

The Complete Predicate and the Simple Predicate, or Verb

A *complete predicate* consists of a verb and all the words that describe the verb and complete its meaning.

8d. A *simple predicate*, or *verb*, is the main word or group of words in the complete predicate.

In the following examples, the vertical lines separate the complete subjects (comp. subj.) from the complete predicates (comp. pred.). The simple predicate, or verb, appears in bold type.

comp. subj. comp. pred.
EXAMPLES The popular movie star | **signed** autographs for hours.

comp. subj. comp. pred.
The trees | **sagged** beneath the weight of the ice.

The Verb Phrase

A simple predicate may be a one-word verb, or it may be a verb phrase. A *verb phrase* consists of a main verb and its

SENTENCES

helping verbs. In the following examples, the simple predicates, which are all verb phrases, appear in bold type.

comp. subj.   comp. pred.
EXAMPLES   Our class | **is reading** the famous novel
                             Frankenstein.

comp. subj.   comp. pred.
The musicians | **have been rehearsing** since noon.

comp. subj.   comp. pred.
These books | **should have been returned** to the
                   library last week.

The words *not* and *never,* which are frequently used with verbs, are not part of a verb phrase. Both of these words are adverbs.

EXAMPLES   She | **did** not **believe** me.
                 The two cousins | **had** never **met.**

 REFERENCE NOTE: For more information about verb phrases, see pages 60–61.

Sometimes the complete predicate appears at the beginning of a sentence.

EXAMPLES   **On the tiny branch perched** a chickadee.
                 At the bottom of the pool were smooth, blue
                 stones.

Part of the predicate may appear on one side of the subject and the rest on the other side.

EXAMPLES   **Before winter** many birds **fly south.**
                 As a matter of fact, she and I **did see that movie.**

 In this book, the term *verb* refers to the simple predicate unless otherwise indicated.

 QUICK CHECK 3   **Identifying Complete Predicates
                                    and Verbs**

Identify the *complete predicate* and the *verb* in each of the following sentences. Keep in mind that parts of the complete predicate may come before and after the complete subject.

[1] Samuel Pepys (pēps) was an English government worker. [2] Between 1660 and 1669, Pepys kept a diary. [3] Presented in the diary is a personal look at life in England during the seventeenth century. [4] For example, in entries during 1666, Pepys gave a detailed account of the Great Fire of London. [5] What other events might be described in the diary?

The Compound Subject

8e. A *compound subject* consists of two or more connected simple subjects that have the same verb. The usual connecting word is *and* or *or*.

EXAMPLES   **Keshia** and **Todd** worked a jigsaw puzzle.
Either **Carmen** or **Ernesto** will videotape the ceremony tomorrow.
Among the guest speakers were an **astronaut,** an **engineer,** and a **journalist.**

The Compound Verb

8f. A *compound verb* consists of two or more verbs that have the same subject.

A connecting word—usually *and, or,* or *but*—is used between the verbs.

EXAMPLES   The dog **barked** and **growled** at the stranger.
We **can go** forward, **go** back, or **stay** right here.
The man **was convicted** but later **was found** innocent of the crime.

Both the simple subject and the verb of a sentence may be compound. In such a sentence, each subject goes with each verb.

SENTENCES

EXAMPLES

$\overset{\text{S}}{}$ $\overset{\text{S}}{}$ $\overset{\text{V}}{}$

The **captain** and the **crew battled** the storm and

$\overset{\text{V}}{}$

hoped for better weather. [The captain battled and hoped, and the crew battled and hoped.]

$\overset{\text{S}}{}$ $\overset{\text{S}}{}$ $\overset{\text{V}}{}$ $\overset{\text{V}}{}$

My **sister** and **I listen** to and **perform** bluegrass. [My sister and I listen to bluegrass, and my sister and I perform it.]

STYLE NOTE Using compound subjects and verbs, you can combine ideas and reduce wordiness in your writing. Compare the examples below.

WORDY   Anne Brontë wrote under a male pen name. Charlotte Brontë wrote under a male pen name. Emily Brontë wrote under a male pen name.

REVISED   **Anne, Charlotte, and Emily Brontë** wrote under male pen names.

 REFERENCE NOTE: See pages 223–229 for more information about sentence combining.

 QUICK CHECK 4   **Identifying Compound Subjects and Compound Verbs**

Identify the compound subjects and the compound verbs in the following paragraph.

[1] Aaron Neville and his brothers (Art, Charles, and Cyril) are the famous Neville Brothers. [2] They formed their act and started singing together in 1977. [3] Before then, the brothers had performed and toured separately. [4] New Orleans gospel sounds and jazz rhythms fill the brothers' songs. [5] *Yellow Moon* and *Brother's Keeper* are two of their most popular albums.

GRAMMAR INVADERS

"It's a new concept in teaching machines. You get 50 points for every grammatical error you blast away!"

GLASBERGEN

© Randy Glasbergen.

✓ *Chapter Review*

A. Identifying Sentences and Sentence Fragments

Identify each group of words as a *sentence* or a *sentence fragment*. If the word group is a sentence fragment, correct it by adding words to make a complete sentence.

EXAMPLES
1. Do you like the U.S. Postal Service's special postage stamps?
1. *sentence*

2. When my parents buy stamps.
2. *sentence fragment—When my parents buy stamps, they ask for new commemorative ones.*

1. I really enjoy collecting postage stamps.
2. A new stamp that features U.S. Senator Dennis Chavez of New Mexico.
3. Chavez worked to improve U.S.-Latin American relations.
4. Some stamps with pictures of animals and famous people.
5. Since I like "Love" stamps and holiday stamps.

SENTENCES

B. Identifying Complete Subjects and Complete Predicates

Label each italicized group of words as the *complete subject* or the *complete predicate* of the sentence.

EXAMPLES **1.** *Anyone searching for the world's highest mountains* must look both on land and under the sea.
    1. *complete subject*

    2. Anyone searching for the world's highest mountains *must look both on land and under the sea.*
    2. *complete predicate*

  6. *Much of the earth's surface and a good deal of the ocean's floors* are mountainous.
  7. Can you *name the world's highest mountain?*
  8. *Mount Everest, located in the Himalayas,* claims that title.
  9. In fact, *seven of the world's highest mountains* are in the Himalayan mountain range.
10. Mount Everest *towers to a height of 29,028 feet above sea level.*
11. *The Atlas Mountains in Africa, the Alps in Europe, the Rockies in North America, and the Andes in South America* are other high mountain ranges.
12. Many high mountains *also have been discovered under the ocean.*
13. Down more than ten thousand miles of the ocean floor runs *the earth's longest continuous mountain range, the Mid-Atlantic Ridge.*
14. The peaks of these undersea mountains *rise above the surface of the water and form islands like Iceland and the Azores.*
15. In the Pacific Ocean, *the islands of Hawaii* are actually the peaks of a 1,600-mile-long chain of submerged mountains.

C. Identifying Simple Subjects and Verbs

Identify the simple subjects and the verbs in each of the following sentences.

EXAMPLE **1.** What festivals and holidays does your family celebrate?

1. *simple subject—family; verb—does celebrate*

16. Brave knights and noblewomen return each year to the medieval festival at Ribeauville, France.
17. During Sweden's Midsommar (Midsummer) Festival, maypoles and buildings bloom with fresh flowers.
18. Wrestling and pole climbing attract crowds to the Tatar Festival of the Plow in Russia.
19. Games, dances, and feasts highlight the Green Corn Dance of the Seminole Indians of the Florida Everglades.
20. In Munich, Germany, floats and bandwagons add color to the Oktoberfest Parade.

SENTENCES

9 COMPLEMENTS

Direct and Indirect Objects, Subject Complements

✓ Checking What You Know

Identifying Complements

Identify each of the italicized words or word groups in the following sentences as a *direct object,* an *indirect object,* a *predicate nominative,* or a *predicate adjective.*

EXAMPLES   **1.** The rancher raised prize-winning *cattle.*
      1. *cattle—direct object*

      2. The rancher became a rich *man.*
      2. *man—predicate nominative*

  1. Pilar caught the *ball* and threw it to first base.
  2. Your cousin seems *nice.*
  3. I'm not the *one* who did that.
  4. The sun grew *hotter* as the day went on.
  5. Mrs. Sato gave *me* a failing grade.
  6. Whoopi Goldberg is *famous* for comedy.
  7. Amy's father and mother are both *truck drivers.*
  8. Have you bought your *tickets* yet?

9. Wear a *helmet* when you ride your trail bike.
10. The irate customer sent the store *manager* a letter of complaint.
11. The nurse gave *Willie* a flu shot.
12. Josh often looks *tired* on Monday mornings.
13. With his calloused hands he cannot feel the *texture* of velvet.
14. My sister's room is always *neater* than mine.
15. Heather, who is new at our school, is the nicest *girl* I know.
16. The Algonquians used *toboggans* to haul goods over snow and ice.
17. Throw *Eric* a long pass.
18. When left to dry in the sun, some plums become *prunes.*
19. Charles Drew, a well-known African American doctor, gave *science* a better way to store blood.
20. Ms. Rosada will be our Spanish *teacher* this fall. ✓

SENTENCES

Recognizing Complements

9a. A *complement* is a word or a group of words that completes the meaning of a verb.

Every sentence has a subject and a verb. Often a verb also needs a complement to make the sentence complete. Each of the following subjects and verbs needs a complement to be a complete sentence.

```
                    S       V
INCOMPLETE   Marlene brought [what?]

                    S       V       C
  COMPLETE   Marlene brought sandwiches.

                  S       V
INCOMPLETE   Carlos thanked [whom?]
```

                   S   V   C

COMPLETE   Carlos thanked **her.**

                   S   V

INCOMPLETE **We were** [*what?*]

                   S   V   C

COMPLETE   We were **hungry.**

As you can see, a complement may be a noun, a pronoun, or an adjective. Complements complete the meanings of verbs in several ways.

EXAMPLES   Jody painted her **room.** [The noun *room* completes the meaning of the verb by telling *what* Jody painted.]

                My uncle sent **me** a **postcard.** [The pronoun *me* and the noun *postcard* complete the meaning of the verb by telling *what* was sent and *to whom* it was sent.]

                The Ephron sisters are **writers.** [The noun *writers* completes the meaning of the verb *are* by identifying the sisters.]

                This story is **exciting.** [The adjective *exciting* completes the meaning of the verb *is* by describing the story.]

An adverb is never a complement.

ADVERB   **The dog is outside.** [*Outside* modifies the verb *is* by telling where the dog is.]

COMPLEMENT **The dog is friendly.** [The adjective *friendly* modifies the subject *dog* by telling what kind of dog.]

A complement is never in a prepositional phrase.

COMPLEMENT   Benjamin is studying his world geography **notes.**

OBJECT OF A   Benjamin is studying for his world geography
PREPOSITION **test.**

☞ REFERENCE NOTE: For more information on prepositional phrases, see pages 148–151.

 *QUICK CHECK 1* **Identifying Subjects, Verbs, and Complements**

Identify the subject, verb, and complement in each sentence in the following paragraph. [Remember: A complement is never in a prepositional phrase.]

[1] During Shakespeare's time, many people watched plays at the most popular playhouse in London—the Globe Theatre. [2] Richard and Cuthbert Burbage built the Globe in 1599. [3] The Globe enclosed an inner courtyard. [4] Some of the audience watched the play from seats around the courtyard. [5] Many playgoers, however, did not have seats during a performance.

Direct Objects

9b. A **direct object** is a noun or a pronoun that receives the action of the verb or that shows the result of the action. A direct object tells *what* or *whom* after a transitive verb.

The **direct object** is one kind of complement. It completes the meaning of a transitive verb.

☞ REFERENCE NOTE: For more information about transitive verbs, see pages 58–59.

EXAMPLES Our history class built a **model** of the Alamo. [The noun *model* receives the action of the transitive verb *built* and tells *what* the class built.]
The freeze hurt **some** of the crops. [The pronoun *some* receives the action of the transitive verb *hurt* and tells *what* the freeze hurt.]
Dorothea Lange photographed **farmers** in the Midwest during the Depression. [The noun *farmers* receives the action of the transitive verb *photographed* and tells *whom* Dorothea Lange photographed.]

SENTENCES

A direct object can never follow a linking verb because a linking verb does not express action.

LINKING **William Wordsworth became** poet laureate of
VERB England in 1843. [The verb *became* does not express action. Therefore, it has no direct object.]

A direct object is never part of a prepositional phrase.

OBJECT OF A **He walked for miles** in the English country-
PREPOSITION side. [*Miles* is not the direct object of the verb *walked.* It is the object of the preposition *for.*]

 REFERENCE NOTE: For more about linking verbs, see pages 59–60. For more about prepositional phrases, see pages 148–151.

 A direct object may be compound.

EXAMPLE The man wore a white **beard,** a red **suit,** and black **boots.**

Mother Goose and Grimm reprinted by permission: Tribune Media Services.

 QUICK CHECK 2 **Identifying Direct Objects**

Identify the direct object or objects in each of the following sentences.

1. On the plains the Cheyenne hunted buffalo for food and clothing.
2. We watched a performance of African American writer Lorraine Hansberry's *A Raisin in the Sun.*
3. During most of its history, the United States has welcomed refugees from other countries.

4. Mayor Fiorello La Guardia governed New York City during the Great Depression.

5. Have the movie theaters announced the special discount for teenagers or the new weekend matinee times yet?

Indirect Objects

The *indirect object* is another type of complement. Like a direct object, an indirect object helps to complete the meaning of a transitive verb. If a sentence has an indirect object, it always has a direct object also.

> **9c.** An *indirect object* is a noun or a pronoun that comes between the verb and the direct object and tells *to what* or *to whom* or *for what* or *for whom* the action of the verb is done.

EXAMPLES   Dad gave the **horse** an apple. [The noun *horse* tells *to what* Dad gave an apple.]
Luke showed the **class** his collection of comic books. [The noun *class* tells *to whom* Luke showed his collection.]
From an old sock, Kim made her **cat** a toy. [The noun *cat* tells *for what* Kim made a toy.]
Sarita bought **us** a chess set. [The pronoun *us* tells *for whom* Sarita bought a chess set.]

Linking verbs do not have indirect objects. Also, an indirect object, like a direct object, is never in a prepositional phrase.

LINKING VERB   Her mother **was** a collector of rare books. [The linking verb *was* does not express action, so it cannot have an indirect object.]

INDIRECT OBJECT   She sent her **mother** a rare book. [The noun *mother* shows *to whom* the action of the verb was done.]

OBJECT OF A PREPOSITION   She sent a rare book to her **mother.** [The noun *mother* is the object of the preposition *to.*]

SENTENCES

NOTE Like a direct object, an indirect object may be compound.

EXAMPLE   Uncle Alphonso bought my **brother** and **me** an
aquarium.

 QUICK CHECK 3   **Identifying Direct Objects and
Indirect Objects**

Identify the direct objects and the indirect objects in the
following sentences. [Note: Not every sentence has an indirect object.]

1. The speaker showed the audience the slides of
Zimbabwe.
2. Juan would not deliberately tell you and me a lie.
3. The art teacher displayed the students' paintings.
4. Latoya's parents shipped her the books and the magazines she had forgotten.
5. In most foreign countries, United States citizens must
carry their passports for identification.

Subject Complements

A *subject complement* completes the meaning of a linking
verb and identifies or describes the subject.

Common Linking Verbs					
appear	become	grow	remain	smell	stay
be	feel	look	seem	sound	taste

EXAMPLES   **Alice Eng is a dedicated teacher.** [The noun
teacher follows the linking verb *is* and identifies
the subject *Alice Eng.*]
The lemonade tastes sour. [*Sour* follows the linking verb *tastes* and describes the subject *lemonade*—sour lemonade.]

 REFERENCE NOTE: For more information about linking verbs,
see pages 59–60.

There are two kinds of subject complements—the *predicate nominative* and the *predicate adjective*.

Predicate Nominatives

9d. A *predicate nominative* is a noun or a pronoun that follows a linking verb and identifies the subject or refers to it.

EXAMPLES   My aunt's dog is a **collie**. [*Collie* is a predicate nominative that identifies *dog*.]

Enrique is **one** of the best players. [*One* is a predicate nominative that refers to the subject *Enrique*.]

The exchange students from Germany are **they**. [The word *they* is a predicate nominative that refers to the subject *exchange students*.]

NOTE Expressions such as *It is I* and *That was he* sound odd even though they are correct. In everyday speech, you would probably say *It's me* and *That was him*. Such nonstandard expressions may one day become acceptable in writing as well as in speech. For now, however, it is best to follow the rules of standard English in your writing.

Like subjects and objects, predicate nominatives never appear in prepositional phrases.

EXAMPLES   The prize was a **pair** of tickets to the movies. [The word *pair* is a predicate nominative that identifies the subject *prize*. *Tickets* is the object of the preposition *of*, and *movies* is the object of the preposition *to*.]

An invertebrate is an **animal** without a backbone. [*Animal* is the predicate nominative that identifies the subject. *Backbone* is the object of the preposition *without*.]

NOTE Predicate nominatives may be compound.

EXAMPLE   Hernando de Soto was a **soldier** and a **diplomat**.

 *QUICK CHECK 4*   **Identifying Predicate Nominatives**

Identify the predicate nominative in each of the following sentences.

1. Robert A. Heinlein is one of America's most important science fiction writers.
2. Many of Heinlein's "future history" stories have become classics.
3. Heinlein's novels for young people and adults remain top sellers.
4. Published in 1961, *Stranger in a Strange Land* is a novel still enjoyed by many readers.
5. Heinlein was the winner of several Hugo Awards for his writing.

Predicate Adjectives

9e. A *predicate adjective* is an adjective that follows a linking verb and describes the subject.

EXAMPLES   An atomic reactor is very **powerful.** [The adjective *powerful* follows the linking verb *is* and describes the subject *reactor.*]
This ground looks **swampy.** [The adjective *swampy* follows the linking verb *looks* and describes the subject *ground.*]

NOTE   Predicate adjectives may be compound.

EXAMPLE   A computer can be **entertaining** and **helpful,** but sometimes **frustrating.**

Some verbs, such as *look, grow,* and *feel,* may be used as either linking verbs or action verbs.

LINKING VERB   The sailor **felt** tired. [*Felt* is a linking verb because it links the adjective *tired* to the subject *sailor.*]

ACTION VERB   The sailor **felt** the cool breeze. [*Felt* is an action verb because it is followed by the direct object *breeze,* which tells what the sailor felt.]

REFERENCE NOTE: See page 60 for more information about verbs that may be used as either linking or action verbs.

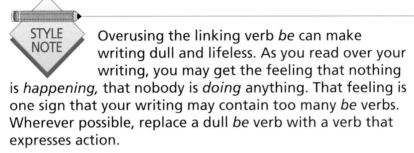

STYLE NOTE Overusing the linking verb *be* can make writing dull and lifeless. As you read over your writing, you may get the feeling that nothing is *happening*, that nobody is *doing* anything. That feeling is one sign that your writing may contain too many *be* verbs. Wherever possible, replace a dull *be* verb with a verb that expresses action.

BE VERB	Edgar Allan Poe **was** a writer of poems and frightening short stories.
ACTION VERB	Edgar Allan Poe **wrote** poems and frightening short stories.

 QUICK CHECK 5 **Identifying Predicate Adjectives**

Identify the predicate adjectives in the sentences below.

1. San Francisco's Chinatown is colorful and inviting.
2. The great stone creatures that guard the entrance to Chinatown look very powerful.
3. The streets there are crowded and full of activity.
4. The special foods at the tearooms and restaurants smell spicy and delicious.
5. San Francisco's Chinese community is large.

COMPUTER NOTE The overuse of *be* verbs is a problem that a computer can help you solve. Use the computer's "Search" function to find and highlight each occurrence of *am, are, is, was, were, be, been,* and *being.* For each case, decide whether the *be* verb is needed or whether it could be replaced with an action verb for greater variety.

SENTENCES

✓ Chapter Review

Identifying Complements

Identify each italicized word in the following paragraphs as a *direct object,* an *indirect object,* a *predicate nominative,* or a *predicate adjective.*

EXAMPLES   I enjoy [1] cooking but it can be hard [2] work.
1. cooking—direct object
2. work—predicate nominative

My dad has been giving [1] *me* cooking [2] *lessons* since last summer. At first, I was [3] *reluctant* to tell the guys because some of them think that cooking is a girl's [4] *job.* But Dad told me to remind them that we guys eat [5] *meals* just as often as girls do. He also said that cooking is an excellent [6] *way* for us to do our share of the work around the house.

When I began, I could hardly boil [7] *water* without fouling up, but Dad remained [8] *patient* and showed [9] *me* the correct and easiest ways to do things. For example, did you know that water will boil faster if it has a little [10] *salt* in it or that cornstarch can be an excellent thickening [11] *agent* in everything from batter to gravy?

My first attempts tasted [12] *awful,* but gradually I've become a fairly good [13] *cook.* Probably my best complete meal is [14] *chicken stew.* Although stew doesn't require the highest [15] *grade* of chicken, a good baking hen will give [16] *it* a much better taste. I am always very [17] *careful* about picking out the vegetables, too. Our grocer probably thinks that I am too [18] *picky* when I demand the best [19] *ingredients.* I don't care, though, because when I serve my [20] *family* my stew, they say it is their favorite dish.

10 KINDS OF SENTENCES

Sentence Structure and Purpose

✓ *Checking What You Know*

A. Identifying the Four Kinds of Sentence Structure

Identify each of the following sentences as *simple, compound, complex,* or *compound-complex.*

EXAMPLE **1.** We bought a new computer program that helps with spelling and grammar.
   1. *complex*

1. When the rabbit saw us, it ran into the bushes.
2. In 1967, Thurgood Marshall became the first African American named to the U.S. Supreme Court.
3. You can either buy a new bicycle tire or fix the old one.
4. There was no way that we could tell what had really happened.

5. Mercedes Rodriguez of Miami, Florida, entered and won the Ms. Wheelchair America contest.
6. Do you know who wrote this note and left it on my desk?
7. Nobody is worried about that, for it will never happen.
8. Whatever you decide will be fine with me.
9. Is the movie that we want to see still playing in theaters, or is it available on videocassette?
10. Rammel knew the play, and he assigned each of us a part.
11. Amphibians and some insects can live both on the land and in the water.
12. The tornado cut across the edge of the housing development yesterday morning, and seven homes were destroyed.
13. By July of 1847, the Mormons had reached the Great Salt Lake valley.
14. Before the game started, all the football players ran out onto the field, and everyone cheered.
15. My father stopped to help the family whose car had broken down on the highway.

B. Classifying Sentences According to Purpose

Classify each of the following sentences as *declarative, interrogative, imperative,* or *exclamatory.* Then, write the last word of each sentence, and supply the correct end punctuation.

EXAMPLE   **1. Please tell me whether the sea horse is a fish**
                1. *imperative—fish.*

16. The sea horse is a very unusual kind of fish
17. What a beautiful butterfly that is
18. Can you believe that most bears hibernate
19. Daniel, find out how many miles per hour a rabbit can hop
20. Some jack rabbits can hop forty miles per hour ✓

Sentences Classified by Structure

Sentences may be classified according to *structure*—the kinds and the number of clauses they contain. The four kinds of sentences are *simple, compound, complex,* and *compound-complex.*

 REFERENCE NOTE: Sentences may also be classified according to purpose. See pages 210–212.

The Simple Sentence

10a. A *simple sentence* has one independent clause and no subordinate clauses.

EXAMPLES
          S   V
The **hairstylist gave** Latrice a new look.

      S   V
Ernesto has volunteered to organize the recycling campaign.

A simple sentence may have a compound subject, a compound verb, or both.

EXAMPLES
      S   S   V
Beth Heiden and **Sheila Young won** Olympic medals. [compound subject]

      S   V   V
Lawrence caught the ball but then **dropped** it. [compound verb]

      S   S   V
The **astronomer** and her **assistant studied** the

      V
meteor and **wrote** reports on their findings. [compound subject and compound verb]

REFERENCE NOTE: For more information about compound subjects and compound verbs, see pages 185–186.

 QUICK CHECK 1 | **Identifying Subjects and Verbs in Simple Sentences**

Identify the subjects and the verbs of the following simple sentences. [Note: Some sentences have compound subjects or compound verbs.]

1. Throughout history, people have invented and used a variety of weapons.
2. To protect themselves from such weapons, warriors in battle needed special equipment.
3. In Assyria, soldiers wore armor made of leather and metal.
4. By 1800 B.C., the Greeks had made the first metal armor out of bronze.
5. Before and during the Middle Ages, European knights and foot soldiers often dressed in shirts of chain mail.

The Compound Sentence

10b. A *compound sentence* has two or more independent clauses but no subordinate clauses.

The independent clauses are usually joined by a coordinating conjunction: *and, but, for, nor, or, so,* or *yet.*

EXAMPLES **According to legend, Betsy Ross made our first**
$\quad$ S $\quad\quad\quad\quad$ V

$\quad\quad$ V $\quad\quad\quad\quad$ S
flag, but there is little evidence of this. [two independent clauses joined by the conjunction *but*]

$\quad\quad$ S $\quad$ V $\quad\quad$ S $\quad$ V $\quad\quad\quad$ S
The whistle blew, the drums rolled, and the crowd
$\quad\quad$ V
cheered. [three independent clauses, the last two joined by the conjunction *and*]

REFERENCE NOTE: For more information about independent clauses, see page 164. For information on the use of commas in compound sentences, see page 264.

 NOTE Do not confuse a compound sentence with a simple sentence that contains a compound subject, a compound verb, or both.

	S S V
SIMPLE SENTENCE	**Alberto** and **Jared increased** their speed
	V
	and **passed** the other runners. [compound subject and compound verb]

	S V S
COMPOUND SENTENCE	**Alberto led** half the way, and then **Jared**
	V
	took the lead. [two independent clauses]

The independent clauses in a compound sentence may also be joined by a semicolon.

                                S   V

EXAMPLE   Many mathematical **concepts originated** in

                              S   V

              North Africa; the ancient **Egyptians used** these concepts in building the pyramids.

 REFERENCE NOTE: For more information on using semicolons in compound sentences, see pages 271–274.

 QUICK CHECK 2   **Identifying Subjects, Verbs, and Conjunctions in Compound Sentences**

Each of the sentences in the following paragraph is a compound sentence. Identify the subjects and the verbs of the independent clauses in each sentence. Then give the coordinating conjunction or the mark of punctuation that joins the independent clauses.

[1] The director of a theater-in-the-round visited our class, and we listened to his stories for almost an hour.

[2] According to him, the workers in charge of properties are usually alert and careful, yet they still make mistakes sometimes. [3] For example, in one production of *Romeo and Juliet,* the character Juliet prepared to kill herself with a dagger, but there was no dagger on the stage. [4] Audiences at theaters-in-the-round can also be a problem, for they sit very close to the stage. [5] During one mystery drama, a spectator became too involved in the play; he leaped onto the stage and tackled the villain.

The Complex Sentence

10c. A *complex sentence* has one independent clause and at least one subordinate clause.

EXAMPLE   When I watch Martha Graham's performances, I feel like studying dance.

                                     S V

Independent Clause   **I feel** like studying dance

                                     S   V

Subordinate Clause   When **I watch** Martha Graham's performances

EXAMPLE   Some of the sailors who took part in the mutiny on the British ship *Bounty* settled Pitcairn Island, in the South Pacific.

                                  S   V

Independent Clause   **Some** of the sailors **settled** Pitcairn Island, in the South Pacific

                                   S V

Subordinate Clause   **who took** part in the mutiny on the British ship *Bounty*

EXAMPLE   In Isaac Bashevis Singer's story "The Washwoman," although an old washwoman is deathly ill, she recovers so that she can finish her work.

Independent Clause	In Isaac Bashevis Singer's story "The

S   V

Washwoman," **she recovers**

S   V

Subordinate Clause	although an old **washwoman is** deathly ill

S   V

Subordinate Clause	so that **she can finish** her work

Notice in the examples above that a subordinate clause can appear at the beginning, in the middle, or at the end of a complex sentence.

 REFERENCE NOTE: For more information on clauses, see pages 163–173. For information on punctuating complex sentences, see pages 170 and 269.

 *QUICK CHECK 3* **Identifying Independent Clauses and Subordinate Clauses in Complex Sentences**

Identify each of the clauses in the following sentences as *independent* or *subordinate*. Be prepared to give the subject and the verb of each clause. [Note: Two sentences have more than one subordinate clause.]

1. China is a largely agricultural country that has a population of more than one billion people.
2. A group of popular singers, who donated their time, recorded a song that made people aware of the problems in Ethiopia.
3. The nineteenth-century Hawaiian ruler who wrote the famous farewell song *"Aloha Oe"* ("Farewell to Thee") was Queen Liliuokalani.
4. While the crew was building the sets, the performers continued their rehearsal, which went on into the night.
5. Although she had had polio as a child, Wilma Rudolph became a top American Olympic athlete.

SENTENCES

The Compound-Complex Sentence

10d. A *compound-complex sentence* has two or more independent clauses and at least one subordinate clause.

EXAMPLE   Yolanda began painting only two years ago, but already she has been asked to hang one of her paintings at the art exhibit that is scheduled for next month.

Independent Clause   **Yolanda began** painting only two years ago

Independent Clause   already **she has been asked** to hang one of her paintings at the art exhibit

Subordinate Clause   **that is** scheduled for next month

EXAMPLE   I have read several novels in which the main characters are animals, but the novel that I like best is *Animal Farm*.

Independent Clause   **I have read** several novels

Independent Clause   the **novel is** *Animal Farm*

Subordinate Clause   in which the main **characters are** animals

Subordinate Clause   that **I like** best

EXAMPLE   When Bill left, he locked the door, but he forgot to turn off the lights.

Independent Clause   **he locked** the door

		S	V
Independent Clause		**he forgot** to turn off the lights	

		S	V
Subordinate Clause		When **Bill left**	

 REFERENCE NOTE: To show how the parts of a compound-complex sentence go together, be sure to use marks of punctuation correctly. See pages 264–269 for guidelines on using commas. See pages 271–274 for information about semi-colons.

 QUICK CHECK 4

Identifying Clauses in Compound-Complex Sentences

Identify each of the clauses in the following sentences as *independent* or *subordinate*.

1. Before we conducted the experiment, we asked for permission to use the science lab, but the principal insisted on teacher supervision of our work.
2. Inside the old trunk up in the attic, which is filled with boxes and toys, we found some dusty photo albums; one of them contained pictures from the early 1900s.
3. We told them that their plan wouldn't work, but they wouldn't listen to us.
4. Every expedition that had attempted to explore that region had vanished without a trace, yet the young adventurer was determined to map the uncharted jungle because he couldn't resist the challenge.
5. The smoke, which grew steadily thicker and darker, billowed through the dry forest; and the animals ran ahead of it as the fire spread quickly.

STYLE NOTE When you revise your writing, pay attention both to the words you choose and to the types of sentences you use. By using a number of different sentence structures, you can make your writing clearer and more interesting.

Simple sentences are best used to express single ideas. To describe more complicated ideas and to show how the ideas fit together, use compound, complex, and compound-complex sentences.

SIMPLE SENTENCES	Yesterday I visited my friend Amy. Then I went to Willa's house. We worked on our dance steps.
COMPOUND-COMPLEX SENTENCE	After I visited my friend Amy yesterday, I went to Willa's house, and we worked on our dance steps.

 REFERENCE NOTE: For more information on improving sentence style, see pages 229–232.

COMPUTER NOTE A computer can help you look at your writing for sentence length and structure. Programs are now available that will tell you the average number of words in your sentences. Such programs will also tell you how many different kinds of sentences you used. You can compare your numbers with the averages for students at your grade level. In this way, you can easily see which sentence structures you've mastered and which ones you'll need to work on.

Sentences Classified by Purpose

In addition to being classified by structure, a sentence is also classified according to its purpose. The four kinds of sentences are *declarative, interrogative, imperative,* and *exclamatory.* They each serve a different purpose.

10e. A ***declarative sentence*** makes a statement. It is followed by a period.

EXAMPLES   Miriam Colón founded the Puerto Rican Traveling Theatre.
Curiosity is the beginning of knowledge.

10f. An *interrogative sentence* asks a question. It is followed by a question mark.

EXAMPLES What do you know about glaciers?
Was the game exciting?

10g. An *imperative sentence* gives a command or makes a request. It is followed by a period. A strong command is followed by an exclamation point.

EXAMPLES Do your homework each night.
John, please close the door.
Watch out!

In an imperative sentence, the "understood" subject is always *you*.

EXAMPLES (You) Do your homework each night.
John, (you) please close the door.
(You) Watch out!

10h. An *exclamatory sentence* shows excitement or expresses strong feeling. It is followed by an exclamation point.

EXAMPLES What a sight the sunset is!
Sarah won the VCR!

Hi & Lois reprinted with special
permission of King Features
Syndicate, Inc.

SENTENCES

Many people overuse exclamation points. In your own writing, save exclamation points for sentences that really do show strong emotion. When it is overused, this mark of punctuation loses its impact.

OVERUSED I went to our city's nature center yesterday, and I saw their birds of prey! Some had been abandoned by their owners! Others had been hit by cars! I'm glad the nature center makes a home for these beautiful birds!

IMPROVED I went to our city's nature center yesterday, and I saw their birds of prey. Some had been abandoned; others had been hit by cars. I'm glad the nature center takes care of these beautiful birds!

 REFERENCE NOTE: For more information about the different end marks of punctuation, see pages 257–260.

 QUICK CHECK 5 **Classifying Sentences**

Classify each of the following sentences according to its purpose.

1. Let no man pull you so low as to make you hate him.
> Booker T. Washington, from *I Have a Dream*

2. The art of war is simple enough.
> Ulysses S. Grant, *On the Art of War*

3. What happens to a dream deferred?
> Langston Hughes, "Harlem"

4. I know not what course others may take; but as for me, give me liberty or give me death!
> Patrick Henry, speech to the Virginia Convention of 1775

5. Join the union, girls, and together say *Equal Pay for Equal Work.*
> Susan B. Anthony, The Revolution (October 8, 1868)

✓ *Chapter Review 1*

A. Identifying the Four Kinds of Sentence Structure

Identify each sentence in the following paragraphs as *simple, compound, complex,* or *compound-complex.*

EXAMPLE   [1] When my grandmother came to visit, she taught us how to make our own holiday ornaments.

    1. *complex*

[1] Last year my grandmother came to stay with us from the middle of December until my brother's birthday in January. [2] While we were getting out the holiday decorations, Mom and Grandma told us all about how people used to make their own decorations. [3] Mom said that she remembered making beautiful decorations and that it used to be a lot of fun, so we decided to try making some of our own.

[4] My dad, my brother, and I drove out to the woods to gather pine cones. [5] We had forgotten to ask what size to get, and since Dad had never made decorations, he didn't know. [6] We decided to play it safe and get all different sizes, which was easy to do because there were pine cones everywhere. [7] My brother picked up all the little ones, and my dad and I threw a bunch of medium and big ones into the trunk of the car. [8] When Mom and Grandma saw how many we had, they laughed and said we had enough to decorate ten houses.

[9] First, we sorted the cones; the little ones went into one pile, and the bigger ones into another. [10] Dad and I painted the little ones silver, and Mom and Grandma painted stripes, dots, and all sorts of other designs on them. [11] Then we tied strings to the tops of the cones, and later, when we put them up, they made great ornaments.

[12] We painted the bigger pine cones all different colors and glued on cranberries and beads, which made each

cone look like a miniature fir tree. [13] We saved some smaller ones for the dining room table, and we put most of the others all around the house. [14] My brother took some to school, too.

[15] Besides the pine-cone decorations, we made some strings to decorate the mantel. [16] My mom got needles and a spool of heavy thread out of her sewing basket, and we strung the rest of the cranberries on six-foot lengths of the thread.

[17] Mom and Grandma cut several more long pieces of thread, and we used them to make strings of popcorn, just like our strings of cranberries. [18] We left some of the popcorn strings white, painted the others different colors, and hung them around the living room and dining room.

[19] Decorating was even more fun than usual, and I think that the whole house looked prettier, too, with all our homemade ornaments. [20] From now on, we're going to make decorations every year.

B. Classifying Sentences According to Purpose

Classify each of the following sentences as *declarative, interrogative, imperative,* or *exclamatory.* Then write the last word of each sentence, and provide the appropriate end punctuation.

EXAMPLE   **1.** Write your name and the date at the top of your paper
     1. *imperative—paper.*

21. Juana plans to study architecture at the state university after she graduates
22. This isn't the right answer, is it
23. No, it definitely is not
24. Clean up your room this instant, and don't make any excuses or try to get out of it
25. I can't right now, Mom, because everybody is waiting for me at Andy's house

✓ *Chapter Review 2*

Writing a Variety of Sentence Structures

Write ten original sentences according to the following instructions.

EXAMPLE   **1.** a compound sentence with two independent clauses joined by *and*

          1. *My mother usually gives us tacos for supper once a week, and she makes the best tacos in the world.*

1. a simple sentence with a compound subject
2. an imperative sentence with a compound verb
3. a compound sentence with two independent clauses joined by *but*
4. an interrogative sentence with a compound subject
5. a complex sentence with a subordinate clause that begins with *that*
6. an exclamatory sentence with a single subject and a single verb
7. a complex sentence with a subordinate clause at the beginning of the sentence
8. a complex sentence with a subordinate clause at the end of the sentence
9. a declarative sentence with two subordinate clauses
10. a compound-complex sentence

SENTENCES

11 WRITING EFFECTIVE SENTENCES

Revising for Completeness and Style

✓ Checking What You Know

A. Finding and Revising Sentence Fragments

Revise each fragment to make a complete sentence. You may need to change the punctuation and capitalization, too. If the word group is already a complete sentence, write *S*.

EXAMPLE   **1.** After the sun rose.
           1. *We walked to the beach after the sun rose.*

1. People near the water.
2. Two little children were playing in the wet sand.
3. Whenever the waves broke.
4. My sister and I on a red inflatable raft.
5. Tried to ride the waves as they came in.

B. Identifying and Revising Run-on Sentences

Revise each run-on sentence that follows by making two separate sentences or by using a comma and a coordinating conjunction. If the group of words is already correct, write *C*.

EXAMPLE **1.** The Louvre is the largest museum in the world it is also one of the oldest.

    1. *The Louvre is the largest museum in the world. It is also one of the oldest.*

 6. The first works of art in the Louvre were bought by the kings of France each ruler added more treasures.

 7. King Francis I was a great supporter of the arts he bought *La Gioconda,* better known as the *Mona Lisa.*

 8. As other French rulers made additions, the Louvre grew.

 9. The Louvre is now a state-owned museum, its new pieces are either bought or received as gifts.

10. Each year, about one and a half million people from all over the world come to see the artwork at the Louvre.

C. Combining Sentences

Combine each of the following pairs of sentences. To make a smoother combination, you may need to delete, change, or rearrange words.

EXAMPLE **1.** Young Louis Armstrong first showed his talent on the streets of New Orleans. His talent was for music.

    1. *Young Louis Armstrong first showed his musical talent on the streets of New Orleans.*

11. Armstrong became a jazz musician. He received acclaim for his music.

12. Louis Armstrong had a deep voice. It was rough.

13. During the first fifty years of its history, tennis was largely a pastime. It was a pastime of the wealthy.

14. Prominent tennis players competed in professional promotions. They toured with their managers.

15. Australians produce many cattle products. Australians consume many cattle products.

16. Beef is popular in Australia. Lamb is popular there, too.

17. The metric system was developed in France. The system became popular in many countries.

SENTENCES

18. We can keep the old system of measurement. We can switch to the metric system.
19. The Aztecs practiced a religion. It affected every part of their lives.
20. Aztec craftworkers made drums and rattles. Drums and rattles were their main musical instruments.

D. Revising Stringy and Wordy Sentences

Decide which of the following sentences are *stringy* or *wordy*. Then revise them to make them clearer and more precise. If a sentence is effective as it is, write C.

EXAMPLE   **1.** Harriet Ross grew up as a slave in Maryland, and she worked on a plantation there, but in 1844 she married John Tubman, and he was a freed slave.

   1. *Stringy—Harriet Ross grew up as a slave in Maryland and worked on a plantation there. In 1844, she married John Tubman, a freed slave.*

21. Harriet Tubman did not believe that people should be slaves, and she decided to escape, and late one night she began her dangerous trip to the North.
22. Traveling at night, she made the long journey to Philadelphia, Pennsylvania.
23. Most wasps are helpful to humanity because of the fact that they eat harmful insects.
24. Social wasps are the type that live together as groups and work as a team to build their nest.
25. Social wasps make their nests from old wood and tough plant fibers. ✓

Writing Clear Sentences

One of the easiest ways to make your writing clear is to use complete sentences. A *complete sentence* is a word group that meets the following requirements.

- The word group has a subject.
- The word group has a verb.
- The word group expresses a complete thought.

EXAMPLES   Dolphins communicate with one another by
                making clicking and whistling sounds.
                When a dolphin is in trouble, it can give off a
                distress call.
                Help!

Each of these examples meets all the requirements of a sentence. At first glance, the third example may not appear to have a subject. The subject, *you,* is understood in the sentence even though it isn't stated: "(You) Help!"

 REFERENCE NOTE: For more information about subjects and verbs, see pages 181–186. For information on the different kinds of sentences, see **Chapter 10: Kinds of Sentences.**

Two of the stumbling blocks to the development of clear sentences are *sentence fragments* and *run-on sentences.*

Sentence Fragments

11a. Avoid using sentence fragments.

A *sentence fragment* is a part of a sentence that has been punctuated as if it were a complete sentence.

FRAGMENT   Looked something like a sewing machine. [The
                subject is missing. *What* looked like a sewing
                machine?]
SENTENCE   The first typewriter looked something like a
                sewing machine.
FRAGMENT   Christopher Sholes the typewriter in 1867. [The
                verb is missing. What did Sholes *do* in 1867?]
SENTENCE   Christopher Sholes invented the typewriter in
                1867.
FRAGMENT   After Mark Twain typed one of his manuscripts
                on a Sholes typewriter. [This group of words has
                a subject and a verb, but it does not express a

SENTENCES

complete thought. *What happened* after Mark Twain typed one of his manuscripts on a Sholes typewriter?]

SENTENCE   After Mark Twain typed one of his manuscripts on a Sholes typewriter, the invention began to attract public attention.

 NOTE Often, fragments result when you write in a hurry or are a little careless. For example, you might accidentally chop off part of a sentence by putting in a period and a capital letter too soon. In the following example, notice that the fragment in dark type is actually a part of the sentence that comes before it.

> The ballgame ended. **When the only ball disappeared into the stands.**

You can correct the fragment by attaching it to the sentence it belongs with.

> The ballgame ended **when the only ball disappeared into the stands.**

 A computer can help you check your writing for sentence fragments. Some style-checking programs will find and highlight sentence fragments for you. These programs aren't perfect, however. It's still a good idea for you to check each sentence that you write. Be certain that it has a subject and a verb and that it expresses a complete idea.

 REFERENCE NOTE: For more about sentences and sentence fragments, see pages 179–180.

Run-on Sentences

11b. Avoid using run-on sentences.

If you run together two complete sentences as if they were one sentence, you get a *run-on sentence.*

RUN-ON   Margaret Bourke-White was a famous news photographer she worked for *Life* magazine during World War II.

CORRECT   Margaret Bourke-White was a famous news photographer. She worked for *Life* magazine during World War II.

RUN-ON   Bourke-White traveled all over the world taking photographs she went underground to photograph miners in South Africa.

CORRECT   Bourke-White traveled all over the world taking photographs. She went underground to photograph miners in South Africa.

To spot run-ons, try reading your writing aloud. A natural pause in your voice usually marks the end of one thought and the beginning of another. If you pause at a place where you don't have any end punctuation, you may have found a run-on sentence.

Shoe, by Jeff MacNelly, reprinted by permission:
Tribune Media Services.

NOTE A comma does mark a brief pause in a sentence, but it does not show the end of a sentence. If you use just a comma between two complete sentences, you create a run-on sentence.

RUN-ON Our dog finally came home late last night, she was dirty and hungry.

CORRECT Our dog finally came home late last night. She was dirty and hungry.

 REFERENCE NOTE: For more about commas, see pages 261–271 and 279.

Revising Run-on Sentences

There are several ways you can revise run-on sentences. Here are two of them.

1. You can make two sentences.

RUN-ON Kite building is an ancient art the Chinese made the first kites around three thousand years ago.

CORRECT Kite building is an ancient art. The Chinese made the first kites around three thousand years ago.

2. You can use a comma and the coordinating conjunction *and, but,* or *or.*

RUN-ON The Chinese sometimes used kites in religious ceremonies, they usually used them for sport.

CORRECT The Chinese sometimes used kites in religious ceremonies, **but** they usually used them for sport.

 *QUICK CHECK 1* **Revising to Correct Fragments and Run-ons**

The following paragraph is confusing because it contains fragments and run-ons. First, identify the *fragments* and *run-ons*. Then revise each fragment and run-on to make the paragraph clearer.

[1] *Godzilla* a movie about a huge reptile. [2] Godzilla looks like a dinosaur he breathes fire like a dragon. [3] When an atomic bomb wakes him up. [4] Godzilla can melt steel with his atomic breath he is big enough to knock down huge buildings. [5] In the film, he destroys the city of Tokyo he is defeated at the end.

Combining Sentences

Sometimes a short sentence can express your meaning perfectly. But a long, unbroken series of short sentences will make your writing sound choppy.

11c. Improve choppy sentences by combining them into longer, smoother sentences.

CHOPPY   George Lucas's films are famous. They are famous for their plots and special effects. The plots are suspenseful. The special effects are thrilling. *Star Wars* became a success in the late 1970's. Lucas wrote and directed it. Its success was international. Lucas later teamed up with director Steven Spielberg. They created *Raiders of the Lost Ark*. The movie was popular.

To make the paragraph more interesting, the writer combined sentences to eliminate some repeated words and ideas.

REVISED   George Lucas's films are famous for their suspenseful plots and thrilling special effects. *Star Wars,* which Lucas wrote and directed, became an international success in the late 1970's. Lucas later teamed up with director Steven Spielberg to create the popular *Raiders of the Lost Ark.*

Combining by Inserting Words

One way to combine short sentences is to pull a key word from one sentence and insert it into another sentence.

SENTENCES

Sometimes you will need to change the form of the key word before you can insert it.

INSERTING WITHOUT A CHANGE	
ORIGINAL	Louis Armstrong was a famous musician. He was a jazz musician.
COMBINED	Louis Armstrong was a famous **jazz** musician.

INSERTING WITH A CHANGE	
ORIGINAL	Armstrong was an easygoing person. He was a friend to many people.
COMBINED	Armstrong was an easygoing, **friendly** person.

NOTE When you change the forms of words, you often add endings such as *–ed, –ing,* and *–ly* to make adjectives and adverbs.

EXAMPLES need   need**ed**
          sing   sing**ing**
          fortunate   fortunate**ly**

 REFERENCE NOTE: For more information about adjectives and adverbs, see pages 53–56 and 62–64. For more about using adjectives and adverbs, see pages 131–137.

Combining by Inserting Phrases

A *phrase* is a group of words that doesn't have a subject and a verb. You can combine sentences by taking a phrase from one sentence and inserting it into the other sentence.

ORIGINAL Brown bears gather in groups. They gather around riverbanks.

COMBINED Brown bears gather in groups **around riverbanks.**

 REFERENCE NOTE: For more information about phrases, see **Chapter 6: Phrases.**

Sometimes you will need to put commas around the phrase you are inserting. Ask yourself whether the phrase renames or explains a noun or pronoun in the sentence. If it does, use a comma or commas to set off the phrase from the rest of the sentence.

ORIGINAL   Alaska is home to the big brown bears. The big brown bears are the largest kind of bear.

COMBINED   Alaska is home to the big brown bears, **the largest kind of bear.**

 REFERENCE NOTE: For more about using commas to set off phrases, see pages 265–269.

Often, you can change the verb in a sentence to make a phrase. You change the verb by adding *–ing* or *–ed* or by putting the word *to* in front of it. You can then use the phrase to modify a word in another sentence.

ORIGINAL   The bear prepares his winter retreat. He digs a burrow in a bank.

COMBINED   **Digging a burrow in a bank,** the bear prepares his winter retreat. [*Digging a burrow in a bank* modifies *bear.*]

ORIGINAL   Bears dig in soil. Digging is how they find roots and sweet bulbs.

COMBINED   Bears dig in soil **to find roots and sweet bulbs.** [*To find roots and sweet bulbs* modifies *dig.*]

STYLE NOTE   Be careful to place verb forms ending in *–ed* or *–ing* right next to the words they modify. Otherwise, you may create a confusing sentence.

MISPLACED   I could see the hummingbird at our feeder looking through the binoculars. [Was the hummingbird looking through the binoculars?]

REVISED   **Looking through the binoculars,** I could see the hummingbird at our feeder.

 REFERENCE NOTE: For more information about verb forms using *–ing*, *–ed*, or *to*, see pages 152–157. For more about the correct placement of verb forms using *–ing* or *–ed*, see pages 139–140.

SENTENCES

SENTENCES

Combining by Using *And, But,* or *Or*

You can also combine sentences by using the conjunction *and, but,* or *or.* With one of these connecting words, you can form a *compound subject,* a *compound verb,* or a *compound sentence.*

Compound Subjects and Verbs

Sometimes two sentences have the same verb with different subjects. You can combine the sentences by linking the two subjects with *and* or *or.* When you do this, you create a *compound subject.*

ORIGINAL Kangaroos carry their young in pouches. Koalas carry their young in pouches.

COMBINED **Kangaroos and koalas** carry their young in pouches.

If two sentences have the same subject with different verbs, you can link the verbs with *and, but,* or *or* to form a *compound verb.*

ORIGINAL Kangaroos can hop on their hind legs. They can walk on all four legs.

COMBINED Kangaroos **can hop** on their hind legs **or walk** on all four legs.

 NOTE When you form a compound subject, make sure that it agrees with the verb in number.

ORIGINAL Tasmania is in Australia. Queensland is in Australia.

REVISED **Tasmania and Queensland are** in Australia.
[The plural subject takes the verb *are.*]

 REFERENCE NOTE: For more information about agreement of subjects and verbs, see pages 77–87.

Compound Sentences

Sometimes you may want to combine two sentences and give equal emphasis to both ideas. You can connect the two sentences by using a comma and the conjunction *and,* *but,* or *or.* When you link sentences in this way, you create a *compound sentence.*

ORIGINAL   Many nations throughout the world use the metric system. The United States still uses the old system of measurement.

COMBINED   Many nations throughout the world use the metric system, **but** the United States still uses the old system of measurement.

STYLE NOTE

Before you create a compound sentence out of two simple sentences, make sure the thoughts in the sentences are closely related to each other. If you combine two sentences that are not closely related, you will confuse your reader.

UNRELATED   Kim chopped the vegetables, and I liked the soup.

RELATED   Kim chopped the vegetables, and I stirred the soup.

SENTENCES

Combining by Using a Subordinate Clause

A *clause* is a word group that contains a verb and its subject. An *independent clause* can stand alone as a sentence. A *subordinate clause* cannot stand alone as a sentence because it doesn't express a complete thought.

SENTENCE   Henry David Thoreau was living alone in the woods when he wrote *Walden.*

                     S   V

INDEPENDENT   Henry David Thoreau was living alone in the
CLAUSE   woods [can stand alone as a sentence]

                     S V

SUBORDINATE   when he wrote *Walden* [can't stand alone as
CLAUSE   a sentence]

If two sentences are closely related but unequal in emphasis, you can combine them by using a subordinate clause. Just make the idea that you want to emphasize the independent clause. The subordinate clause will give additional information about the idea expressed in the independent clause.

ORIGINAL   For two years, Thoreau lived in a simple hut. He built the hut at Walden Pond.

COMBINED   For two years, Thoreau lived in a simple hut **that he built at Walden Pond.**

or

At Walden Pond, Thoreau built a simple hut **that he lived in for two years.**

 REFERENCE NOTE: For more information about sentences that contain subordinate clauses, see pages 206–209.

Clauses Beginning with *Who, Which,* or *That*

You can make a short sentence into a subordinate clause by inserting *who, which,* or *that* in place of the subject.

ORIGINAL   The Aztecs were Native American people. They once ruled a mighty empire in Mexico.

COMBINED   The Aztecs were Native American people **who once ruled a mighty empire in Mexico.**

or

The Aztecs, **who were Native American people,** once ruled a mighty empire in Mexico.

Clauses Beginning with Words of Time or Place

You can also make a subordinate clause by adding a word that tells time or place. Words that tell time or place include *after, before, where, wherever, when, whenever,* and *while.*

ORIGINAL   The capital city of the Aztec empire was in central Mexico. Mexico City stands in that spot today.

COMBINED The capital city of the Aztec empire was in central Mexico, **where Mexico City stands today.**

or

Mexico City stands today in the spot **where the capital city of the Aztec empire was.**

 NOTE If you put your clause of time or place at the beginning of the sentence, you'll need to put a comma after the clause.

ORIGINAL The Aztec empire grew. Aztec warriors conquered nearby territories.
COMBINED **When Aztec warriors conquered nearby territories,** the Aztec empire grew.

 REFERENCE NOTE: For more information about using commas after clauses of time or place, see pages 170 and 269.

 QUICK CHECK 2 **Revising a Paragraph by Combining Sentences**

The following paragraph sounds choppy because it has too many short sentences. Use the methods you've learned in this section to combine some of the sentences.

[1] The Arctic is a cold region. [2] It is around the North Pole. [3] The Arctic may seem like a barren place. [4] But berries actually do manage to grow in a few places. [5] Vegetables actually grow in a few places. [6] The area also has rich mineral deposits. [7] Mines in Alaska and Canada produce gold and copper. [8] Mines in arctic Russia produce tin. [9] Early explorers revealed that the Arctic is far from worthless. [10] They discovered many natural resources in the area.

Improving Sentence Style

11d. Improve *stringy* and *wordy sentences* by making them shorter and more precise.

Revising Stringy Sentences

Stringy sentences have too many independent clauses strung together with words like *and* or *but.*

STRINGY   I dreamed I was in a big castle, and I turned a corner, and I could see a young princess, and she waved at me, but then she ran up the stairs, and she ran into the darkness.

To fix a stringy sentence, you can

- break the sentence into two or more sentences
- turn some of the independent clauses into phrases or subordinate clauses

REVISED   I dreamed I was in a big castle. When I turned a corner, I could see a young princess. She waved at me, but then she ran up the stairs into the darkness.

NOTE When you revise a stringy sentence, you may decide to keep *and* or *but* between two independent clauses. If you do, be sure to add a comma before the *and* or *but* to show a pause between the two thoughts.

ORIGINAL   She waved at me but then she ran up the stairs into the darkness.

REVISED   She waved at me, but then she ran up the stairs into the darkness.

 REFERENCE NOTE: For more information about using commas in compound sentences, see page 264.

Revising Wordy Sentences

You can revise wordy sentences in three different ways.

1. Replace a group of words with one word.

WORDY   Our snow sculpture was the biggest and best on the block due to the fact that we had spent over three hours making it.

REVISED   Our snow sculpture was the biggest and best on the block **because** we had spent over three hours making it. [*Because* replaces *due to the fact that.*]

WORDY   With great suddenness, our beautiful snow sculpture began to melt.

REVISED   **Suddenly,** our beautiful snow sculpture began to melt. [*Suddenly* replaces *with great suddenness.*]

2. Replace a clause with a phrase.

WORDY   When the play had come to an end, we walked to a restaurant and treated ourselves to pizza.

REVISED   **After the play,** we walked to a restaurant and treated ourselves to pizza. [*After the play* replaces *when the play had come to an end.*]

WORDY   I ordered a slice with mushrooms, which is my favorite topping.

REVISED   I ordered a slice with mushrooms, **my favorite topping.** [*My favorite topping* replaces *which is my favorite topping.*]

3. Take out a whole group of unnecessary words.

WORDY   What I mean to say is that Carlos did not go to the movie with us.

REVISED   Carlos did not go to the movie with us.

WORDY   We all liked the movie because it had some very funny scenes that were the kinds of scenes that make you laugh.

REVISED   We all liked the movie because it had some very funny scenes.

STYLE NOTE   Extra words and phrases tend to make writing sound awkward and unnatural. As you revise your writing, read your sentences aloud to check for wordiness or a stringy style. If you run out of breath before the end of a sentence, chances are it is stringy, wordy, or both.

SENTENCES

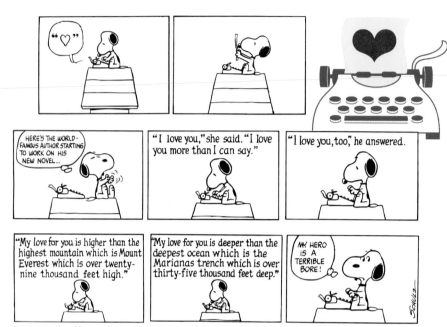

Peanuts reprinted by permission of UFS, Inc.

 QUICK CHECK 3

Revising Stringy and Wordy Sentences

The following paragraph is hard to read because it contains stringy and wordy sentences. First, label each sentence as *stringy* or *wordy*. Then revise the sentences to improve the style of the paragraph.

[1] On Halloween night in 1938, an amazing event took place that was very surprising. [2] Many families were gathered around their radios, and they were listening to music, and then they heard that Martians had invaded Earth. [3] Actually, the fact is that the news report was a radio version of H. G. Wells's novel *The War of the Worlds*. [4] But Orson Welles, who was the producer of this famous hoax, made the show very realistic. [5] Thousands of Americans were frightened and upset, and many people

jumped in cars to escape from the aliens, and some people even reported seeing the Martians and spaceships.

✓ Chapter Review

A. Finding and Revising Sentence Fragments

Some of the following groups of words are sentence fragments. Revise each fragment to make a complete sentence. You may need to change the punctuation and capitalization. If the word group is already a complete sentence, write *S*.

EXAMPLE   **1.** The cat sitting in the window.
            1. *The cat sitting in the window looked longingly at the bird outside.*

1. A huge wave flipped over the raft.
2. Because we were good swimmers.
3. We were ready to go back in the water after we rested in the sun for a while.
4. Ran by and kicked sand on our blanket.
5. The family next to us a sand sculpture of a dragon.

B. Identifying and Revising Run-on Sentences

Decide which of the following groups of words are run-ons. Then revise each run-on to make it correct. If the group of words is already correct, write *C*.

EXAMPLE   **1.** Have you ever heard of the Louvre it is the most famous art museum in Paris.
            1. *Have you ever heard of the Louvre? It is the most famous art museum in Paris.*

6. The buildings of the Louvre form a rectangle there are courtyards and gardens inside the rectangle.
7. The Louvre covers about forty acres, it has about eight miles of gallery space.
8. Over one million works of art are exhibited in the Louvre.

9. Many of the buildings of the Louvre have been expanded and modernized, the most recent additions are the glass pyramids designed by I. M. Pei.

10. In the Jeu de Paume Museum, an annex of the Louvre, is housed the finest collection of impressionist paintings in the world.

C. Combining Sentences

Combine each of the following pairs of sentences. To make a smooth combination, you may need to delete, change, or rearrange words.

EXAMPLE   1. Television networks have made professional tennis a popular sport. They show all the major tournaments.
   1. *Showing all the major tournaments, television networks have made professional tennis a popular sport.*

11. Rod Laver won the Wimbledon men's singles title in 1961. Rod Laver was an Australian.

12. Women players organized themselves. They organized so that they could demand equal prize money.

13. Louis Armstrong sang jazz. His singing was brilliant.

14. Armstrong started playing at a New Orleans night spot. He played the cornet.

15. Many Australians grill their meat. Many Australians also roast their meat.

16. Potatoes are often served with the meat. Other vegetables are often served with the meat, too.

17. The kilogram is the basic unit of weight in the metric system. The meter is the basic unit of length in the metric system.

18. The old system of measurement has more than twenty basic units of measurement. The metric system has only seven.

19. The Aztec empire was destroyed by the Spanish. The Spanish conquered it in 1521.

20. There was very little left of the Aztec civilization. The Spanish invaders tore down all the Aztec buildings.

D. Revising Stringy and Wordy Sentences

Label each of the following sentences as *stringy* or *wordy*. Then revise them to make them clearer and more precise. If a sentence is effective as it is, write C.

EXAMPLE   **1.** What I want to say is that wasps do far more good then harm.
         1. *wordy—Wasps do far more good than harm.*

21. According to some historians, the Chinese invented paper after watching wasps make it.
22. Wasps chew wood and wasps chew plant fiber until the mixture they make becomes all pasty and mushy.
23. A wasp colony lasts only through the summer.
24. Harriet Tubman never learned to read or write, but she was a powerful speaker, and she spoke at many anti-slavery meetings.
25. The Civil War broke out, and Tubman volunteered to help the Union army, and she served as a cook and a nurse, and later she became a spy.

SENTENCES

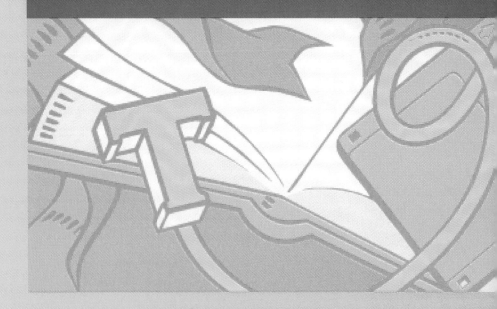

MECHANICS

12 CAPITAL LETTERS

Rules for Capitalization

✓ *Checking What You Know*

Proofreading Sentences for Correct Capitalization

Each of the following sentences contains at least one error in capitalization. Correct the errors by changing capitals to lowercase letters or lowercase letters to capitals.

EXAMPLE   **1.** The Maxwells enjoyed visiting the southwest, particularly the alamo in San Antonio.
        1. *Southwest; Alamo*

1. Is dr. Powell's office at Twenty-First street and Oak drive?
2. On labor day we went to Three Trees State Park.
3. We invited aunt Mae and my cousins to go with us.
4. Our junior high school had a much more successful carnival than lakeside junior high school did.
5. Did you know that the folk tale "cinderella," which is included in *grimm's fairy tales,* is similar to a tale from ninth-century china?
6. Abe's cousin joined the Peace corps and lived in a small village on the west coast of africa.

7. No fish live in the Great salt lake in Utah.
8. I found out that I could save money by shopping at Al's discount city.
9. We have studied Japanese Culture, including the shinto religion.
10. This semester I have English, American History, Spanish, and Industrial Arts I in the afternoon.
11. On saturday and sunday, my mother and i are going to a family reunion in the town where she grew up.
12. The Robinsons live near route 41, not far from Memorial Parkway on the South side of town.
13. At our Wednesday Night meeting, the reverend Terry Witt gave a talk on the beliefs of Lutherans.
14. We salute you, o Caesar!
15. Did you know that thursday was named after the Norse God Thor?
16. The Winter air chilled the scouts to the bone.
17. Dale Evans and Roy Rogers always sang "happy trails to you" at the end of their television programs.
18. Thurgood Marshall was the first african american appointed to the Supreme court.
19. My Uncle served in the U.S. Army during the Vietnam war.
20. The American revolution took place toward the end of the Age of Enlightenment in the 1700's. ✓

12a. Capitalize the first word in every sentence.

EXAMPLES　**M**ore and more people are discovering the benefits of exercise. **D**aily workouts at the gymnasium or on the running track strengthen the heart.

The first word of a sentence that is a direct quotation is capitalized even if the quotation begins within a sentence.

EXAMPLE　In his *Sacred Meditations,* Francis Bacon states, "**K**nowledge is power."

MECHANICS

Traditionally, the first word in a line of poetry begins with a capital letter.

EXAMPLE

Hold fast to dreams
For if dreams die
Life is a broken-winged bird
That cannot fly.

Langston Hughes, "Dreams"

Some modern poets and writers do not follow this style. When you are quoting, follow the capitalization used in the source of the quotation.

 REFERENCE NOTE: For more about using capital letters in quotations, see pages 285–286.

12b. Capitalize the pronoun *I.*

EXAMPLE

They took my lover's tallness off to war,
Left me lamenting. Now I cannot guess
What I can use an empty heart-cup for.

Gwendolyn Brooks,
from "The Sonnet-Ballad"

12c. Capitalize the interjection *O.*

The interjection *O* is most often used on solemn or formal occasions. It is usually followed by a word in direct address.

EXAMPLES

O our Mother the Earth, O our Father the Sky,
Your children are we, and with tired backs
We bring you the gifts you love.

from a traditional song of the
Tewa people

Protect us in the battle, O great Athena!

The interjection *oh* requires a capital letter only at the beginning of a sentence.

EXAMPLE   **Oh, I wish I could tell you how lonely I felt.**

Rudolfo A. Anaya, from *Tortuga*

Otherwise, *oh* is not capitalized.

EXAMPLE   We felt tired but, **oh,** so victorious.

 QUICK CHECK 1   **Correcting Sentences by Capitalizing Words**

Most of the following sentences contain errors in capitalization. If a sentence is correct, write *C*. If there are errors in the use of capitals, correct the word or words that should be changed.

1. If i need a ride, i will give you a call.
2. Loretta is spending her vacation in Maine, but Oh, how she would like to visit Paris.
3. Ana exclaimed, "oh no, I left my backpack on the bus!"
4. Please accept these gifts, o Lord.
5. Have I told you that my grandmother teaches karate?

12d. Capitalize proper nouns.

A *common noun* is a general name for a person, a place, a thing, or an idea. A *proper noun* names a particular person, place, or thing.

 REFERENCE NOTE: For more about common and proper nouns, see pages 47–48.

A common noun is capitalized only when it begins a sentence or is part of a title. A proper noun, however, is always capitalized.

COMMON NOUNS	PROPER NOUNS
athlete	Florence Griffith Joyner
river	Nile
month	February
team	Los Angeles Dodgers

Some proper nouns consist of more than one word. In these names, short prepositions (those of fewer than five letters) and articles (*a, an, the*) are not capitalized.

EXAMPLES   Statue **of** Liberty, Alexander **the** Great

MECHANICS

(1) Capitalize the names of persons and animals.

PERSONS	Alice Walker, Franklin Chang-Díaz, Ms. Sandoz
ANIMALS	Lassie, Trigger, Shamu, Socks

NOTE Some names consist of more than one part. The different parts may begin with capital letters only or with a combination of capital and lowercase letters. If you are not sure about the spelling of a name, ask the person, or check a reference source.

EXAMPLES   Van den Akker, McEnroe, La Fontaine, de la Garza, ibn-Saud

COMPUTER NOTE   You may be able to use your spelling checker to help you capitalize people's names correctly. Make a list of the names you write most often. Be sure that you have spelled and capitalized each name correctly. Then add this list to your computer's dictionary or spelling-check feature.

(2) Capitalize geographical names.

TYPE OF NAME	EXAMPLES	
Towns, Cities	Jamestown San Diego	Montreal St. Louis
Counties, States	Cook County Georgia	Orange County New Hampshire
Countries	Germany Mexico	Japan New Zealand
Islands	Wake Island Isle of Wight	Attu Molokai
Bodies of Water	Lake Erie Tampa Bay	Kentucky River Indian Ocean
Forests, Parks	Sherwood Forest Palmetto State Park	Yellowstone National Park
Streets, Highways	Madison Avenue Interstate 75	Route 44 West Fourth Street

NOTE In a hyphenated street number, the second part of the number is not capitalized.

EXAMPLE East Seventy-**e**ighth Street

TYPE OF NAME	EXAMPLES	
Mountains	Mount Washington Big Horn Mountains	Sawtooth Range Pikes Peak
Continents	Europe North America South America	Asia Africa Australia
Regions	the Middle East New England the West Coast	the North the Midwest the Great Plains

Peanuts reprinted by permission of UFS, Inc.

 NOTE Words such as *north, east,* and *southwest* are not capitalized when they indicate direction.

EXAMPLES flying **s**outh for the winter
northeast of Atlanta

(3) Capitalize the names of planets, stars, and other heavenly bodies.

EXAMPLES **J**upiter, **S**aturn, **S**irius, the **M**ilky **W**ay,
the **B**ig **D**ipper, **H**alley's **C**omet

 NOTE The word *earth* is not capitalized unless it is used along with the names of other heavenly bodies. The words *sun* and *moon* are not capitalized.

MECHANICS

EXAMPLES   Water covers more than seventy percent of the surface of the **earth**.

Mercury and Venus are closer to the sun than **Earth** is.

(4) Capitalize the names of teams, organizations, businesses, institutions, and government bodies.

TYPE OF NAME	EXAMPLES	
Teams	**Detroit Pistons**	**Pittsburgh Pirates**
	Seattle Seahawks	**Southside Raiders**
Organizations	**African Studies Association**	
	Future Farmers of America	
	National Football League	
Businesses	**Wilson's Vacuum World**	
	Levi Strauss Associates	
	Kellogg Company	
Institutions	**Cary Memorial Hospital**	
	Hillcrest Junior High School	
	Antioch College	
Government Bodies	**Air National Guard**	
	Department of Agriculture	
	Governor's Council on Equal Opportunity	

NOTE   Do not capitalize the words *democratic* or *republican* when they refer to principles or forms of government. Capitalize these words only when they refer to political parties.

EXAMPLES   **democratic** reforms   **Republican** candidate

The word *party* following the name of a political party is usually not capitalized. Some writers, however, do capitalize it. Either way is correct.

EXAMPLE   **Democratic party** [*or* Party]

 REFERENCE NOTE: Many of the names of organizations and government bodies are often abbreviated. For more on abbreviations, see pages 417–420.

(5) Capitalize the names of historical events and periods, special events, and calendar items.

TYPE OF NAME	EXAMPLES	
Historical Events	Revolutionary War Battle of Bunker Hill	Crusades Yalta Conference
Historical or Prehistoric Eras	Great Depression Paleozoic Era	Middle Ages Renaissance
Special Events	World Series Olympic Games	Oklahoma State Fair Cannes Film Festival
Calendar Items	Friday October	Memorial Day Fourth of July

NOTE The name of a season is not capitalized unless it is part of a proper name.

EXAMPLES   the last day of **s**ummer
the Oak Ridge **W**inter Carnival

(6) Capitalize the names of nationalities, races, and peoples.

EXAMPLES   **Greek, Asian, African American, Caucasian, Hispanic, Lakota Sioux**

NOTE The words *black* and *white* may or may not be capitalized when they refer to races.

EXAMPLE   The first edition of the first **b**lack [*or* Black] newspaper, *Freedom's Journal,* was published on Friday, March 16, 1827.

(7) Capitalize the names of religions and their followers, holy days, sacred writings, and specific deities.

TYPE OF NAME	EXAMPLES		
Religions and Followers	Christianity Zen Buddhism	Muslim Amish	Hindu Judaism
Holy Days	Lent Easter	Ramadan Passover	el Día de la Virgen Guadalupe
Sacred Writings	Koran Talmud	the Bible New Testament	Tao Te Ching Veda
Specific Deities	God Allah	Holy Spirit Jehovah	Brahma Vishnu

MECHANICS

NOTE The word *god* is not capitalized when it refers to a god of ancient mythology. The names of specific gods, however, are capitalized.

EXAMPLE The trickster **g**od in many Native American tales is called **C**oyote.

(8) Capitalize the names of buildings and other structures.

EXAMPLES **W**orld **T**rade **C**enter, **G**olden **G**ate **B**ridge, **S**hubert **T**heater, **P**laza **H**otel, **H**oover **D**am, **E**iffel **T**ower

(9) Capitalize the names of monuments and awards.

TYPE OF NAME	EXAMPLES	
Monuments	**Washington Monument** **Statue of Liberty**	**Vietnam Veterans Memorial**
Awards	**Academy Award** **Pulitzer Prize**	**Newbery Medal** **Purple Heart**

(10) Capitalize the names of trains, ships, airplanes, and spacecraft.

TYPE OF NAME	EXAMPLES	
Trains	*Silver Rocket*	*Orient Express*
Ships	**USS** *Nimitz*	*Santa María*
Airplanes	the *Spirit of St. Louis*	*Air Force One*
Spacecraft	*Apollo 11*	*Columbia*

REFERENCE NOTE: For more information about using italics (underlining) with the names of vehicles, see pages 282–283.

(11) Capitalize the brand names of business products.

EXAMPLES **N**ike shoes, **B**uick station wagon, **W**rangler jeans
[Notice that the names of the types of products are not capitalized.]

MECHANICS

QUICK CHECK 2   **Using Capital Letters Correctly**

Correct each of the following expressions, using capital letters as needed.

1. decisions of the united states supreme court
2. the apaches of the southwest
3. power produced at boulder dam
4. the tomb of the unknown soldier
5. 512 west twenty-fourth street
6. pictures of saturn sent by *voyager 2*
7. maui, one of the islands that make up hawaii
8. the great lakes
9. monday, april 29
10. the stone age

12e. Capitalize proper adjectives.

A *proper adjective* is formed from a proper noun and is almost always capitalized.

PROPER NOUN	PROPER ADJECTIVE
Africa	African imports
China	Chinese doctor
Islam	Islamic culture
King Arthur	Arthurian legend
Mars	Martian year
Rome	Roman army

 REFERENCE NOTE: For more about proper nouns and proper adjectives, see pages 47–48 and 55.

12f. Do *not* capitalize the names of school subjects, except language classes and course names followed by a number.

EXAMPLES   I have tests in **E**nglish, **L**atin, and **m**ath.
You must pass **A**rt I before taking **A**rt II.
Ms. Anello teaches **C**ivics I and history.

MECHANICS

QUICK CHECK 3 **Using Capital Letters Correctly**

Correct each of the following expressions, using capital letters as needed.

1. a lesson in spanish
2. this valuable elizabethan manuscript
3. a program on japanese customs
4. problems in geometry I
5. studying german, chemistry, and government II

STYLE NOTE Misusing a capital letter or a lowercase letter at the beginning of a word can confuse the meaning of a sentence.

CONFUSING   We used the heavy-duty Jack at Ben's garage to lift my brother's mustang. [The sentence means, *We used the strong person at the garage at Ben's house to lift my brother's horse.*]

CLEAR   We used the heavy-duty jack at Ben's Garage to lift my brother's Mustang. [The meaning of the sentence is, *We used the equipment at Ben's auto repair shop to lift my brother's car.*]

You may be able to use such double meanings effectively in poetry or in other creative writing. But most of the time, you should follow the rules of standard capitalization.

12g. Capitalize titles.

(1) Capitalize the title of a person when it comes before a name.

EXAMPLES   There will be a short address by **G**overnor Halsey.
Report to **L**ieutenant Engstrom, please.
Does **Ms.** Tam know **Dr.** Politi?
The **R**everend Henry Ward Beecher preached here.
How many terms did **P**resident Theodore Roosevelt serve?

MECHANICS

REFERENCE NOTE: For more about abbreviations such as *Mrs.* and *Dr.*, see page 259 and pages 417–418.

(2) Capitalize a title used alone or following a person's name only when you want to emphasize the position of someone holding a high office.

EXAMPLES   Will the **S**ecretary of **L**abor hold a news conference this afternoon?
The secretary of our scout troop has the measles.
The crowd grew quiet as the **R**abbi rose to speak at the town meeting.
Is he the rabbi at the new synagogue on the corner?

In direct address, a title used without a proper name is usually capitalized.

EXAMPLES   Is the patient resting comfortably, **N**urse?
What is your name, **S**ir [*or* sir]?

(3) Capitalize a word showing a family relationship when the word is used before or in place of a person's name.

EXAMPLES   I received a letter from **A**unt Christina and **U**ncle Garth.
When will **M**om and **D**ad be home?

Do not capitalize a word showing a family relationship when a possessive comes before the word.

EXAMPLE   Angela's **m**other and my **a**unt Daphne coach the softball team.

(4) Capitalize the first and last words and all important words in titles of books, magazines, newspapers, poems, short stories, historical documents, movies, television programs, works of art, and musical compositions.

Unimportant words in titles include

- prepositions of fewer than five letters (such as *at, of, for, from, with*)

MECHANICS

- coordinating conjunctions (*and, but, for, nor, or, so, yet*)
- articles (*a, an, the*)

 REFERENCE NOTE: For a list of prepositions, see pages 65–66.

 NOTE The article *the* before a title is not capitalized unless it is the first word of the title.

> EXAMPLES Is that the late edition of the *Chicago Sun-Times*?
>
> I read an interesting story in *The New Yorker*.

TYPE OF NAME	EXAMPLES	
Books	*Dust Tracks on a Road* *A Jar of Dreams* *The Red Badge of Courage*	*Johnny Tremain* *Sounder*
Magazines	*Sports Illustrated* *Woman's Day* *Essence*	*Latin American* *Literary Review* *Popular Science*
Newspapers	*Boston Herald* *Houston Chronicle* *The Miami Herald*	*St. Petersburg Times* *San Francisco Examiner*
Poems	"Refugee Ship" "Mother to Son"	"With Eyes at the Back of Our Heads"
Short Stories	"The Tell-Tale Heart" "Gorilla, My Love" "El Mago"	"My Wonder Horse" "Uncle Tony's Goat" "Marigolds"
Historical Documents	Bill of Rights Treaty of Ghent Magna Carta	Emancipation Proclamation Mayflower Compact
Movies	*Stand and Deliver* *Jurassic Park*	*Back to the Future* *Coneheads*
Television Programs	*The Wonder Years* *A Different World*	*FBI: The Untold Stories*
Works of Art	*Mona Lisa* *Birth of Venus* *The Old Guitarist*	*Bird in Space* *I and the Village*
Musical Compositions	*West Side Story* *Rhapsody in Blue* *The Marriage of Figaro*	"In the Name of Love" "On Top of Old Smoky"

MECHANICS

REFERENCE NOTE: For information on when to italicize (underline) a title, see pages 282–283. For information on using quotation marks for titles, see page 289.

 Certain abbreviations are capitalized.

EXAMPLES **Mr.** **Ms.** **U.S.** **TV** **Fla.** **NAACP**
B.A. **B.S.** **Ph.D.** **SOS** **FL**

However, some abbreviations, especially those for measurements, are not capitalized.

EXAMPLES **in.** **ft** **lb** **cc** **ml**
etc. **e.g.** **i.e.** **b.**

 REFERENCE NOTE: For information on using periods with abbreviations, see pages 258–260. For a list of state abbreviations, see pages 419–420. For information on using abbreviations, see pages 417–420.

 QUICK CHECK 4 | **Correcting Sentences by Capitalizing Words**

Most of the following sentences contain words that should be capitalized. Correct the words requiring capitals. If a sentence is correct, write C.

1. When my aunt Inez visited Mexico, she met several of grandmother Villa's brothers and sisters for the first time.
2. All of these pronunciations are correct according to both the *american heritage dictionary* and *webster's new world dictionary.*
3. Did you hear commissioner of education smathers's speech recommending a longer school day and year-round school?
4. After the secretary read the minutes from the last meeting, the treasurer reported on the club's current budget situation.
5. Did you know that dr. Santos subscribed to *field and stream*?

MECHANICS

✓ Chapter Review

A. Proofreading Sentences for Correct Capitalization

Each of the following sentences contains at least one error in capitalization. Correct the errors by changing capitals to lowercase letters or lowercase letters to capitals.

EXAMPLE   **1.** The shubert Theater is located at 225 West Forty-Fourth Street in New York.
           1. *Shubert; Forty-fourth*

1. The planet mars was named for the roman God of war.
2. In History class we memorized the state Capitals.
3. Uncle Dave owns one of the first honda Motorcycles that were sold in north America.
4. My cousin gave me a terrific book, *rules of the game,* which illustrates the rules of all sorts of games.
5. Rajiv Gandhi, who was then the prime minister of India, visited Washington, d.c., in June of 1985.
6. The Indus river flows down from the Himalaya mountains to the Arabian sea.
7. The writings and television appearances of dr. Carl Sagan have increased public interest in Science.
8. In the afternoons i help Mrs. Parkhurst deliver the *Evening Independent,* a local Newspaper.
9. Many people have left Northern states and moved to the south and west.
10. The Writer Ernest Hemingway served in the red cross during World war I.
11. Could you please tell me how to get to the chrysler Factory on highway 21 and riverside road?
12. For father's day, let's buy Dad a new power saw.
13. In 1978, the president of egypt and the prime minister of israel shared the nobel peace prize.
14. After we read "fire and ice" by Robert Frost, i wanted to read more of the Poet's work.
15. At Cam's house, i tried a vietnamese noodle dish.

B. Proofreading Paragraphs for Correct Capitalization

Most of the sentences in the following paragraphs contain errors in capitalization. Proofread the paragraphs, adding or omitting capital letters as necessary. If a sentence is correct, write C.

EXAMPLE   [1] The national park service celebrated its seventy-fifth Anniversary in 1991.
1. *National Park Service; anniversary*

[16] The national park service was set up as a Bureau of the department of the interior on august 15, 1916. [17] However, the beginnings of today's system of National parks go back to 1872, when congress established Yellowstone national park in idaho, montana, and wyoming. [18] In 1906, president Theodore Roosevelt signed the Antiquities act, which authorized the president to declare spanish missions and ancient native american villages as monuments. [19] Of the more than three hundred areas now under the Agency's protection, the one located farthest North is Noatak national preserve in northern Alaska. [20] Farthest east is the Buck Island National Monument on st. Croix, in the u.s. Virgin islands. [21] One park is both the farthest South and the farthest west: the national park of american Samoa, in the South pacific.

[22] Continuing to expand its services to visitors, the national park service in 1991 began compiling a computerized directory of the 3,500,000 civil war Soldiers. [23] The Directory will eventually be installed at all twenty-eight civil war sites maintained by the national park service. [24] It should be popular with the 11,000,000 people who visit those sites each year. [25] Historians estimate that one half of all United States citizens have Relatives who fought in the Civil War, and the question "did my Great-great-grandfather fight here?" is the one visitors to civil war sites ask most often.

MECHANICS

SUMMARY STYLE SHEET

Names of Persons

Lupe Serrano	a ballet dancer
Neil A. Armstrong	an astronaut
Martin Luther King, Jr.	a civil rights leader

Geographical Names

Twenty-second Street	a one-way street
Salt Lake City	a city in Utah
in the East, Northwest	traveling east, northwest
Denmark	a country in Europe
Philippine Islands	a group of islands
Pacific Ocean	the largest ocean
Redwood National Park	a park in California
Blue Ridge Mountains	camping in the mountains

Names of Heavenly Bodies

Mars, Pluto, Uranus, Earth	the surface of the earth
North Star	a bright star

Names of Organizations, Businesses, Institutions, Government Bodies

Clarksville Computer Club	the members of the club
Eastman Kodak Company	employed by the company
Pine Bluff High School	a large high school
Department of Transportation	a department of government

Names of Historical Events and Periods, Special Events, Calendar Items

Boston Tea Party	an afternoon tea party
Stone Age	at the age of fourteen
National Chess Tournament	an annual tournament
Memorial Day	a national holiday

Names of Nationalities, Races, Religions

Japanese	a nationality
Caucasian	a race
Christianity	a religion
God	a god of Greek mythology

Names of Buildings, Monuments, Awards

the John Hancock Building	an insurance building
Aladdin Motel	a motel in Miami
Mount Rushmore National Memorial	a national monument
Pulitzer Prize	winning a prize

(continued)

SUMMARY STYLE SHEET *(continued)*

Names of Trains, Ships, Airplanes, Spacecraft

Golden Arrow	a train
Andrea Doria	a ship
the *Spirit of St. Louis*	an airplane
Apollo 11	a spacecraft

Brand Names

Timex watch	a digital watch
Huffy bicycle	a ten-speed bicycle

Names of Languages, School Subjects

English, German, French, Spanish	a native language
Algebra I, Science II, Art 101	algebra, science, art

Titles

Governor Martínez	a former governor
the President of the United States	the president of the club
Grandfather Bennett	my grandfather
Thank you, Grandfather.	
The War of the Worlds	a book
People Weekly	a magazine
the *Dallas Morning News*	a newspaper
"Casey at the Bat"	a poem
"The Gift of the Magi"	a short story
Declaration of Independence	a historical document
West Side Story	a play, a movie
The Cosby Show	a television program
American Gothic	a painting
"The Star-Spangled Banner"	a national anthem

MECHANICS

13 Punctuation

End Marks, Commas, Semicolons, Colons

Correcting Sentences by Adding End Marks, Commas, Semicolons, and Colons

Write the following sentences, inserting end marks, commas, semicolons, and colons as needed.

EXAMPLE
1. Have you seen our teacher Ms. O'Donnell today
1. *Have you seen our teacher, Ms. O'Donnell, today?*

1. Cortez Peters the world's fastest typist can type 250 words per minute and he has won 13 international typing contests
2. We made a salad with the following vegetables from our garden lettuce cucumbers and cherry tomatoes
3. Running after the bus Dr Sloan tripped and fell in a puddle

4. My first pet which I got when I was six was a beagle I named it Bagel

5. Come in Randy and sit down

6. The soft subtle colors of this beautiful Navajo rug are produced from natural vegetable dyes

7. Well I do know John 3 16 by heart

8. Does anyone know where the crank that we use to open the top windows is

9. The chickens clucked and the ducks squawked however the dogs didn't make a sound

10. Now I recognize her She's in my math class

11. Wow That's the longest home run I've ever hit

12. After the rain stopped the blue jays searched for worms

13. Wasn't President John F Kennedy assassinated in Dallas Texas on November 22 1963

14. Soy sauce which is made from soybeans flavors many traditional Chinese and Japanese foods

15. Everybody had told her of course that she couldn't succeed if she didn't try

16. Preparing for takeoff the huge jetliner rolled slowly toward the runway

17. In one of the barns we found an old butter churn

18. Did you see the highlights of the Cinco de Mayo Fiesta on the 6 00 PM news

19. Her address is 142 Oak Hollow Blvd Mendota CA 93640

20. To get a better view of the fireworks Josh and I rode our bikes to Miller's Hill ✓

MECHANICS

End Marks

An *end mark* is a mark of punctuation placed at the end of a sentence. The three kinds of end marks are the *period,* the *question mark,* and the *exclamation point.*

13a. Use a period at the end of a statement.

EXAMPLES   Kristi Yamaguchi is a world-champion figure skater.

"I live in a world of such beautiful stories that I have to write one every now and then."

from an interview with Pearl Crayton

13b. Use a question mark at the end of a question.

EXAMPLES   What is the capital of Canada?
Did Shel Silverstein or Gordon Parks write *The Learning Tree*?

13c. Use an exclamation point at the end of an exclamation.

EXAMPLES   What an exciting time we had!
Wow! What a view!

Animal Crackers reprinted by permission: Tribune Media Services.

13d. Use a period or an exclamation point at the end of a request or a command.

EXAMPLES   Please give me the scissors. [a request]
Give me the scissors! [a command]

13e. Use a period after most abbreviations.

TYPES OF ABBREVIATIONS	EXAMPLES			
Personal Names	Pearl S. Buck W.E.B. DuBois		I. M. Pei H. D. (Hilda Doolittle)	
Titles Used with Names	Mr. Sr.	Mrs. Jr.	Ms. Dr.	
States	Ky. Mass.	Fla. N. Dak.	Tenn. N.Y.	Calif. S.C.

NOTE A two-letter state abbreviation without periods is used only when it is followed by a ZIP Code.

EXAMPLE   Austin, **TX** 78741

 REFERENCE NOTE: For a complete list of state abbreviations, see pages 419–420.

TYPES OF ABBREVIATIONS	EXAMPLES			
Addresses	St.	Rd.	Blvd.	P.O. Box
Organizations and Companies	Co. Ltd.	Inc. Org.	Corp.	Assn.

NOTE Abbreviations for government agencies and some widely used abbreviations are written without periods. Each letter of the abbreviation is capitalized.

EXAMPLES   UN, FBI, PTA, NAACP, PBS, CNN, YMCA, VHF

 REFERENCE NOTE: For information about capitalizing abbreviations, see page 251.

TYPES OF ABBREVIATIONS	EXAMPLES
Times	A.M. (*ante meridiem,* used with times from midnight to noon) P.M. (*post meridiem,* used with times from noon to midnight) B.C. (before Christ) A.D. (*anno Domini,* in the year of the Lord)

MECHANICS

STYLE NOTE ▷ The abbreviations *A.D.* and *B.C.* need special attention. Place *A.D.* before the number and *B.C.* after the number.

EXAMPLES   31 B.C.   A.D. 540

There is only one exception to this rule. For centuries expressed in words, place both *A.D.* and *B.C.* after the century.

EXAMPLES   sixth century B.C.
           third century A.D.

NOTE   Abbreviations for most units of measure are written without periods.

EXAMPLES   cm, kg, ml, ft, lb, mi, oz, qt

The abbreviation for *inch* (*in.*) takes a period to prevent confusion with the word *in*. If you're not sure when to use periods with abbreviations, look in a dictionary.

When an abbreviation with a period ends a sentence, another period is not needed. However, a question mark or an exclamation point is used if needed.

EXAMPLES   This is my friend J.R.
           Have you met Nguyen, J.R.?

 QUICK CHECK 1   **Correcting Sentences by Adding End Marks**

Write the following sentences, adding end marks where they are needed.

1. Have you ever heard of Little Tokyo
2. It's a neighborhood in Los Angeles, Calif, bordered by First St, Third St, Alameda St, and Los Angeles St
3. Our friends from Los Angeles, Mr and Mrs Albert B Cook, Sr, and their son, Al, Jr, introduced us to the area

MECHANICS

4. They met our 11:30 AM flight from Atlanta, Ga, and took us to lunch at a restaurant in the Japanese Plaza Village

5. What a great day we had exploring Japanese culture

Commas

An end mark is used to separate complete thoughts. A *comma* is used to separate words or groups of words *within* a complete thought.

Items in a Series

13f. Use commas to separate items in a series.

Words, phrases, and clauses in a series are separated by commas to show the reader where one item in the series ends and the next item begins.

WORDS IN A SERIES
Hammock, canoe, and *moccasin* are three of the words that English-speaking people owe to Native Americans. [nouns]
Always stop, look, and listen before crossing railroad tracks. [verbs]
In the morning, the lake looked cold, gray, and calm. [adjectives]
PHRASES IN A SERIES
Tightening the spokes, checking the tire pressure, and oiling the gears, Carlos prepared his bike for the race. [participial phrases]
We found seaweed in the water, on the sand, under the rocks, and later in our shoes. [prepositional phrases]
Clearing the table, washing the dishes, and putting everything away took almost an hour. [gerund phrases]
CLAUSES IN A SERIES
We didn't know where we were going, how we would get there, or when we would arrive. [subordinate clauses]
The lights dimmed, the curtain rose, and the orchestra began to play. [short independent clauses]

MECHANICS

NOTE Only *short* independent clauses in a series may be separated by commas. Independent clauses in a series are usually separated by semicolons.

EXAMPLE As the flood waters rose, Uncle Luke moved the farm animals to higher ground; Aunt Rose, Jenny, and I piled bags of sand around the house; and my cousin Bill filled pitchers with drinking water.

Always be sure that there are at least three items in a series; two items do not need a comma between them.

INCORRECT Workers will be collecting gifts of food, and clothing.

CORRECT Workers will be collecting gifts of food and clothing.

In your reading, you will find that some writers leave out the comma before the *and* joining the last two items in a series. But you should use a comma before the *and* so that the meaning will be clear.

Notice how the comma affects the meaning in the following examples.

EXAMPLES Luanne, Zack and I are going. [Luanne is being told that two people are going.]

Luanne, Zack, and I are going. [Three people are going.]

If all items in a series are joined by *and* or *or*, do not use commas to separate them.

EXAMPLES I voted for Corey **and** Mona **and** Ethan.

For your report you may want to read Jean Toomer's *Cane* **or** Ralph Ellison's *Invisible Man* **or** Richard Wright's *Native Son.*

13g. Use a comma to separate two or more adjectives that come before a noun.

EXAMPLES An Arabian horse is a fast, beautiful animal.

Many ranchers depended on the small, tough, sure-footed mustang.

MECHANICS

Sometimes the final adjective in a series is closely linked to the noun. When the adjective and the noun are linked in such a way, do not use a comma before the final adjective.

EXAMPLE   Training a frisky colt to become a gentle, dependable **riding horse** takes great patience. [not *dependable, riding horse*]

If you aren't sure whether the final adjective and the noun are linked, use this test. Insert the word *and* between the adjectives. If *and* makes sense, use a comma. In the example, *and* makes sense between *gentle* and *dependable*. *And* doesn't make sense between *dependable* and *riding*. Therefore, *dependable* and *riding* should not be separated by a comma.

A comma should never be used between an adjective and the noun immediately following it.

INCORRECT   Mary O'Hara wrote a tender, exciting, story about a young boy and his colt.

CORRECT   Mary O'Hara wrote a tender, exciting story about a young boy and his colt.

QUICK CHECK 2   **Correcting Sentences by Adding Commas**

Write the following sentences, adding commas where they are needed.

1. Someday I would like to visit Thailand Nepal China and Japan.
2. Charlayne Hunter-Gault's skillful probing interviews have made her a respected broadcast journalist.
3. The California condor the ocelot the brown pelican and the red wolf are only some of the endangered mammals in North America.
4. This book describes the harsh isolated lives of pioneer women in Kansas.
5. We now know what we will write about where we will find sources and how we will organize our reports.

MECHANICS

Compound Sentences

13h. Use a comma before *and, but, or, nor, for, so,* or *yet* when it joins independent clauses.

EXAMPLES The musical comedy started as an American musical form**, and** its popularity has spread throughout the world.

I enjoyed *The King and I***, but** *Oklahoma!* is still my favorite musical.

When the independent clauses are very short, the comma before *and, but,* or *or* may be omitted.

EXAMPLES Oscar Hammerstein wrote the words and Richard Rodgers wrote the music.

I'm tired but I can't sleep.

The cat can stay inside or it can go out.

A comma is always used before *nor, for, so,* or *yet* joining independent clauses.

EXAMPLES We will not give up**, nor** will we fail.

Everyone seemed excited**, for** it was time to begin.

No one else was waiting in line at the theater**, so** we left.

The water was deep and cold**, yet** it looked inviting.

NOTE Don't be misled by a simple sentence with a compound verb. A simple sentence has only one independent clause.

SIMPLE SENTENCE Margo likes golf but doesn't enjoy archery. [compound verb]

COMPOUND SENTENCE Margo likes golf**,** but she doesn't enjoy archery. [two independent clauses]

REFERENCE NOTE: For more about compound sentences, see pages 204–205. For more about simple sentences with compound verbs, see page 203.

MECHANICS

QUICK CHECK 3

Correcting Compound Sentences by Adding Commas

For each of the following sentences, identify the two words that should be separated by a comma. Include the comma. If a sentence is correct, write C.

1. Human beings must study to become architects yet some animals build amazing structures by instinct.
2. The male bowerbird builds a complex structure and he decorates it carefully to attract a mate.
3. This bird constructs a dome-shaped garden in a small tree and underneath the tree he lays a carpet of moss covered with brilliant tropical flowers.
4. Then he gathers twigs and arranges them in a three-foot-wide circle around the display.
5. Tailor ants might be called the ant world's high-rise workers for they gather leaves and sew them around tree twigs to make nests.

Interrupters

13i. Use commas to set off an expression that interrupts a sentence.

Two commas are needed if the expression to be set off comes in the middle of the sentence. One comma is needed if the expression comes first or last.

EXAMPLES   My favorite gospel singers, BeBe and CeCe Winans, were on TV last night.
Yes, I'll call back later.
How did you do in karate class today, Kami?

(1) Use commas to set off a *nonessential* participial phrase or a *nonessential* subordinate clause.

A ***nonessential*** (or ***nonrestrictive***) phrase or clause adds information that the reader doesn't need to understand the

MECHANICS

meaning of the sentence. Such a phrase or clause can be omitted without changing the main idea of the sentence.

NONESSENTIAL
PHRASES

The spider web, **shining in the morning light,** looked like sparkling lace.
Harvard College, **founded in 1636,** is the oldest college in the United States.

NONESSENTIAL
CLAUSES

Kareem Abdul-Jabbar, **who retired from professional basketball in 1989,** holds several NBA records.
Joshua eventually overcame his acrophobia, **which is the fear of being in high places.**

Do not set off an *essential* (or *restrictive*) phrase or clause. Since such a phrase or clause tells *which one(s),* it cannot be omitted without changing the meaning of the sentence.

ESSENTIAL
PHRASES

All farmers **growing the new hybrid corn** should have a good harvest. [Which farmers?]
The discoveries **made by Albert Einstein** have changed the way people think about the universe. [Which discoveries?]

ESSENTIAL
CLAUSES

The book **that you recommended** is not in the library. [Which book?]
Often, someone **who does a good deed** gains more than the person **for whom the deed is done.** [Which someone? Which person?]

 NOTE A clause beginning with *that* is usually essential.

 REFERENCE NOTE: For more information about participial phrases, see pages 152–154. For more information about subordinate clauses, see pages 165–173.

(2) Use commas to set off an appositive or an appositive phrase that is nonessential.

APPOSITIVES

My best friend, **Nancy,** is studying ballet.
We're out of our most popular flavor, **vanilla.**

APPOSITIVE PHRASES — Nancy, **my best friend,** has won a dance scholarship.

The Rio Grande, **one of the major rivers of North America,** forms the border between Texas and Mexico.

The Rio Grande runs along the southern border of Big Bend, **a national park in West Texas.**

Do not set off an appositive that tells *which one(s)* about the word it identifies. Such an appositive is essential to the meaning of the sentence.

EXAMPLE — My ancestor **Alberto Pazienza** immigrated to America on the ship *Marianna.* [Which ancestor? Which ship?]

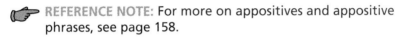 REFERENCE NOTE: For more on appositives and appositive phrases, see page 158.

(3) Use commas to set off words used in direct address.

EXAMPLES — **Mrs. Clarkson,** this package is addressed to you.
Do you know, **Elena,** when the next bus is due?

(4) Use commas to set off a parenthetical expression.

A *parenthetical expression* is a side remark that adds information or relates ideas.

EXAMPLES — The president said, **of course,** that he was deeply disappointed.
In my opinion, the movie was too violent.
I will invite Samantha, **I think.**

Commonly Used Parenthetical Expressions		
after all	generally speaking	nevertheless
at any rate	on the other hand	of course
by the way	I believe (hope,	on the contrary
for example	suppose, think)	however
for instance	in my opinion	therefore

MECHANICS

Some of these expressions are not always used as interrupters. Use commas only when the expressions are parenthetical.

EXAMPLES **What, in your opinion,** is the best solution?
[parenthetical]
I have faith **in your opinion.** [not parenthetical]
Traveling by boat may take longer, **however.**
[parenthetical]
However you go, it will be a delightful trip. [not parenthetical]

 *QUICK CHECK 4* **Using Commas to Set Off Interrupters**

Write each of the following sentences, using commas to set off expressions that interrupt the sentence. If a sentence is correct, write *C*.

1. My favorite performer is Gloria Estefan who is the lead singer with the Miami Sound Machine.
2. Harper Lee well-known author of *To Kill a Mockingbird* is from Alabama.
3. Have you signed up for a baseball team yet Aaron?
4. The main character in many of Agatha Christie's mystery novels is the Belgian detective Hercule Poirot.
5. *Cilantro* by the way is the Spanish name for the herb coriander.

Introductory Words, Phrases, and Clauses

13j. Use a comma after certain introductory elements.

(1) Use a comma after *yes, no,* or any mild exclamation such as *well* or *why* at the beginning of a sentence.

EXAMPLES Yes, I understand the problem.
Well, I think we should ask for help.

(2) Use a comma after an introductory prepositional phrase if the phrase is long or if two or more phrases appear together.

EXAMPLES   **Underneath the moss-covered rock,** we found a shiny, fat earthworm.

At night in the desert, the temperature falls rapidly.

At the bottom of the card for Drew, Julie wrote, "Happy Birthday, Kiddo."

NOTE   If the introductory prepositional phrase is short, a comma may or may not be used.

EXAMPLE   **In the morning,** [*or* In the morning] we'll tour the Caddo burial mounds.

(3) Use a comma after a verbal phrase that introduces a sentence.

PARTICIPIAL   **Forced onto the sidelines by a sprained ankle,**
PHRASES   Carlos was restless and unhappy.

Using all of her energy, Seema rode her bike to the top of the hill.

INFINITIVE   **To defend the honor of King Arthur's knights,**
PHRASE   Sir Gawain bravely accepted the Green Knight's challenge.

(4) Use a comma after an introductory adverb clause.

EXAMPLES   **When March came,** the snow fort began to melt and break down.

Because I had a sore throat, I could not audition for the school play.

So that she wouldn't forget to return her library book, Rachel left it on the table next to the front door.

NOTE   An adverb clause that comes at the end of a sentence does not usually need a comma.

REFERENCE NOTE: For more information on prepositional phrases, see pages 148–151. For more about verbal phrases, see pages 152–157. For more about adverb clauses, see pages 169–172.

Using Commas in Sentences with Introductory Words, Phrases, or Clauses

If a sentence needs a comma, identify the word it should follow, and add the comma.

1. Issued in 1991 a stamp honoring American inventor Jan Matzeliger became part of the U.S. Postal Service's Black Heritage series.
2. Since the Postal Service began issuing the series in 1978 the stamps have become popular collectors' items.
3. Why more than twenty million people in the United States alone enjoy stamp collecting.
4. To attract collectors the Postal Service produces limited numbers of special stamps.
5. With their treasures safely in albums collectors enjoy examining their first stamps as well as their newest ones.

Conventional Situations

13k. Use commas in certain conventional situations.

(1) Use commas to separate items in dates and addresses.

EXAMPLES   The delegates to the Constitutional Convention signed the Constitution on September 17, 1787, in Philadelphia, Pennsylvania.
The Kentucky Derby is held in Louisville, Kentucky, on the first Saturday in May.
Passover begins on Wednesday, April 14.
My address is 68 Lee Road, Chicago, IL 60607.

A comma separates the last item in a date or in an address from the words that follow it. A comma does *not* separate a month and a day (*April 14*), a house number and a street name (*6448 Higgins Road*), or a state abbreviation and a

ZIP Code (*IL 60607*). Nor does a comma separate a month and a year if no day is given (*June 1992*).

 NOTE If a preposition is used between items of an address, a comma is not necessary.

> EXAMPLE   He lives at 144 Smith Street **in** Moline, Illinois.

(2) Use a comma after the salutation of a friendly letter and after the closing of any letter.

EXAMPLES   Dear Aunt Margaret,
              Sincerely yours,

☞ **REFERENCE NOTE:** For information on punctuating the salutation of a business letter, see page 276. For more about all kinds of letters, see pages 407–415. For a summary of comma uses, see page 279.

Peanuts reprinted by permission of UFS, Inc.

 *QUICK CHECK 6*   **Using Commas in Dates, Addresses, and Parts of Letters**

Write the following items, inserting commas as needed.

1. 11687 Montana Avenue Los Angeles CA 90049
2. Dresser Road at North First Street in Lynchburg Virginia
3. from December 1 1991 to March 15 1992
4. Dear Joanne
5. Yours truly

Semicolons

A *semicolon* looks like a period and a comma combined, and that's just what it is. A semicolon separates complete thoughts as a period does. A semicolon also separates items within a sentence as a comma does.

131. Use a semicolon instead of a comma between independent clauses when they are not joined by *and, but, or, nor, for, so,* or *yet.*

EXAMPLES On our first trip to Houston I wanted to see the Astrodome; my little brother wanted to visit the Johnson Space Center.

Our parents settled the argument for us; they took us to both places.

Use a semicolon rather than a period between independent clauses only when the ideas in the clauses are closely related.

EXAMPLE I called Leon. He will be here in ten minutes.

I called Leon; he will be here in ten minutes.

 Very short independent clauses without conjunctions may be separated by commas.

EXAMPLE The leaves whispered, the sun beamed, the brook glittered.

 Semicolons do a better job if you don't use too many. Sometimes it is better to make two sentences out of a compound sentence or a sentence with several commas, rather than to use a semicolon.

ACCEPTABLE In the jungles of South America, it rains every day, sometimes all day; the plants there, some of which are found nowhere else in the world, are rich, thick, and fast-growing.

BETTER In the jungles of South America, it rains every day, sometimes all day. The plants there, some of which are found nowhere else in the world, are rich, thick, and fast-growing.

MECHANICS

13m. Use a semicolon between independent clauses joined by a conjunctive adverb or a transitional expression.

A *conjunctive adverb* or a *transitional expression* shows how the independent clauses that it joins are related.

EXAMPLES Mary Ishikawa decided not to stay at home; **instead,** she went to the soccer game with friends.

English was Louise's most difficult subject; **accordingly,** she gave it more time than any other subject.

The popular names of certain animals are misleading; **for example,** the koala bear is not a bear.

Many words in English come from American Indian languages; **for instance,** the word *toboggan* comes from the Algonquian language.

Commonly Used Conjunctive Adverbs

accordingly	furthermore	instead	nevertheless
besides	however	meanwhile	otherwise
consequently	indeed	moreover	therefore

Commonly Used Transitional Expressions

as a result	for example	for instance	that is
in addition	in spite of	in conclusion	in fact
of course	in other words	on the other hand	

NOTE When a conjunctive adverb or a transitional expression *joins* clauses, it is preceded by a semicolon and followed by a comma. When it *interrupts* a clause, however, it is set off by two commas.

EXAMPLES You are entitled to your opinion; **however,** you can't ignore the facts.

You are entitled to your opinion; you can't, **however,** ignore the facts.

A computer can help you check your writing for the correct punctuation of conjunctive adverbs and transitional expressions. Use the computer's "Search" function to find and highlight conjunctive adverbs and transitional expressions. Then look at each one carefully to see how it is used. Does it join clauses? Does it interrupt a clause? Or does it have another use in the sentence? Add commas and semicolons correctly, using the rule on page 273.

13n. A semicolon rather than a comma may be needed to separate clauses joined by a coordinating conjunction when there are commas within the clauses.

EXAMPLES   A tall, heavy woman entered the large, drafty room; and a short, slim, blond woman followed her.

We will practice Act I on Monday, Act II on Wednesday, and Act III on Friday; and on Saturday we will rehearse the entire play.

 *QUICK CHECK 7*   **Correcting Sentences by Adding Semicolons and Commas**

Write the following sentences, adding semicolons and commas as needed.

1. Scientists have explored almost all areas of the earth they are now exploring the floors of the oceans.
2. Some scientists predict the development of undersea cities however other scientists question this prediction.
3. St. Augustine Florida was the first European settlement in the United States the Spanish founded it in 1565.
4. In 1991 Mike Powell set a world record for the long jump his leap of 29 feet, $4\frac{1}{2}$ inches beat Bob Beamon's 1968 record by 2 inches.

MECHANICS

5. Some reptiles like a dry climate others prefer a wet climate.

Colons

13o. Use a colon before a list of items, especially after expressions like *as follows* or *the following.*

EXAMPLES Needed equipment for camping includes these items: sleeping bag, pots and pans for cooking, forks to eat with, warm clothing, sturdy shoes, and rope.

Beyond talent lie all the usual words: discipline, love, luck, but, most of all, endurance.

James Baldwin, from *The Writer's Chapbook*

NOTE Never use a colon directly after a verb or a preposition. Leave out the colon, or reword the sentence.

INCORRECT This sauce is made of: tomatoes, bay leaves, onions, oregano, and garlic.

CORRECT This sauce is made of the following ingredients: tomatoes, bay leaves, onions, oregano, and garlic.

INCORRECT My stepsister's favorite sports are: basketball, tennis, swimming, and bowling.

CORRECT My stepsister's favorite sports are basketball, tennis, swimming, and bowling.

CORRECT My stepsister's favorite sports are the following ones: basketball, tennis, swimming, and bowling.

13p. Use a colon before a statement that explains or clarifies a preceding statement.

When a list of words, phrases, or subordinate clauses follows a colon, the first word of the list is lowercase. When an independent clause follows a colon, the first word of the clause begins with a capital letter.

EXAMPLES My opinion of beauty was clearly expressed by Margaret Wolfe Hungerford in her novel *Molly Bawn*: "Beauty is in the eye of the beholder."

He could think of but one course of action: He would have to admit he had lied to his father.

13q. Use a colon in certain conventional situations.

(1) Use a colon between the hour and the minute.

EXAMPLES 11:30 P.M.
4:08 A.M.

(2) Use a colon after the salutation of a business letter.

EXAMPLES Dear Ms. Gonzalez:
Dear Sir or Madam:
Dear Sales Manager:
To Whom It May Concern:

(3) Use a colon between chapter and verse in referring to passages from the Bible.

EXAMPLES John 3:16
Matthew 6:9–13

 *QUICK CHECK 8* **Correcting Sentences by Adding Colons**

Write each of the following sentences, inserting a colon as needed.

1. During the field trip our teacher pointed out the following trees sugarberry, papaw, silver bell, and mountain laurel.
2. The first lunch period begins at 11 00 A.M.
3. This is my motto Laugh and the world laughs with you.
4. In Ruth 1 16, Ruth pledges her loyalty to Naomi, her mother-in-law.
5. The artist showed me how to make a pale peach color Simply mix white, yellow, and a little red.

✓ *Chapter Review*

Correcting Sentences by Adding End Marks, Commas, Semicolons, and Colons

Write the following paragraphs, inserting end marks, commas, semicolons, and colons as needed.

EXAMPLE [1] Did I ever tell you how our washing machine which usually behaves itself once turned into a foaming monster

1. *Did I ever tell you how our washing machine, which usually behaves itself, once turned into a foaming monster?*

[1] "Oh no The basement is full of soapsuds" my younger sister Sheila yelled [2] When I heard her I could tell how upset she was [3] Her voice had that tense strained tone that I know so well [4] To see what had alarmed her I ran down to the basement [5] Imagine the following scene The washing machine the floor and much of my sister were completely hidden in a thick foamy flow of bubbles [6] I made my way gingerly across the slippery floor fought through the foam and turned off the machine

[7] Turning the switch of course merely stopped the flow [8] Sheila and I now had to clean up the mess for we didn't want Mom and Dad to see it when they got home [9] We mopped up soapsuds we sponged water off the floor we dried the outside of the washing machine [10] After nearly an hour of steady effort at the task we were satisfied with our work and decided to try the washer

[11] Everything would have been fine if the machine had still worked however it would not even start [12] Can you imagine how upset we both were then [13] Thinking things over we decided to call a repair shop

[14] We frantically telephoned Mr Hodges who runs the appliance-repair business nearest to our town [15] We told him the problem and asked him to come to 21 Crestview Drive Ellenville as soon as possible

[16] When he arrived a few minutes after 4 00 Mr Hodges inspected the machine asked us a few questions and said that we had no real problem [17] The wires had become damp they would dry out if we waited a day before we tried to use the machine again

[18] Surprised and relieved we thanked Mr Hodges and started toward the stairs to show him the way out [19] He stopped us however and asked whether we knew what had caused the problem with the suds [20] We didn't want to admit our ignorance but our hesitation gave us away [21] Well Mr Hodges suggested that from then on we measure the soap instead of just pouring it into the machine

[22] Looking at the empty box of laundry powder I realized what had happened [23] It was I believe the first time Sheila had used the washing machine by herself she hadn't followed the instructions on the box

[24] This incident occurred on November 10 1992 and we have never forgotten it [25] Whenever we do the laundry now we remember the lesson we learned the day the washer overflowed

SUMMARY OF USES OF THE COMMA

13f   Use commas to separate items in a series—words, phrases, and clauses.

13g   Use a comma to separate two or more adjectives that come before a noun.

13h   Use a comma before *and, but, for, or, nor, so,* or *yet* when it joins independent clauses.

13i   Use commas to set off expressions that interrupt sentences.

   (1) Use commas to set off nonessential participial phrases and nonessential clauses.

   (2) Use commas to set off appositives and appositive phrases that are nonessential.

   (3) Use commas to set off words used in direct address.

   (4) Use commas to set off parenthetical expressions.

13j   Use a comma after certain introductory elements.

   (1) Use a comma after *yes, no,* or any mild exclamation such as *well* or *why* at the beginning of a sentence.

   (2) Use a comma after two or more introductory prepositional phrases.

   (3) Use a comma after an introductory verbal phrase.

   (4) Use a comma after an introductory adverb clause.

13k   Use commas in certain conventional situations.

   (1) Use commas to separate items in dates and addresses.

   (2) Use a comma after the salutation of a friendly letter and after the closing of any letter.

MECHANICS

14 PUNCTUATION

Italics and Quotation Marks

Proofreading Sentences for the Correct Use of Quotation Marks and Underlining (Italics)

Each of the following sentences contains at least one error in the use of quotation marks or underlining (italics). Write each sentence correctly.

EXAMPLE **1.** Marcella asked, "Did you read Robert Frost's poem Nothing Gold Can Stay in class?"
1. *Marcella asked, "Did you read Robert Frost's poem 'Nothing Gold Can Stay' in class?"*

1. Uncle Ned reads The Wall Street Journal every day.
2. Fill in all the information on both sides of the form, the secretary said.
3. How many times have you seen the movie of Frances H. Burnett's novel The Secret Garden?

MECHANICS

280

4. Many of the students enjoyed the humor in O. Henry's short story The Ransom of Red Chief.
5. My little sister asked, Why can't I have a hamster?
6. Please don't sing I've Been Working on the Railroad again.
7. Last summer my older sister played in a band on a Caribbean cruise ship named Bright Coastal Star.
8. "Read James Baldwin's essay Autobiographical Notes, and answer both of the study questions," the teacher announced.
9. Dudley Randall's poem Ancestors asks why people always seem to believe that their ancestors were aristocrats.
10. "That artist," Mr. Russell said, was influenced by the Cuban painter Amelia Pelaez.
11. The magazine rack held current issues of National Wildlife, Time, Hispanic, Jewish Monthly, and Sports Illustrated.
12. Please hold my backpack for a minute, Dave, Josh said. I need to tie my shoelace.
13. Elise, do you know who said, The only thing we have to fear is fear itself? asked the teacher.
14. The final number will be a medley of excerpts from George Gershwin's opera Porgy and Bess.
15. Hey, Jason, said Chen, you play the drums like an expert!
16. When President Lincoln heard of the South's defeat, he requested that the band play Dixie.
17. The plays Les Misérables and Cats were hits on Broadway and are now on national tours.
18. I've read, Phil said, that the Yoruba people of Nigeria are fantastic artists.
19. Cary asked, What's pita bread?
20. The latest issue of National Geographic has a long article on rain forests.

Underlining (Italics)

Italics are printed letters that lean to the right, such as *the letters in these words.* In your handwritten or typewritten work, indicate italics by underlining. If your work were to be printed for publication, the underlined words would appear in italics. For example, if you were to write or type, the title would look like this:

Born Free is the story of a lioness that became a pet.

Born Free is the story of a lioness that became a pet.

The printed version of the title would look like this:

Born Free is the story of a lioness that became a pet.

COMPUTER NOTE If you use a computer, you may be able to set words in italics yourself. Most word-processing programs and many printers can produce italic type.

14a. Use underlining (italics) for titles of books, plays, periodicals, works of art, films, television programs, recordings, long musical compositions, trains, ships, aircraft, and spacecraft.

TYPE OF TITLE	EXAMPLES	
Books	*Storyteller* *Barrio Boy*	*House Made of Dawn* *River Notes*
Plays	*The Piano Lesson* *Macbeth*	*Visit to a Small Planet*
Periodicals	*Hispanic* *The Atlantic*	*The New York Times*

NOTE The article *the* before the title of a magazine or a newspaper is only italicized and capitalized when it is part of

MECHANICS

the official title. The official title of a newspaper or magazine appears on the *masthead.* The masthead is a boxed listing of the publication's publishers, owners, editors, and address. It usually appears on a newspaper's editorial page and near the front of a magazine.

EXAMPLES My parents get **the** *San Francisco Chronicle.*
On Sundays, we all share ***The New York Times.***

TYPE OF TITLE	EXAMPLES	
Works of Art	*The Thinker* *The Last Supper*	*American Gothic* *Bird in Space*
Films	*Stand and Deliver* *Casablanca*	*Malcolm X* *Into the West*
Television Programs	*Life Goes On* *Home Improvement*	*Wall Street Week*
Recordings	*Unforgettable* *No Fences*	*Into the Light* *Man of Steel*
Long Musical Compositions	*Don Giovanni* *A Sea Symphony*	*The Four Seasons* *Peer Gynt Suite*
Ships	*Calypso* *Pequod*	USS *Nimitz* *Queen Elizabeth 2*
Trains	*Orient Express* *Garden State Special*	*City of New Orleans*
Aircraft	*Enola Gay* *Spruce Goose*	*Spirit of St. Louis*
Spacecraft	*Apollo 12* *Voyager I*	USS *Enterprise* *Sputnik II*

 REFERENCE NOTE: For examples of titles that are not italicized but enclosed in quotation marks, see page 289.

14b. Use underlining (italics) for words, letters, and figures referred to as such.

EXAMPLES What is the difference between the words *affect* and *effect*?
Don't forget to drop the final *e* before you add *-ing* to that word.
Is the last number a *5* or an *8*?

✓ *QUICK CHECK 1* **Using Underlining (Italics) in Sentences**

Write and underline the words that should be italicized in each of the following sentences.

1. Sometimes I forget to put the first o in the word thorough, and by mistake I write through.

2. Picasso's painting Guernica is named for a Spanish town that was destroyed by German planes during the Spanish Civil War.

3. My father reads the Washington Post because he likes Carl Rowan's column.

4. The British movie My Left Foot celebrates the accomplishments of a writer and artist who has serious disabilities.

5. Janice finally found her mistake; the 4 was in the wrong column.

STYLE NOTE Now and then, writers will use italics (underlining) for emphasis, especially in written dialogue. The italic type shows how the sentence is supposed to be spoken. Read the following sentences aloud. Notice that by italicizing different words, the writer can change the meaning of the sentence.

EXAMPLES "Are you *certain* that he's the new exchange student?" asked Martha. [Are you certain, not just guessing?]

"Are you certain that *he's* the new exchange student?" asked Martha. [Is he, not that other boy, the new exchange student?]

"Are you certain that he's the new *exchange* student?" asked Martha. [Is he the new exchange student, not a new transfer student?]

Italicizing (underlining) words for emphasis is a handy technique that should not be overused. It can quickly lose its impact.

MECHANICS

Quotation Marks

14c. Use quotation marks to enclose a *direct quotation*—a person's exact words.

Be sure to place quotation marks both before and after a person's exact words.

EXAMPLES   "Has anyone in the class swum in the Great Salt Lake?" asked Ms. Estrada.
       "I swam there last summer," said Peggy Ann.

Do not use quotation marks for an *indirect quotation*—a rewording of a direct quotation.

DIRECT   Kaya asked, "What do you think Langston
QUOTATION Hughes's poem means?"

INDIRECT Kaya asked what I thought Langston Hughes's
QUOTATION poem meant.

DIRECT   As Barbara Jordan said in her speech to the
QUOTATION Democratic National Convention in 1976, "We are willing to suffer the discomfort of change in order to achieve a better future."

INDIRECT Barbara Jordan said that people will put up
QUOTATION with the discomfort of change to have a better future.

14d. A direct quotation begins with a capital letter.

EXAMPLES   Brandon shouted, "Let's get busy!"
       Abraham Lincoln said, "Those who deny freedom to others deserve it not for themselves."

14e. When the expression identifying the speaker interrupts a quoted sentence, the second part of the quotation begins with a small letter.

EXAMPLES   "What are some of the things," asked Mrs. Perkins, "that the astronauts discovered on the moon?"

> "One thing they found," answered Gwen, "**wa**s that the moon is covered by a layer of dust."
> "Gee," Angelo added, "**m**y room at home is a lot like the moon, I guess."

Notice in the examples above that each part of a divided quotation is enclosed in a set of quotation marks. In addition, the interrupting expression is followed by a comma.

When the second part of a divided quotation is a sentence, it begins with a capital letter.

EXAMPLE   "Any new means of travel is exciting," remarked Mrs. Perkins. "**S**pace travel is no exception."

Notice that a period, not a comma, follows the interrupting expression.

14f. A direct quotation is set off from the rest of the sentence by a comma, a question mark, or an exclamation point, but not by a period.

Set off means "separated." If a quotation comes at the beginning of a sentence, a comma follows it. If a quotation comes at the end of a sentence, a comma comes before it. If a sentence in quotation marks is interrupted, a comma follows the first part and comes before the second part.

EXAMPLES   "I've just finished reading a book about Narcissa Whitman**,**" Alyssa said.
Mark said**,** "I've never heard of her."
"Alyssa**,**" begged Janet**,** "will you please tell the rest of us who she was?"

When a quotation ends with a question mark or with an exclamation point, no comma is needed.

EXAMPLES   "Wasn't she one of the early settlers in the Northwest**?**" asked Delia.
"What an adventure**!**" exclaimed Iola.

14g. A period or a comma is always placed inside the closing quotation marks.

EXAMPLES Ramón said, "Hank Aaron was a better baseball player than Babe Ruth because Aaron hit more home runs in his career."
"But Hank Aaron never hit sixty homers in one year," Paula responded.

14h. A question mark or an exclamation point is placed inside the closing quotation marks when the quotation itself is a question or an exclamation. Otherwise, it is placed outside.

EXAMPLES "Is the time difference between Los Angeles and Chicago two hours?" asked Ken. [The quotation is a question.]
Linda exclaimed, "I thought everyone knew that!" [The quotation is an exclamation.]
What did Jade Snow Wong mean in her story "A Time of Beginnings" when she wrote "Like the waves of the sea, no two pieces of pottery art can be identical"? [The sentence, not the quotation, is a question.]
I'm angry that Mom said, "You are not allowed to stay out past 10 P.M. on Friday night"! [The sentence, not the quotation, is an exclamation.]

When both the sentence and the quotation at the end of the sentence are questions (or exclamations), only one question mark (or exclamation point) is used. It is placed inside the closing quotation marks.

EXAMPLE Did Elizabeth Barrett Browning write the poem that begins with "How do I love thee?"

14i. When you write dialogue (conversation), begin a new paragraph each time you change speakers.

EXAMPLE "No," I answered, "I do not fish for carp. It is bad luck."
"Do you know why?" he asked and raised an eyebrow.

> "No," I said and held my breath. I felt I sat on the banks of an undiscovered river whose churning, muddied waters carried many secrets.
>
> "I will tell you a story," Samuel said after a long silence, "a story that was told to my father . . ."
>
> Rudolfo A. Anaya, *Bless Me, Ultima*

14j. When a quotation consists of several sentences, place quotation marks at the beginning and at the end of the whole quotation.

EXAMPLE   **"**Memorize all your lines for Monday. Have someone at home give you your cues. Enjoy your weekend!**"** said Ms. Goodwin.

 QUICK CHECK 2   **Correcting Paragraphs by Adding Punctuation**

Revise the following paragraphs by adding commas, end marks, and quotation marks where necessary.

[1] Gordon, do you ever think about pencils Annie asked

[2] I'm always wondering where I lost mine Gordon replied

[3] Well said Annie let me tell you some of the things I learned about pencils

[4] Sure Gordon said I love trivia

[5] People have used some form of pencils for a long time Annie began [6] The ancient Greeks and Romans used lead pencils [7] However, pencils as we know them weren't developed until the 1500's, when people started using graphite

[8] What's graphite asked Gordon

[9] Graphite is a soft form of carbon Annie explained that leaves a mark when it's drawn over most surfaces

[10] Thanks for the information, Annie Gordon said Now, do you have a pencil I can borrow?

14k. Use single quotation marks to enclose a quotation within a quotation.

EXAMPLES   "Excuse me, but did you just say, 'Hearts are wild'?"

"I said, 'Wednesday's quiz will cover Chapter 3 of Unit 2 and your special reports,'" repeated Mr. Allyn.

"What Christina Rossetti poem begins with the line 'My heart is like a singing bird'?" Carol asked.

14l. Use quotation marks to enclose titles of short works such as short stories, poems, articles, songs, episodes of television programs, and chapters and other parts of books.

TYPE OF TITLE	EXAMPLES
Short Stories	"Raymond's Run" "The Rule of Names" "The Tell-Tale Heart"
Poems	"Mother to Son" "The Road Not Taken" "Calling in the Cat"
Articles	"Free Speech and Free Air" "How to Sharpen Your Wit" "Marriage in the '90s"
Songs	"La Bamba" "Amazing Grace" "The Streets of Laredo"
Episodes of Television Programs	"Heart of a Champion" "The Trouble with Tribbles" "An Englishman Abroad"
Chapters and Other Parts of Books	"Learning About Reptiles" "English: Origins and Uses" "Creating a Federal Union"

MECHANICS

REFERENCE NOTE: For examples of titles that are italicized, see pages 282–283.

 *QUICK CHECK 3* **Correcting Sentences by Adding Quotation Marks**

Revise the following sentences by supplying quotation marks as needed.

1. Has anyone read the story To Build a Fire? asked the teacher.
2. I have, said Eileen. It's a terrific story, and it was written by Jack London.
3. Do you know the poem To Make a Prairie?
4. Our chorus will sing When You Wish upon a Star at the recital.
5. In the chapter of our social studies book called Workers' Rights, the author discusses Cesar Chavez's efforts to help migrant workers.

"WOULD YOU STOP PUTTING QUOTES AROUND EVERYTHING I SAY!"

© Leo Cullum 1993.

✓ *Chapter Review*

Proofreading Sentences for the Correct Use of Quotation Marks and Underlining (Italics)

Each of the following sentences requires underlining (italics), quotation marks, or both. Write each sentence correctly.

EXAMPLE   1. Ted, can you answer the first question? Ms. Simmons asked.

1. *"Ted, can you answer the first question?" Ms. Simmons asked.*

1. The best chapter in our vocabulary book is the last one, More Word Games.
2. "I answered all the questions, Todd said, but I think that some of my answers are wrong."
3. Star Wars was more exciting on the big movie screen than it was on our small television set.
4. Mr. Washington asked Connie, "Which flag also included the slogan Don't Tread on Me?"
5. There is a legend that the band on the Titanic played the hymn Nearer My God to Thee as the ship sank into the icy sea.
6. Play the Freddie Jackson tape again, Sam, Rebecca called from her room.
7. Wendy wrote an article called Students, Where Are You? for our local newspaper, the Morning Beacon.
8. In the short story Thank You, M'am, by Langston Hughes, a woman helps a troubled boy.
9. "Can I read Treasure Island for my book report? Carmine asked.
10. Every Christmas Eve my uncle recites 'Twas the Night Before Christmas for the children in the hospital.
11. The first battle between ironclad ships took place between the Monitor and the Merrimack in 1862.
12. Run! Run! cried the boys. A tornado is headed this way!

MECHANICS

13. We sang Greensleeves for the assembly.
14. Have you read the adventure novel The Call of the Wild?
15. Mom, will you take us to soccer practice? asked Libby.
16. I've read, Connie said, that Thomas Jefferson loved Italian food and ordered pasta from Italy.
17. What can have happened to Francine this time? Didn't she say, I'll be home long before you're ready to leave? Justin asked.
18. Jerry Spinelli won the Newbery Medal for his book Maniac Magee, which is about an unusual athlete.
19. Did you read the article about runner Jackie Joyner-Kersee in USA Weekend? Lynn asked.
20. Won't you stay? pleaded Wynnie. There will be music and refreshments later.

15 PUNCTUATION

Apostrophes, Hyphens, Parentheses, and Dashes

 Checking What You Know

Proofreading Sentences for the Correct Use of Apostrophes, Hyphens, Parentheses, and Dashes

Each of the following sentences contains at least one mistake in the use of apostrophes, hyphens, parentheses, or dashes. Write each sentence correctly.

EXAMPLE
    1. Alices mother said shes read that tomatoes are native to Peru.
    1. *Alice's mother said she's read that tomatoes are native to Peru.*

1. Marsha is this years captain of the girls basketball team.
2. Susan B. Anthony 1820–1906 worked to get women the right to vote in the United States.
3. Id never heard of a Greek bagpipe before, but Mr. Karras played one during the folk festival.

4. We couldnt have done the job without you're help.
5. Hes strict about being on time.
6. On my older brothers next birthday, he will turn twenty one years old.
7. Wed have forgotten to turn off the computer if Maggie hadnt reminded us.
8. The recipe said to add two eggs, a teaspoon of salt, and one quarter cup of milk.
9. My mothers office is on the twenty second floor of the Rialto Building.
10. Our dog he's a giant schnauzer is gentle and very well behaved.
11. Last weeks travel story was about Mindanao, the second-largest island of the Philippines.
12. Isnt the preface to that edition of *Frankenstein* twenty four pages long?
13. The house cat Latin name: *Felis cattus* is one of the most popular pets.
14. They cant come with us; theyre studying.
15. From Fifty third Street down to Forty fifth Street, there are ninety seven businesses.
16. Paul Revere he imported hardware made beautiful jewelry and utensils.
17. That trucks taillights are broken.
18. Shelly said that shes always wanted to read Maya Angelou's book *I Know Why the Caged Bird Sings.*
19. Your capital *I*s and *J*s are hard to tell apart.
20. At the family reunion I sat beside my great-grandfather Wylie Clyde.

✓

Apostrophes

An *apostrophe* is used to form the possessive case of nouns and some pronouns, to indicate in a contraction where letters have been left out, and to form some plurals.

Possessive Case

The *possessive case* of a noun or a pronoun shows ownership or relationship.

OWNERSHIP	RELATIONSHIP
Sandra's boat	an **hour's** time
Mother's job	**Julio's** father
your book	**everyone's** choice

15a. To form the possessive case of a singular noun, add an apostrophe and an *s*.

EXAMPLES   a dog's collar
a moment's notice
one dollar's worth
Charles's typewriter

NOTE A proper name ending in *s* may take only an apostrophe to form the possessive case if adding *'s* would make the name hard to pronounce.

EXAMPLES   Marjorie Kinnan Rawlings' novels
Hercules' feats
Buenos Aires' population

15b. To form the possessive case of a plural noun ending in *s*, add only the apostrophe.

EXAMPLES   students' records   doctors' opinions
citizens' committee   hostesses' invitations

15c. To form the possessive case of a plural noun that does not end in *s*, add an apostrophe and an *s*.

EXAMPLES   women's suits   geese's noise
mice's tracks   children's voices

NOTE Do not use an apostrophe to form the *plural* of a noun.

INCORRECT The passenger's showed their tickets to the flight attendant.

CORRECT The **passengers** showed their tickets to the
flight attendant. [plural]

CORRECT The flight attendant checked the **passengers'**
tickets. [plural possessive]

15d. Do not use an apostrophe with possessive personal pronouns.

EXAMPLES These keys are **yours,** not **mine.**
Are these tapes **ours** or **theirs**?
His pantomime was good, but **hers** was better.
My bicycle is older than **hers.**

NOTE The possessive case form of *it* is *its*. The expression *it's* is a contraction of the words *it is* or *it has*.

 REFERENCE NOTE: For more about the difference between
its and *it's,* see page 21.

15e. To form the possessive case of some indefinite pronouns, add an apostrophe and an *s*.

EXAMPLES everyone**'s** opinion
no one**'s** fault
somebody**'s** umbrella

 REFERENCE NOTE: For more about possessive personal pronouns, see pages 116–117. For information about indefinite pronouns used as adjectives, see page 53.

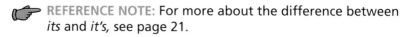 QUICK CHECK 1 **Forming Possessives**

Give the correct possessive form for each of the following expressions. If an expression is correct, write *C*.

EXAMPLE **1.** a day work
1. *a day's work*

1. everybody favorite
2. women careers
3. friend comments
4. three days homework
5. it muffler

6. the Joneses cabin
7. men shoes
8. one of theirs
9. cities mayors
10. oxen yokes

Contractions

15f. To form a contraction, use an apostrophe to show where letters have been left out.

A *contraction* is a shortened form of a word, a figure, or a group of words. The apostrophe in a contraction indicates where letters or numerals have been left out.

Common Contractions	
I am . . . . I'm	they had . . . . they'd
1995 . . . . '95	where is . . . . . . where's
let us . . . . let's	we are . . . . we're
of the clock . . . . o'clock	he is . . . . he's
she would . . . . . . she'd	you will . . . . you'll

The word *not* can be shortened to *n't* and added to a verb, usually without changing the spelling of the verb.

EXAMPLES
is not . . . . isn't	has not . . . . hasn't
are not . . . . . . aren't	have not . . . . . haven't
does not . . . . doesn't	had not . . . . . . hadn't
do not . . . . don't	should not . . shouldn't
was not . . . . . wasn't	would not . . wouldn't
were not . . . weren't	could not . . . couldn't

EXCEPTIONS will not . . . . . . won't   cannot . . . . can't

Do not confuse contractions with possessive pronouns.

CONTRACTIONS	POSSESSIVE PRONOUNS
It's snowing. [*It is*] **It's** been a long time. [*It has*]	**Its** front tire is flat.
Who's next in line? [*Who is*] **Who's** been helping you? [*Who has*]	**Whose** idea was it?
There's only one answer. [*There is*] **There's** been a change in plans. [*There has*]	This trophy is **theirs**.
They're not here. [*They are*] **You're** a good friend. [*You are*]	**Their** dog is barking. **Your** writing has improved.

MECHANICS

Plurals

 15g. Use an apostrophe and an *s* to form the plurals of letters, numerals, and signs, and of words referred to as words.

EXAMPLES The word has two *d*'s, not one.
Your *2*'s look like *5*'s.
Jazz became quite popular in the 1920's.
Don't use *&*'s in place of *and*'s.

NOTE In your reading, you may notice that an apostrophe is not always used in forming these four kinds of plurals. Nowadays, many writers leave out the apostrophe if the plural meaning is clear without it. However, to make sure that your writing is clear, always use an apostrophe.

© 1993 by Sidney Harris.

 QUICK CHECK 2 **Correcting Sentences by Adding Apostrophes**

Write the correct form of each item that requires an apostrophe in the following sentences.

1. Dorothy usually gets all As and Bs on her report card.
2. It isnt correct to use &s in your compositions.
3. Many of the scores on the test were in the 80s and 90s.

4. If its all right to tell them where were going, theyll meet us later.
5. Whos signed up for the talent show?

Hyphens

15h. Use a hyphen to divide a word at the end of a line.

EXAMPLES   How long had the new bridge been under construction before it was opened?
You can probably find the answer in the alma-
nac in the library.

When dividing a word at the end of a line, remember the following rules:

(1) Divide a word only between syllables.

INCORRECT   Lisa wrote her science report on the tyra-
nnosaurs, the largest meat-eating dinosaurs.
CORRECT   Lisa wrote her science report on the tyran-
nosaurs, the largest meat-eating dinosaurs.

☞ REFERENCE NOTE: If you are not sure how to divide a word into syllables, check in a dictionary.

(2) Do not divide a one-syllable word.

INCORRECT   The fans stood and sang while the band played the school song.
CORRECT   The fans stood and sang while the band played
the school song.

(3) Divide an already hyphenated word only at a hyphen.

INCORRECT   I went to the fair with my sister and my broth-
er-in-law.
CORRECT   I went to the fair with my sister and my brother-
in-law.

MECHANICS

(4) Do not divide a word so that one letter stands alone.

INCORRECT   On their way to Chicago last week, they stayed o-
vernight in Cincinnati.

CORRECT   On their way to Chicago last week, they stayed
overnight in Cincinnati.

COMPUTER NOTE   Some word-processing programs will automatically break a word at the end of a line and insert a hyphen. Sometimes, such a break will break one of the rules given above. Always check a printout of your writing to see how the computer has hyphenated words at the ends of lines. If a hyphen is used incorrectly, revise the line by moving the word or by rebreaking the word and inserting a "hard" hyphen (one that the computer cannot move).

15i. Use a hyphen with compound numbers from *twenty-one* to *ninety-nine* and with fractions used as adjectives.

EXAMPLES   **thirty-five** students
one-half cup of milk
forty-eighth state

When a fraction is a noun, do not use a hyphen.

EXAMPLE   **two thirds** of the earth's surface

STYLE NOTE   Hyphens are often used in compound names. In such cases, the hyphen is thought of as part of the name's spelling.

PEOPLE   Daniel Day-Lewis   Rolando Hinojosa-Smith
Abdul-Hamid II   Jackie Joyner-Kersee

PLACES   Hesse-Darmstadt   Stratford-upon-Avon
                          [region]   [borough]
                          Put-in-Bay [inlet]   Schleswig-Holstein [state]
                          Wilkes-Barre [city]   Kut-al-Imara [city]

If you are not sure whether a compound name is hyphenated, ask the person, or look in a reference source.

 QUICK CHECK 3   **Hyphenating Numbers and Fractions**

Write the following expressions, inserting hyphens as needed. If an expression is correct, write *C*.

1. a two thirds majority
2. one half of the coconut
3. one hundred thirty five pages
4. Forty second Street
5. twenty two Amish quilts

Parentheses

15j. Use parentheses to enclose material that is added to a sentence but is not considered of major importance.

EXAMPLES   Mohandas K. Gandhi **(1869–1948)** led India's struggle for independence from British rule.
               Ms. Matsuo served us the sushi **(so͞o′shē)** that she had prepared.

Material placed in parentheses may range from a single word or number to a short sentence. A short sentence in parentheses may stand by itself or be contained within another sentence.

EXAMPLES   Fill in the order form carefully. **(Do not use a pencil.)**

MECHANICS

> My great-uncle Chester **(he's Grandma's brother)** will stay with us during the holidays.

STYLE NOTE   Too many parenthetical expressions in a piece of writing can keep readers from seeing the main idea. Keep your meaning clear by limiting the number of parenthetical expressions you use.

 *QUICK CHECK 4*   **Writing Sentences with Parentheses**

For each of the following sentences, insert parentheses where they are needed. Be sure not to enclose any words or marks of punctuation that do not belong inside the parentheses.

1. The old fort it was used during the Civil War has been rebuilt and is open to the public.
2. Yellowstone National Park established in 1872 covers territory in Wyoming, Idaho, and Montana.
3. The writer Langston Hughes 1902–1967 is best known for his poetry.
4. Alligators use their feet and tails to dig water holes also called "gator holes" in marshy fields.
5. On the Sabbath we eat braided bread called challah pronounced "khä´ lə."

Dashes

Many words and phrases are used *parenthetically;* that is, they break into the main thought of a sentence. Most parenthetical elements are set off by commas or parentheses.

EXAMPLES   The tomato, **however,** is actually a fruit, not a vegetable.

The outcome **(which candidate would be elected governor?)** was in the hands of the voters.

 REFERENCE NOTE: For more information on using commas with parenthetical expressions, see page 267–268. For more information on using parentheses, see pages 301–302.

Sometimes parenthetical elements demand a stronger emphasis. In such cases, a dash is used.

15k. Use a dash to indicate an abrupt break in thought or speech.

EXAMPLES Ms. Alonzo—she just left—will be one of the judges of the talent show.
"Right over here—oh, excuse me, Mr. Mills—you'll find the reference books," said the librarian.
The murderer is—but I don't want to give away the ending.

 QUICK CHECK 5 **Writing Sentences with Dashes**

For each of the following sentences, insert dashes where they are needed.

1. A beautiful grand piano it was once played by Chopin was on display in the museum.
2. "I'd like the red no, give me the blue cycling shorts," said Josh.
3. Frederic Remington he was an artist, historian, and lover of the western frontier painted the West as it really was.
4. In 1993, Ruth Bader Ginsburg she's the second woman associate justice was nominated to the U.S. Supreme Court.
5. Cheryl wondered aloud, "Where oh, my poor Muffy could that hamster be?"

MECHANICS

✓ Chapter Review

Proofreading Sentences for the Correct Use of Apostrophes, Hyphens, Parentheses, and Dashes

Each of the following sentences contains at least one mistake in the use of apostrophes, hyphens, parentheses, or dashes. Write each sentence correctly.

EXAMPLE   **1.** The judges were impressed with Antonios project.

       1. *The judges were impressed with Antonio's project.*

1. One third of Hollys allowance goes into the bank.
2. The boys didnt say when theyd be back.
3. Twenty six student council members (more than a two thirds majority voted to change the school song.
4. Emily Brontë 1818–1848 is probably best known for her novel *Wuthering Heights.*
5. If your going to the football game, remember to take a-long a stadium blanket.
6. Dont those 2s look like zs to you?
7. Jeromes dream is to have a palomino.
8. Mr. Zapata dont—I mean, doesn't want us to climb in his fruit trees.
9. Lets find out when the next game is.
10. Victor Hugo 1802–1885 wrote articles, poems, plays, and novels.
11. Boater's on the Missouri River may not know that *Missouri* means "people of the big canoes."
12. Have you heard Kentuckys state song by Stephen Foster?
13. The committee voted to help keep the walkway clear of ice during the winter.
14. I cant remember I wonder how many people have this same problem how many rs are in the word *embarrass.*

15. Everybodys favorite tour stops in Virginia were Mount Vernon, George Washingtons home, and Monticello, Thomas Jefferson's home.
16. Don't you remember they're story about catching twenty two fireflies?
17. Three-fourths of the class couldnt pronounce the name *Monongahela* until we broke it into syllables *Mo-non-ga-he-la*.
18. His painting of the sunset was good, but her's was better.
19. Ricardos guidebook the one he ordered last month states that the Everglades is Floridas most precious resource.
20. Shes lived in Massachusetts for thirty one years but has never been to Cape Cod.

16 SPELLING AND VOCABULARY

Improving Your Spelling and Vocabulary; Choosing the Appropriate Word

Improving Your Spelling

As your vocabulary grows, you may have difficulty spelling some of the new words. You can improve your spelling by using the following methods.

1. **Pronounce words correctly.** Pronouncing words carefully can often help you to spell them correctly.

   EXAMPLES athlete: ath•lete [not ath•e•lete]
   probably: prob•a•bly [not pro•bly]
   library: li•brar•y [not li•ba•ry]

2. **Spell by syllables.** When you have trouble spelling long words, divide them into syllables. A *syllable* is a word part that can be pronounced by itself. Learning to spell the syllables of a word one at a time will help you master the spelling of the whole word.

MECHANICS

EXAMPLES gymnasium: gym•na•si•um [four syllables]
          representative: rep•re•sent•a•tive
          [five syllables]

3. **Use a dictionary.** When you are not sure about the
   spelling of a word, look in a dictionary. A dictionary
   will also tell you the correct pronunciations and syllable
   divisions of words.

STYLE NOTE   In some names, marks that show how to say a
                 word are as important as the letters are.

PEOPLE   Alemán   Böll
           Ibáñez   Khayyám
           Janácek   Eugène
PLACES   Açores   Bogotá
           Camagüey   Gîza
           Köln   Sainte-Thérèse

If you're not sure about the spelling of a name, ask the
name's owner or check in a dictionary.

4. **Keep a spelling notebook.** The best way to master
   words that give you difficulty is to list the words and
   review them frequently. Divide each page of a notebook
   into four columns.

   COLUMN 1 Write correctly the words you frequently mis-
             spell.
   COLUMN 2 Write the words again, dividing them into syl-
             lables and marking the accents. (If you are
             not sure how to do this, look in a dictionary
             for examples.)
   COLUMN 3 Write the words again, circling the parts that
             give you trouble.
   COLUMN 4 Jot down any comments that may help you
             remember the correct spelling.

MECHANICS

EXAMPLE

Correct Spelling	Syllable and Accents	Trouble Spots	Comments
escape	es•cape′	e(sc)ape	Pronounce correctly.
calendar	cal′•en•dar	calend(a)r	Think of <u>days</u> marked on the cal<u>e</u>ndar.
casually	cas′•u•al•ly	casua(lly)	Study rule 16e.

5. **Proofread for careless spelling errors.** Whenever you write, proofread your paper for errors in spelling. By slowly rereading what you have written, you can correct careless errors such as uncrossed *t*'s, undotted *i*'s, and crossed *l*'s.

B.C. by Johnny Hart. By permission of Johnny Hart and Creators Syndicate.

COMPUTER NOTE A computer can help you catch spelling mistakes. Use the computer's spelling checker whenever you proofread your writing. Remember, though, that a computer's spelling checker only points out misspellings. For example, if you use *their* when you should use *there*, a spelling checker won't catch the mistake.

Using Word Parts

A *base word* can stand alone. It is a complete word by it-self, although other word parts can be added to it to make new words. Many English words are made up of several word parts: roots, prefixes, and suffixes.

Roots

The *root* of a word is the part that carries the word's main meaning. However, a word root can't stand alone. It is al-ways combined with one or more word parts. Sometimes a root has more than one form.

COMMONLY USED ROOTS		
WORD ROOT	**MEANING**	**EXAMPLES**
-bio-	life	antibiotic, biology
-dem-	people	democrat, democracy
-dict-	speak	dictation, dictionary
-duc-, -duct-	lead	educate, conductor
-gen-	birth, kind, origin	genuine, genetic
-graph-	write, writing	autograph, biography
-ject-	throw	eject, reject
-liber-	free	liberty, liberate
-mal-	bad	malady, malice
-mit-, -miss-	send	omit, mission
-ped-	foot	pedal, pedestrian
-pend-	hang, weigh	suspend, dependent
-port-	carry	portable, transport
-spec-	look	spectator, spectacles
-struct-	build	construct, destruction
-vid-, -vis-	see	videotape, invisible
-voc-	call	vocal, vocation

Prefixes

A *prefix* is one or more than one letter or syllable added to the beginning of a root or base word to make a new word with a different meaning.

MECHANICS

COMMONLY USED PREFIXES		
PREFIX	**MEANING**	**EXAMPLES**
anti-	against	antiwar, anticlimax
bi-	two	bimonthly, bilingual
co-	with, together	coexist, codependent
de-	away, from, off, down	debone, debug
dis-	away, from, opposing	disarm, disconnect
extra-	beyond, outside	extralegal, extraordinary
fore-	before, front part of	forehead, foreshadow
hyper-	over, extremely	hypercritical, hypersensitive
in-	not	inappropriate, ineffective
inter-	between, among	interpersonal, interact
mis-	badly, not, wrongly	misbehave, misfortune
non-	not	nonprofit, nonsense
over-	above, extremely	overstate, overhead
post-	after, following	postwar, postgraduate
pre-	before	prepayment, preexist
re-	back, again	rebuild, reclaim
semi-	half, partly	semiannual, semiprecious
sub-	under, beneath	submarine, substandard
trans-	across, beyond	transplant, transpacific
un-	not, opposite of	unlock, uneven

Suffixes

A *suffix* is one or more than one letter or syllable added to the end of a root or base word to make a new word with a different meaning.

COMMONLY USED SUFFIXES		
SUFFIX	**MEANING**	**EXAMPLES**
-able	able, likely	readable, lovable
-ance, -ancy	act, quality	admittance, constancy
-ate	become, cause	captivate, activate
-dom	state, condition	kingdom, freedom
-en	make, become	darken, weaken
-ence	act, condition	conference, excellence
-esque	in the style of, like	picturesque, statuesque
-ful	full of, characteristic of	joyful, truthful
-fy	make, cause	identify, simplify

(continued)

COMMONLY USED SUFFIXES *(continued)*		
SUFFIX	**MEANING**	**EXAMPLES**
-hood	condition, quality	childhood, sisterhood
-ible	able, likely	flexible, digestible
-ity	state, condition	reality, sincerity
-ize	make, cause to be	socialize, motorize
-less	without	penniless, hopeless
-ly	characteristic of	urgently, rigidly
-ment	result, action	judgment, fulfillment
-ness	quality, state	peacefulness, sadness
-or	one who	actor, editor
-ous	characterized by	dangerous, furious
-ship	condition, state	friendship, hardship
-tion	action, condition	rotation, selection
-ty	quality, state	safety, certainty
-y	condition, quality	dirty, jealousy

 REFERENCE NOTE: For guidelines on spelling when adding prefixes and suffixes, see pages 313–315.

Spelling Rules

ie and *ei*

16a. Except after *c,* write *ie* when the sound is long *e.*

EXAMPLES achieve   believe   chief   field   piece
               ceiling   conceit   deceit   deceive   receive

EXCEPTIONS either   leisure   neither
                protein seize   weird

16b. Write *ei* when the sound is not long *e,* especially when the sound is long *a.*

EXAMPLES foreign   forfeit   height heir their
               freight   neighbor reign veil weigh

EXCEPTIONS ancient conscience fierce
                friend   mischief siege

MECHANICS

This time-tested poem may help you remember the *ie* rule.
> I before *e*
> Except after *c*
> Or when sounded like *a*,
> As in *neighbor* and *weigh*.

 NOTE The poem above and rules 16a and 16b apply only when the *i* and the *e* are in the same syllable.

 QUICK CHECK 1   **Writing Words with ie and ei**

Add the letters *ie* or *ei* to spell each of the following words correctly.

1. conc . . . ted
2. . . . ght
3. p . . . ce
4. shr . . . k
5. fr . . . ght
6. n . . . ther
7. fr . . . nd
8. misch . . . f
9. r . . . gn
10. sh . . . k

-cede, -ceed, and -sede

16c. The only word ending in *-sede* is *supersede*. The only words ending in *-ceed* are *exceed*, *proceed*, and *succeed*. All other words with this sound end in *-cede*.

EXAMPLES   con**cede**   inter**cede**   pre**cede**   re**cede**   se**cede**

 QUICK CHECK 2   **Proofreading Misspelled Words Ending in -cede, -ceed, and -sede**

The following sentences contain five misspelled words ending in *-cede*, *-ceed*, and *-sede*. Identify the errors and spell the words correctly.

1. Clarence Leo Fender succeded in changing the music business in the 1950's.
2. He improved the design of electric guitars, which quickly superceded acoustic guitars in popular music.

3. The success of Fender's invention probably exceded his wildest dreams.

4. Music critics consede that a new era began with the invention of the electric guitar.

5. Concerts that preceeded Fender's invention were not nearly as loud as modern ones.

Adding Prefixes

16d. When adding a prefix to a word, do not change the spelling of the word itself.

EXAMPLES   mis + spell = **mis**spell   il + logical = **il**logical
            over + see = **over**see   in + exact = **in**exact

 QUICK CHECK 3   **Spelling Words with Prefixes**

Spell each of the following words, adding the prefix given.

1. im + migrate   **3.** un + certain   **5.** semi + circle
2. re + settle   **4.** il + legal

Adding Suffixes

16e. When adding the suffix *-ly* or *-ness* to a word, do not change the spelling of the word itself.

EXAMPLES   slow + ly = slow**ly**   dark + ness = dark**ness**
           usual + ly = usual**ly**   eager + ness = eager**ness**
           shy + ly = shy**ly**   shy + ness = shy**ness**

EXCEPTIONS For words ending in *y* and having two or more syllables, change the *y* to *i* before adding *-ly* or *-ness*.

           happy + ly = happ**ily**   lazy + ness = laz**iness**

16f. Drop the final silent *e* before a suffix beginning with a vowel.

EXAMPLES   approve + al = approv**al**   line + ing = lin**ing**
            desire + able = desir**able**   tape + ed = tap**ed**

MECHANICS

EXCEPTIONS **Keep the final silent e**

- in a word ending in *ce* or *ge* before a suffix beginning with *a* or *o:*

  notice + *able* = *noticeable*
  courage + *ous* = *courageous*

- in *dye* before *-ing*: *dyeing*
- in *singe* before *-ing*: *singeing*
- in *mile* before *-age*: *mileage*

 When adding *-ing* to words that end in *ie,* drop the *e* and change the *i* to *y.*

EXAMPLES lie + ing = lying   die + ing = dying

16g. Keep the final silent e before a suffix beginning with a consonant.

EXAMPLES hope + less = hope**less**
care + ful = care**ful**
awe + some = aw**esome**
love + ly = lov**ely**
nine + ty = nin**ety**
amuse + ment = amus**ement**
false + hood = fals**ehood**
same + ness = sam**eness**

EXCEPTIONS nine + th = nin**th**
argue + ment = argu**ment**
true + ly = tru**ly**
judge + ment = judg**ment**
whole + ly = whol**ly**
awe + ful = aw**ful**

16h. For words ending in y preceded by a consonant, change the y to i before any suffix that does not begin with i.

EXAMPLES try + ed = tr**ied**   cry + ing = cry**ing**
easy + ly = eas**ily**   baby + ish = bab**yish**
duty + ful = dut**iful**

16i. For words ending in *y* preceded by a vowel, keep the *y* when adding a suffix.

EXAMPLES pray + ing = pray**ing**   pay + ment = pay**ment**
obey + ed = obey**ed**   boy + hood = boy**hood**
buoy + ing = buoy**ing** play + ful = play**ful**

EXCEPTIONS day + ly = da**ily**   lay + ed = la**id**
say + ed = sa**id**   pay + ed = pa**id**

16j. Double the final consonant before a suffix beginning with a vowel if the word

(1) has only one syllable or has the accent on the last syllable

and

(2) ends in a single consonant preceded by a single vowel.

EXAMPLES sit + ing = si**tt**ing   occur + ed = occu**rr**ed
swim + er = swi**mm**er begin + er = begi**nn**er
drop + ed = dro**pp**ed forbid + en = forbi**dd**en

EXCEPTIONS Do not double the final consonant in words ending in *w* or *x.*

mow + ing = mo**w**ing wax + ed = wa**x**ed
saw + ed = sa**w**ed   ox + en = o**x**en

    Otherwise, the final consonant is usually not doubled before a suffix beginning with a vowel.

EXAMPLES sing + er = singer   final + ist = finalist
speak + ing = speaking center + ed = centered

NOTE In some cases, the final consonant may or may not be doubled.

EXAMPLES cancel + ed = canceled *or* cancelled
travel + er = traveler *or* traveller

Most dictionaries list both of these spellings as correct. When you are not sure about the spelling of a word, it is best to check in a dictionary.

QUICK CHECK 4 **Spelling Words with Suffixes**

Spell each of the following words, adding the suffix given.

1. dry + ness   **6.** lucky + ly
2. jog + er   **7.** display + ed
3. carry + ed   **8.** trace + able
4. advantage + ous   **9.** refer + al
5. trim + ing   **10.** natural + ly

Forming the Plurals of Nouns

16k. For most nouns, add *-s.*

SINGULAR	desk	idea	shoe
	friend	camera	Wilson
PLURAL	desk**s**	idea**s**	shoe**s**
	friend**s**	camera**s**	Wilson**s**

16l. For nouns ending in *s, x, z, ch,* or *sh,* add *-es.*

| SINGULAR | gas | fox | waltz | inch | dish | Suarez |
| PLURAL | gas**es** | fox**es** | waltz**es** | inch**es** | dish**es** | Suarez**es** |

16m. For nouns ending in *y* preceded by a vowel, add *-s.*

| SINGULAR | decoy | highway | alley | Riley |
| PLURAL | decoy**s** | highway**s** | alley**s** | Riley**s** |

16n. For nouns ending in *y* preceded by a consonant, change the *y* to *i* and add *-es.*

SINGULAR	army	country	city
	pony	ally	daisy
PLURAL	arm**ies**	countr**ies**	cit**ies**
	pon**ies**	all**ies**	dais**ies**

EXCEPTIONS For proper nouns ending in *y,* just add *-s.*
       Brady—Bradys   Murphy—Murphys

16o. For some nouns ending in *f* or *fe,* add *-s.* For others, change the *f* or *fe* to *v* and add *-es.*

SINGULAR	belief	thief	sheriff	knife	giraffe
PLURAL	belie**fs**	thie**ves**	sheriff**s**	kni**ves**	giraffe**s**

NOTE When you are not sure about how to spell the plural of a noun ending in *f* or *fe*, look in a dictionary.

16p. For nouns ending in *o* preceded by a vowel, add -*s*.

SINGULAR	radio	patio	stereo	igloo	Matteo
PLURAL	radio**s**	patio**s**	stereo**s**	igloo**s**	Matteo**s**

Born Loser reprinted by permission of NEA, Inc.

16q. For nouns ending in *o* preceded by a consonant, add -*es*.

SINGULAR	tomato	potato	echo	hero
PLURAL	tomato**es**	potato**es**	echo**es**	hero**es**

EXCEPTION For musical terms and proper nouns, add -*s*.

alto—alto**s**   soprano—soprano**s**
Eskimo—Eskimo**s**   Nakamoto—Nakamoto**s**

NOTE To form the plurals of some nouns ending in *o* preceded by a consonant, you may add either -*s* or -*es*.

SINGULAR	domino	mosquito	banjo	flamingo
PLURAL	domino**s**	mosquito**s**	banjo**s**	flamingo**s**
	or	*or*	*or*	*or*
	domino**es**	mosquito**es**	banjo**es**	flamingo**es**

When you are in doubt about the way to form the plural of a noun ending in *o* preceded by a consonant, check the spelling in a dictionary.

MECHANICS

16r. The plurals of a few nouns are formed in irregular ways.

SINGULAR	ox	goose	foot	tooth	woman	mouse
PLURAL	oxen	geese	feet	teeth	women	mice

16s. For most compound nouns, form the plural of the last word in the compound.

SINGULAR	bookshelf	push-up	sea gull	ten-year-old
PLURAL	bookshelves	push-ups	sea gulls	ten-year-olds

16t. For compound nouns in which one of the words is modified by the other word or words, form the plural of the word modified.

SINGULAR	brother-in-law	maid of honor	eighth-grader
PLURAL	brothers-in-law	maids of honor	eighth-graders

☞ REFERENCE NOTE: For more about compound nouns, see page 47.

16u. For some nouns the singular and the plural forms are the same.

SINGULAR AND PLURAL	trout	sheep	Sioux
	deer	moose	Swiss

16v. For numbers, letters, symbols, and words used as words, add an apostrophe and -*s*.

EXAMPLES   The product of two **4's** is twice the sum of four **2's.**
The **1940's** and the **1950's** were decades of great change and growth in the United States.
Notice that the word *committee* has two **m's,** two **t's,** and two **e's.**
Write **$'s** before, not after, amounts of money.
This composition contains too many **so's** and **and's.**

STYLE NOTE In your reading you may notice that some writers do not use apostrophes to form the plurals of numbers, capital letters, symbols, and words used as words.

EXAMPLES   Their music is as popular today as it was in the **1970s.**

When dividing, remember to write **R s** before the remainders in the quotients.

However, using an apostrophe is never wrong. Therefore, it is best always to use the apostrophe.

 QUICK CHECK 5 **Spelling Plurals**

Spell the plural form of each of the following items. [Note: An item may have more than one correct plural form. You need to give only one.]

1. cargo
2. diary
3. Gómez
4. sit-up
5. child

6. car pool
7. hoof
8. Japanese
9. *M*
10. 1900

Spelling Numbers

16w. Spell out a number that begins a sentence.

EXAMPLE   **Fifteen thousand** people went to see the Milton Nascimento concert.

16x. Within a sentence, spell out numbers that can be written in one or two words. Use numerals for other numbers.

EXAMPLES   Do you have **two** nickels for **one** dime?

In all, **fifty-two** people attended the family reunion.

More than **160** people were invited.

MECHANICS

NOTE If you use several numbers, some short and some long, write them all the same way. Usually, it is better to write them all as numerals.

INCORRECT We sold eighty-six tickets to the first dance and 121 tickets to the second dance.

CORRECT We sold **86** tickets to the first dance and **121** tickets to the second dance.

16y. Spell out numbers used to indicate order.

EXAMPLE Our team came in **third** [*not* 3rd] in the regional track meet.

Improving Your Vocabulary

To develop a large vocabulary, you should try to recognize clues to the meanings of unfamiliar words. Learning the meanings of word parts like those on pages 309–311 is also helpful in building your vocabulary. By practicing the following methods, you can increase your knowledge of words and expand your vocabulary.

Developing a Word Bank

An effective way to increase your vocabulary is by starting a word bank. When you encounter an unfamiliar word, enter the word and its definition in a section of your notebook. You might also write a sentence or phrase to illustrate how each word is used. Always check the definition and pronunciation of an unfamiliar word by looking in a dictionary.

Learning New Words from Context

A word's *context* means all of the words around the word and the way in which the word is used. The phrases and sentences around a word often give clues to the word's meaning. The following chart gives examples of the most common types of context clues.

USING CONTEXT CLUES	
TYPE OF CLUE	**EXPLANATION**
Definitions and restatements	Look for words that define the term or restate it in other words. ■ Toshio's ambition is to *circumnavigate*—or sail around—the world.
Examples	Look for examples used in context that reveal the meaning of an unfamiliar word. ■ People use all sorts of *conveyances* such as cars, bicycles, rickshaws, airplanes, boats, and helicopters.
Synonyms	Look for clues showing that an unfamiliar word is the same as or similar to a familiar word or phrase. ■ George seemed *haughty*, but his pride was only a front.
Contrast	Look for clues showing that an unfamiliar word is opposite in meaning to a familiar word or phrase. ■ Donita has become quite *stodgy*, unlike Irene, who has always been easygoing.
Cause and effect	Look for clues showing that an unfamiliar word is related to the cause or the result of an action, feeling, or idea. ■ Because the clouds looked *foreboding*, we decided to cancel the picnic.

Born Loser reprinted by permission of NEA, Inc.

MECHANICS

QUICK CHECK 6 **Using Context Clues**

Use the context clues in sentences 1–5 to match the word or phrase below with the italicized word in each sentence.

a. drinks
b. lack of concern
c. knowledge
d. drifter
e. kindness
f. transformation
g. myths
h. someone who starts a business

1. Leslie Marmon Silko uses Native American *lore,* or teachings, in her writing.
2. We should encourage *compassion* rather than cruelty toward all of the earth's creatures.
3. They have a variety of *beverages,* such as milk, juice, iced tea, and water.
4. Jim Bob's *metamorphosis* was so complete that we barely recognized him.
5. Since Pilar disliked working for others, she decided to become an *entrepreneur.*

Choosing the Right Word

Since many English words have several meanings, you must look at *all* the definitions given for any particular word. When you read or hear an unfamiliar word, think about its context. Then determine the definition that best fits that context.

Some dictionaries include sample contexts to indicate a word's various meanings. Compare the sample contexts given in your dictionary with the context of a new word to make sure you've found the meaning that fits.

Synonyms and Antonyms

A *synonym* is a word that means nearly the same thing as another word. However, words that are synonyms rarely have exactly the same meaning. Two words may have the

MECHANICS

same **denotation,** or dictionary definition, but a different **connotation,** or suggested meaning. For example, the words *chuckle* and *cackle* mean "to laugh." However, *chuckle* has a more friendly connotation than *cackle,* which suggests a harsh, annoying, squawking sound.

When you look up a word in a dictionary, you will often find several synonyms listed. To help you distinguish between synonyms, some dictionaries give *synonym articles*—brief explanations of a word's synonyms and how they differ in meaning. The best book to use to find synonyms is a *thesaurus.* A **thesaurus** is a reference book that has word entries like a dictionary. However, instead of definitions, a thesaurus lists synonyms for its entry words.

Some dictionaries and thesauruses also list *antonyms.* The **antonym** of a word is a word that has nearly the opposite meaning. For example, the words *loud* and *quiet* are antonyms. *Calm* and *nervous* are also antonyms. Knowing the antonym of a word will often help you understand the first word's meaning.

 *QUICK CHECK 7* **Identifying Synonyms and Antonyms**

For each sentence below, decide whether the italicized words are *synonyms* or *antonyms.*

1. My black jacket is made of new *synthetic* cloth, but my shirt is *natural* silk.
2. Under the new *restored* democracy, the citizens had all of their rights *returned.*
3. The cat remained *calm* during the storm, but the dogs became *frantic.*
4. The models wore only the latest *fashion.* Their clothes were always in the latest *style.*
5. I was *embarrassed* when I dropped my lunch tray in the cafeteria, but the applause from other students really *humiliated* me.

Homographs

Homographs are words that are spelled the same but have different meanings. Even though the words look the same, they may not sound the same. For example, the word *sub-ject* (pronounced *sub´ject*) is a noun meaning "a topic," but *subject* (pronounced *sub ject´*) is a verb meaning "to bring under control." To discover the meaning of a homograph in a sentence, read all the meanings listed for it in a dictionary. Then choose the one that best fits the context of your sentence. The more often you see a word in different contexts, the better able you will be to figure out its meaning.

50 Commonly Misspelled Words

ache	guess	though
again	half	through
always	hour	tired
answer	instead	tonight
blue	knew	trouble
built	know	wear
busy	laid	where
buy	meant	which
can't	minute	whole
color	often	women
cough	once	
could	ready	
country	said	
doctor	says	
does	shoes	
don't	since	
early	straight	
easy	sugar	
every	sure	
friend	tear	

250 Spelling Words

The words in the following list are grouped so that you can study them ten at a time. To master words that give you difficulty, follow the five steps given on pages 306–308. If you are not sure what a word means, look it up in a dictionary, and add the word to your word bank.

As you study these words, pay particular attention to the letters in italics. The italicized letters generally cause the greatest difficulty in correctly spelling the words.

aband*o*n	artic*l*e	commer*c*ial
absolut*e*ly	assist*a*nce	co*mmittee*s
a*cc*ept*a*nce	a*u*thority	competition
accident*a*lly	a*w*ful	complet*e*ly
a*cco*mmodate	bas*i*s	conc*ei*ve
a*cc*ompany	begi*nn*ing	conde*mn*
a*cc*omplish	bel*ie*ve	congra*t*ulations
achi*e*ve	ben*e*fit	cons*c*ience
a*c*quaintance	bound*a*ry	cons*c*ious
a*c*quire	bo*uquet*	contro*l*
actu*a*lly	bulle*t*in	conven*i*ence
advertis*e*ment	business	courteous
ag*ai*nst	cancel	critic*i*sm
*a*isle	capacity	c*y*linder
a*m*ount	careless	de*a*lt
anal*y*sis	ca*rr*ier	de*c*ision
anti*c*ipate	c*ei*ling	de*f*ense
anx*ie*ty	challe*n*ge	defin*i*te
apol*o*gy	choi*ce*	defi*n*ition
a*pp*arent	ch*oir*	de*s*cribe
a*pp*ear*a*nce	chorus	de*s*cription
a*pp*lication	cir*cui*t	desir*a*ble
a*pp*reciation	col*o*nel	de*s*pair
a*pp*roach	colu*mn*	develo*p*
arg*u*ment	co*m*ing	d*i*amond

difficulties
disappointment
discipline
discussion
distinction

distribution
doctrine
duplicate
economic
eighth
eligible
embarrass
engineering
enthusiasm
eventually

exactly
exaggerate
excellent
existence
experience
experiment
explanation
fascinating
favorite
February

finally
flu
forty
fourth
friendliness
generally
governor
grammar
gratitude
guarantee

guardian
gymnasium
hatred
height
heir
hesitate
humorous
ignorance
imagination
immediately

incidentally
individual
inferior
initial
inspiration
intelligence
interfere
interrupt
involve
jealous

judgment
knowledge
laboratory
leisure
lengthen
license
lieutenant
loneliness
majority
manufacture

marriage
mechanical
medieval
military
mourn

multiplication
muscular
mystery
naturally
necessary

nickel
nonsense
numerous
obvious
occasionally
occurrence
opinion
opponent
opportunity
orchestra

originally
paid
parallel
parliament
patience
performance
personal
personality
persuade
philosopher

picnicking
planned
pleasant
possess
precede
preferred
prejudice
privilege
probably
procedure

professor
pursuit
qualified
realize
receipt
recognize
recommend
referring
regularly
relieve

repetition
research
response
restaurant
rhythm
satisfied
saucer
schedule
scissors
sense

sentiment
separate
sergeant
shepherd
similar

solemn
source
souvenir
sponsor
straighten

subscription
success
sufficient
suggest
suppress
surprise
surround
suspense
suspicion
tailor

temperament
tendency
theory
therefore
thorough
tobacco
tonsils
tradition
tragedy
transferred

tries
truly
unanimous
unnecessary
unsatisfactory
until
useful
using
utilized
vacuum

variety
various
vein
view
villain
violence
warrant
weird
wholly
writing

COMPOSITION

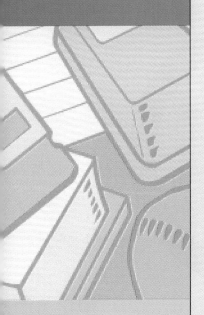

17 THE WRITING PROCESS

Good writing doesn't just happen. For most writers, it comes from following stages in a process. The diagram below shows the stages that writers usually follow. However, the process differs for every writer.

Topic, purpose, and *audience* are also important in the writing process. Sometimes they come together naturally. Your teacher may assign topics, purposes, and audiences. These assignments give you practice for the important writing you will do later on your own.

 *Prewriting*

Finding Ideas for Writing

How do writers find ideas? Often, an everyday experience or a personal interest sparks an idea. But many writers also have special methods they use to find and explore ideas. The following pages show some common ways for finding ideas. Feel free to combine these methods and to experiment with different ways to find ideas.

Writer's Journal

Many writers keep a ***writer's journal*** to record their ideas, experiences, feelings, questions, and thoughts. Your journal can be kept in a notebook or in a file folder. You can put in cartoons, quotations, song lyrics, and poems that have special meaning for you. Here are some suggestions for keeping a writer's journal.

- Try to write daily. Keep your journal handy so you can write down thoughts as they occur to you.
- Let your imagination run free. Write down dreams, songs, poems, story ideas. Include drawings.
- Forget about grammar and punctuation. Only your thoughts matter.

Freewriting

Freewriting is exactly that—writing freely. You can freewrite in your journal, or on a loose piece of paper. You write whatever pops into your head. You don't judge ideas or worry about wording, complete sentences, or mistakes in punctuation. Freewriting can loosen you up for later writing or can give you ideas for topics. When you freewrite, follow these guidelines:

- Set a time limit of three to five minutes and keep writing until the time is up.
- Start with a subject that's important to you—perhaps sports, pioneers, or science fiction.
- If you get stuck, just write anything. The important thing is to keep your pen moving.

One form of freewriting is called *focused freewriting* or *looping.* Here, you choose a word or phrase from your freewriting to use as a starting point. Then you freewrite all over again, using that word or phrase as your subject. This practice helps you to focus your ideas for writing.

Here's an example of freewriting about pioneers.

Pioneers. Worked hard outside. Kids worked hard, too. Remember pictures of Abe Lincoln splitting logs as a child. Simple life. Families close. Good. Close to nature, but hard life. People died young—too hard. No doctors. Kids died, too. Pioneers. Going across plains. Oxen and horses. Wild animals. Built own houses. Wish I was a pioneer. Snakes. Wolves. Glad I wasn't a pioneer.

Brainstorming

In **brainstorming,** you say whatever comes to mind in response to a word. You can brainstorm alone, but group or partner brainstorming is more fun. Hearing other people's ideas helps you think of even more ideas.

■ Write down a subject at the top of a piece of paper. (In a group, use the chalkboard.)

■ List every idea about the subject that comes to mind. (In a group, have one person list the ideas.)

■ Keep going until you run out of ideas.

Here are some brainstorming notes about teen culture.

HERE'S HOW

clothes—how different	relations with parents
groups dress	friends—and enemies
hairstyles	vacation
music	favorite movies
concerts and stars	bad movies
favorite TV shows	Arnold Schwarzenegger
favorite magazines	dating
hangouts—skating rink	peer pressure

Clustering

In *clustering*, sometimes called *webbing*, you brainstorm ideas and connect them with circles and lines. The circles and lines help to show how the ideas are related. To make a cluster diagram, follow the steps below.

■ Write your subject on your paper and circle it.

■ Around the subject, write whatever ideas about it occur to you. Circle these ideas. Draw lines connecting them with the subject.

■ When your ideas make you think of related ideas, connect them with circles and lines.

On the following page is a cluster diagram on "Plains Indians." The two main ideas are *where they lived* and *how they lived.* The details are connected to these main ideas.

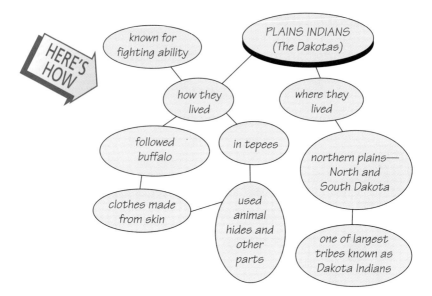

Asking Questions

Reporters often get information for news stories by asking the **5W-How?** questions: *Who? What? Where? When? Why?* and *How?* Not every question word applies to every subject. And sometimes you'll think of more than one question for a particular question word. The point is that by asking questions, you'll cover the basic background information for your writing.

TOPIC:	*How Gorillas Might Be Saved from Extinction*	
WHO?	Who is working on the effort to save gorillas from extinction? (Check at the library for names and addresses of groups.)	
WHAT?	What is needed to save the gorillas? (Read books and articles; interview a zoo director.)	
WHAT?	What is done with money given to save gorillas? (Contact groups working to save gorillas.)	
WHERE?	Where do gorillas live? (Check in an encyclopedia.)	
WHY?	Why are gorillas in danger? (Read books and articles; interview a zoo director.)	
HOW?	How can we save gorillas? (Check in a book, or call the education department at a zoo.)	

Reading and Listening

Sometimes you'll write about things outside your own experience. So how do you get the information you need? You can read and listen.

Reading. Reading sources include books, magazines, newspapers, and brochures. Here are some tips for finding specific information.

- Check the tables of contents and indexes to find the exact pages you need to read.
- Skim the pages until you find something about your topic.
- Slow down and take notes on the main ideas and important details.

Listening. By listening, you can get a lot of information from speeches, radio and TV programs, interviews, audiotapes, or videotapes. Use the following hints when you listen for information.

- Before you listen, make a list of questions about your topic.
- While you listen, take notes on the main ideas and important details.

Imagining

Can you imagine that you are someone else or somewhere else? Can you imagine what it would be like if dinosaurs still roamed the earth? Imagining gives you creative ideas for writing. Trigger your imagination by asking *"What if?"* questions. "What if?" questions can be silly or serious. Here are some examples.

- *What if* I became a grown-up overnight?
- *What if* something in my life—like TV—didn't exist?
- *What if* people could fly like birds?
- *What if* everyone looked exactly alike?
- *What if* I were the principal?

Thinking About Purpose and Audience

Purpose

Before you write, always ask yourself, *Why am I writing?* The first column of the chart shows the basic purposes you might have for writing. The second column lists the forms of writing you might use for these different purposes.

MAIN PURPOSE	FORMS OF WRITING
To express your feelings	Journal entry, letter, personal essay
To be creative	Short story, poem, play
To explain or inform	Science or history writing, news story, biography, autobiography, travel essay
To persuade	Persuasive essay, letter to the editor, advertisement, political speech

Of course, forms and purposes can overlap. For instance, you could write a poem to express how you feel about summer. Or, to persuade people not to pollute the environment, you could write a science fiction short story about a sick planet.

Audience

Before you write, also ask yourself, *Who will read my writing?* Consider your audience—the readers. You want them to understand what you're saying. You don't want to tell them what they already know—that's boring.

Think about how you'll change your writing to suit a specific audience. Ask yourself these questions.

- Why is my audience reading my writing? Do they expect to be entertained, informed, or persuaded?

- What does my audience already know about my topic?
- What does my audience want or need to know about my topic?
- What vocabulary and type of language should I use?

Prewriting

Arranging Ideas

Once you have gathered ideas to write about, the next step is arranging them. You always need to arrange your ideas so that readers can follow them.

Types of Order

The following chart shows four common ways of arranging ideas.

ARRANGING IDEAS		
TYPE OF ORDER	**DEFINITION**	**EXAMPLES**
Chronological	Narration: order that presents events as they happen in time	Story, narrative poem, explanation of a process, history, biography, drama
Spatial	Description: order that describes objects according to location	Descriptions (near to far; left to right; top to bottom)
Importance	Evaluation: order that gives details from least to most important, or the reverse	Persuasive writing; description; explanation (main idea and supporting details); evaluative writing
Logical	Classification: order that relates items and groups	Definitions; classifications; comparisons and contrasts

Calvin & Hobbes copyright 1986 Watterson. Reprinted with permission of Universal Press Syndicate. All rights reserved.

STYLE NOTE Sometimes the order you use depends on the kind of information you want to present. For example, your printed class schedule shows the order in which your classes are held (*chronological order*) because class times are most important. Sometimes it makes sense to describe items close to you first and then to describe items in the distance (*spatial order*). Or you might choose to list your reasons for an opinion with the most important one last. This arrangement focuses the reader's attention on your final, best argument (*order of importance*). When you write, your topic, purpose, and audience help you decide which order is best.

Using Visuals to Organize Ideas

Visuals—such as charts, diagrams, or other graphic layouts—can help you bring order to your prewriting notes.

Charts

To create a chart, think about the different types of information you have. For example, if you gather ideas for a report on gorillas in the wild, you might organize it by making a chart like the following one.

HERE'S HOW

Kind	Location	Number in the Wild
Western lowland gorilla	Western Africa	35,000–45,000
Eastern lowland gorilla	Eastern Zaire	3,000–5,000
Mountain gorilla	Rwanda, Zaire, Uganda	3,000–5,000

COMPOSITION

Diagrams

Venn Diagrams. A *Venn diagram* uses overlapping circles to show how two subjects are similar (comparison) and different (contrast). If you are comparing two subjects, draw two overlapping circles, one for each subject. In the overlapping section, record details shared by both subjects. In the parts that don't overlap, write details that make these subjects different. Here is a Venn diagram that compares and contrasts tornadoes and hurricanes.

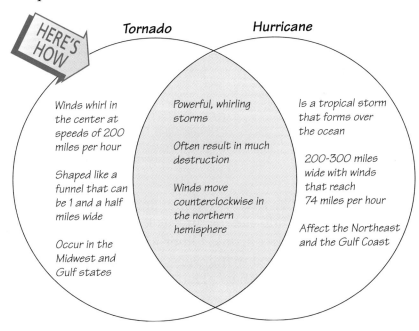

HERE'S HOW

Tornado

Winds whirl in the center at speeds of 200 miles per hour

Shaped like a funnel that can be 1 and a half miles wide

Occur in the Midwest and Gulf states

Powerful, whirling storms

Often result in much destruction

Winds move counterclockwise in the northern hemisphere

Hurricane

Is a tropical storm that forms over the ocean

200-300 miles wide with winds that reach 74 miles per hour

Affect the Northeast and the Gulf Coast

Sequence Chains. A *sequence chain* can help you organize events in chronological order. You can use a sequence chain to show the steps in a process or the main events in a story. The following diagram is a sequence chain for a short story.

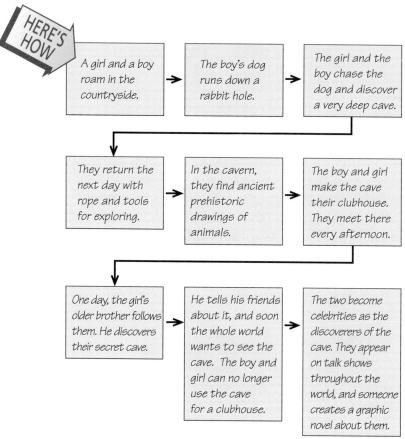

Tree Diagrams. A *tree diagram* is another way of organizing main ideas and details. In this kind of diagram, the main idea is like a tree trunk. Other ideas branch off from the main idea. The following page shows a tree diagram for a report on Matthew Henson, an explorer with Admiral Peary on the first expedition to reach the North Pole.

COMPOSITION

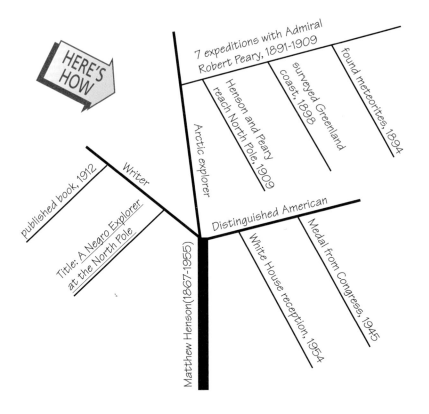

HERE'S HOW

7 expeditions with Admiral Robert Peary, 1891-1909

surveyed Greenland coast, 1898

found meteorites, 1894

Henson and Peary reach North Pole, 1909

Arctic explorer

published book, 1912

Writer

Title: A Negro Explorer at the North Pole

Distinguished American

Matthew Henson (1867-1955)

White House reception, 1954

Medal from Congress, 1945

Writing a First Draft

There's no one way to write a paper. Some people write their first drafts quickly, just trying to get their ideas on paper. Others go slowly, carefully shaping each sentence and paragraph. But whether they write their first drafts quickly or slowly, all writers share something in common. They all are creating something new from separate parts. This process is called *synthesizing*. Writing a first draft is like creating a quilt, writing a song, or making a salad: all of these things are new wholes made from separate parts. To synthesize your first draft, use the following tips:

■ Use your prewriting plan as a guide.

- Think about your main idea. Then write a sentence that states this main idea.
- Write freely. Focus on details that express your main idea.
- As you write, you may discover new ideas. Include these ideas in your draft.
- Don't worry about spelling and grammar errors. You can correct them later.

Here's a first draft of a personal essay. You'll find that there are mistakes in it. Notice that the writer makes a note to check on something. The writer will replace the note with the proper information and will correct mistakes in a later stage of the writing process.

Last year, my family went to the Yucatán Peninsula of Mexico. We stayed in Mérida, which is an ancient city that has many neat buildings. There are big arches and sculptures and parks. The best part of our trip, though, was going to the Chichén Itzá ruins to see the pyramids. I used to think that pyramids were only in Egypt. [Note: look up name] is the biggest pyramid in Chichén Itzá. It has nine levels, and has a temple on top. It was built a thousand years ago over a smaller, older pyramid. Inside the smaller pyramid is a big cat carved out of limestone. After we came home, we all wanted to go back. The cat statue has green jade eyes. I'd never seen such interesting things before. We didn't have enough time to see everything.

STYLE NOTE

A speaking voice is almost like a finger-print—no two are exactly alike. When you write, you have a voice, too. It's made up of the words and kinds of sentences that you use. In your writing, try to have a natural voice—one that sounds like you. Don't use big words or long sentences just because they sound "important." Even when your writing is formal—as in a research report—let your natural voice come through.

Evaluating and Revising

Evaluating and revising are two different steps in improving your writing, although you often do them together.

Evaluating

Evaluating means deciding on the strengths and weaknesses of your paper. You evaluate writing all the time, whether you think about it or not. You like some books and hate others. You find some written directions easy to follow and others hard. You enjoy certain comic strips but not others.

Self-Evaluation

Because you're so close to your own writing, evaluating it is harder than judging someone else's work. These tips may help make the process easier.

- **Read carefully.** Read your paper more than once. First, read for *content* (what you say). Next, read for *organization* (how you order ideas). Finally, read for *style* (how you use words and sentences).
- **Listen carefully.** Read your paper aloud. *Listen* to what you've said. You may notice that the ideas don't flow smoothly or that some sentences sound awkward.
- **Take time.** Set your draft aside. Come back to it later and read through it. You'll find it's easier to be objective about your writing after a little time away.

COMPOSITION

Peer Evaluation

You can get advice from others by sharing your writing with your classmates in a peer-evaluation group. In the group, you'll sometimes be the writer whose work is evaluated. Other times you'll be an evaluator.

EVALUATION GUIDELINES

Guidelines for the Writer

1. Make a list of questions for the peer evaluators. Which parts of your paper worry you?

2. Keep an open mind. Don't take your evaluators' suggestions as personal criticism.

Guidelines for the Peer Evaluator

1. Tell the writer what's good about the paper. Give the writer some encouragement.

2. Focus on content and organization. The writer will catch spelling and grammar errors when proofreading.

3. Be sensitive to the writer's feelings. State your suggestions as questions, such as "What does this mean?" and "Can you give an example?"

After your classmates evaluate your paper, think about the comments. Which comments are most helpful? Remember that the final decisions about changes are yours.

Revising

When you *revise*, you make changes to improve your paper. There are four basic ways to revise your writing: **adding, cutting, replacing,** and **reordering.**

COMPUTER NOTE

If you have a word processor, you'll find revising easier. You can make changes directly on the draft file and print out a new copy.

REVISING	
TECHNIQUE	**EXAMPLE**
1. Add. Add new information. Add words, sentences, and whole paragraphs.	Many of the Amish still live much as their ancestors did, *when they came to the United States more than 250 years ago.*
2. Cut. Take out repeated or unnecessary information and unrelated ideas.	~~They haven't changed much.~~ The women wear long dresses and bonnets; the men wear dark suits and wide-brimmed hats.
3. Replace. Take out weak or awkward wording. Replace with precise words or details.	*modern conveniences,* Many Amish use no ~~new things~~ *not even* ~~like~~ electricity or telephones.
4. Reorder. Move information, sentences, and paragraphs for logical order.	*using* They use mostly horse-drawn ~~machinery and make their living by farming.~~

Handwrite your revisions on your paper. Then write or type a new copy. (If you use a word processor, make your changes on your draft file and print a new copy.)

You'll learn more about evaluating and revising paragraphs, compositions, and research reports in the next two chapters. But the following general guidelines apply to all kinds of writing.

GUIDELINES FOR EVALUATING AND REVISING

EVALUATION GUIDE	REVISION TECHNIQUE
CONTENT	
1 Is the writing interesting?	**Add** examples, an anecdote (brief story), dialogue, and details. **Cut** repeated or boring details.
2 Does the writing achieve its purpose?	**Add** explanations, examples, or details to achieve the purpose.
3 Are there enough details?	**Add** details, facts, or examples to support the main idea.
4 Are there unrelated ideas that distract the reader?	**Cut** the unrelated ideas.
ORGANIZATION	
5 Are ideas and details arranged in an effective order?	**Reorder** ideas and details to make the meaning clear.
6 Are the connections between ideas and sentences clear? (See pages 356–358.)	**Add** transitional words to link ideas: *because, for example,* and so on.
STYLE	
7 Is the meaning clear?	**Replace** unclear wording. Use precise, easy-to-understand words.
8 Does the language fit the audience and purpose?	**Replace** slang and contractions to create a formal tone. **Replace** formal words with less formal ones to create an informal tone.
9 Do sentences read smoothly?	**Reorder** words to vary sentence beginnings. **Reword** to vary sentence structure.

Here's the personal essay from page 342. It has been revised, using the four revision techniques.

Last year, my family went to the Yucatán Peninsula of Mexico. We stayed in Mérida, which is an ancient city that has many ~~neat~~ *beautiful* buildings. There are big arches and sculptures and parks *in the city*. The best part of our trip, though, was going to the Chichén Itzá ruins to see the pyramids. ~~I used to think that pyramids were only in Egypt.~~ *El Castillo* ~~[Note: look up name]~~ is the biggest pyramid in Chichén Itzá. It has nine levels, and has a temple on top. It was built a thousand years ago over a smaller, older pyramid. Inside the smaller pyramid is a *jaguar* ~~big cat~~ carved out of limestone. After we came home, we all wanted to go back. The cat statue has green jade eyes. I'd never seen such interesting things before. We didn't have enough time to see everything.

Proofreading and Publishing

Proofreading

When you *proofread,* you carefully reread your paper. You correct mistakes in grammar, spelling, capitalization, and punctuation. Put your paper aside for awhile. Then focus on one line at a time and read slowly, one word at a time. If you're not sure what's correct, look it up. Afterward, exchange papers with a classmate and proofread each other's paper to try to find errors that need to be corrected.

GUIDELINES FOR PROOFREADING

1. Is every sentence a complete sentence, not a fragment? (See pages 179–180.)
2. Does every sentence begin with a capital letter and end with the correct punctuation mark? (See pages 239–251 and pages 257–260.)
3. Do plural verbs have plural subjects? Do singular verbs have singular subjects? (See pages 77–87.)
4. Are verbs in the right form? Are verbs in the right tense? (See pages 97–109.)
5. Are adjective and adverb forms used correctly in making comparisons? (See pages 131–137.)
6. Are the forms of personal pronouns used correctly? (See page 117.)
7. Does every pronoun agree with its antecedent (the word it refers to) in number and in gender? (See pages 87–93.)
8. Are all words spelled correctly? Are the plural forms of nouns correct? (See pages 311–320.)

Publishing

After you proofread, you're ready to publish, or share your writing. You've worked hard, and you can be proud of your writing. Here are some ways of publishing your work.

- Read what you've written to the class or to a group of friends.
- Illustrate or decorate a copy of your creative writing, and give it to a friend or relative.
- Post your book and movie reviews on a school bulletin board or in the library.
- Keep a folder of your writing. Share it with your family and friends.

- Enter a writing contest. Some contests award prizes. Your teacher may have information about writing contests.
- Send your writing to a newspaper or magazine. Try the school newspaper, yearbook, or magazine. Your local newspaper might publish a letter to the editor. Find out which magazines publish student stories, poems, and essays.

You've worked hard on your writing and should give yourself a pat on the back. Before you share your writing with others, however, follow these guidelines to make sure your paper looks as good as it can.

GUIDELINES FOR MANUSCRIPT FORM

1. Use only one side of a sheet of paper.
2. Write in blue or black ink, type, or use a word processor.
3. Leave margins of about one inch at the top, sides, and bottom of each page.
4. Follow your teacher's instructions for putting your name, the date, your class, and the title on your paper.
5. If you write, do not skip lines. If you type, double-space the lines.
6. Indent the first line of each paragraph.

Shoe, by Jeff MacNelly, reprinted by permission: Tribune Media Services.

COMPOSITION

	SYMBOLS FOR REVISING AND PROOFREADING	
SYMBOL	**EXAMPLE**	**MEANING OF SYMBOL**
(cap) ≡	at Waukesha lake	Capitalize a lowercase letter.
(lc) /	a gift for my Uncle	Lowercase a capital letter.
∧	fifty cost cents	Insert a missing word, letter, or punctuation mark.
	our by their house	Replace something.
	What day is is it?	Leave out a word, letter, or punctuation mark.
∏	recieved	Change the order of letters.
¶	¶The last step is	Begin a new paragraph.
⊙	Please be patient⊙	Add a period.
∧	Yes that's right.	Add a comma.

18 PARAGRAPH AND COMPOSITION STRUCTURE

What Makes a Paragraph?

Paragraphs aren't all alike. Some have just a few sentences. Others go on for a page or more. One paragraph might be persuasive; another, purely descriptive.

Despite their differences, paragraphs have the same basic parts. One part is the *main idea*. A second part consists of *supporting sentences* that give specific details about the main idea. And often, the main idea is stated in a *topic sentence*.

The Main Idea

The *main idea* is the idea around which the entire paragraph is organized. In the following paragraph, the main idea is expressed in the first sentence.

> Because Hopis have no written language, Kachina dolls are used to pass tribal lore and religion down through generations. Given to the young during special dances, Kachina dolls are then hung in the home as constant reminders of Hopi ancestry and heritage.

> Though too young to understand their meaning, infants are given Kachina paddle dolls as toys, so that from birth they are familiar with Hopi custom.
>
> Lonnie Dyer, "Kachinas: Sacred Drama of the Hopis"

The Topic Sentence

The *topic sentence* states the main idea of the paragraph. It can occur anywhere in the paragraph. But usually, it's either the first or second sentence. Sometimes the topic sentence is made up of two sentences.

A topic sentence can come later in the paragraph or even at the end. Sometimes the topic sentence pulls the ideas together and helps the reader see how they are related. Sometimes it summarizes, as in the following paragraph.

> Gray clouds ran a mad race across the sky. The wind howled through the hills, ripping the last of the leaves from the trees. Throughout the morning, the temperature continued to drop, and by noon the puddles along the road were beginning to freeze over. It was the first day of winter.

Sometimes a paragraph has no topic sentence, especially if it is a narrative paragraph that tells about a series of events. The reader has to add the details together to figure out what the main idea is. Look at the following paragraph. What's the main idea?

> When the coyote had finished drinking it trotted a few paces, to above the stepping-stones, and began to eat something. All at once it looked up, directly at me. For a moment it stood still. Then it had turned and almost instantly vanished, back into the shadows that underlay the trees. From behind the

trees, a big black hawklike bird with a red head flapped out and away. Up in the lake, the herons took wing. They, too, circled away from me, angled upriver.

Colin Fletcher, *The Secret Worlds of Colin Fletcher*

Each sentence in this paragraph describes a separate action. But if you put them all together, they suggest the main idea: Colin Fletcher disturbed the animals and they fled.

Even though not all paragraphs have topic sentences, most students find it helpful to use topic sentences in their writing. A topic sentence keeps both the writer and the reader focused on the main idea.

Supporting Sentences

Supporting sentences give specific details that explain or prove the main idea of the paragraph. These sentences may use sensory details, facts, or examples.

Sensory Details. When you use words that appeal to one of your five senses—sight, sound, touch, taste, and smell— you are using *sensory details.* Vivid sensory details help your reader clearly imagine what you're writing about.

Notice the sensory details in this paragraph from *A Wind in the Door.* In the first two sentences, for example, you can "smell" the apples, and you can "feel" the cold wind. What other sensory details can you find?

She moved slowly along the orchard wall. The cidery smell of fallen apples was cut by the wind which had completely changed course and was now streaming across the garden from the north-west, sharp and glittery with frost. She saw a shadow move on the wall and jumped back: Louise the Larger, it must be Louise, and Meg could not climb that wall or cross the orchard to the north pasture until she was sure that neither Louise nor the not-quite-seen shape was lurking there waiting to pounce on her. Her legs felt watery, so she sat on a large, squat pumpkin to wait. The cold wind brushed her cheek; corn tassels hished like ocean waves. She looked warily about. She was seeing, she realized, through lenses streaked and spattered by raindrops blowing from sunflowers and corn, so she took off her spectacles, felt under the poncho for her kilt, and wiped them. Better, though the world was still a little wavery, as though seen under water.

Madeleine L'Engle, *A Wind in the Door*

Facts. A *fact* is a statement that can be proved true by directly observing or by checking a reliable reference source. For example, if you say that Washington, D.C., is the capital of the United States, that's a fact. It can be proved. But if you say that it's the best city in the world, that's an opinion. Opinions can't be proved.

Look at how the facts in the following paragraph support the main idea that a volcano was erupting. In the first sentence, for example, facts include the date and time of the boom, as well as the height of the peak. Can you find other facts?

Those who camped overnight on March 28 atop 3,926-foot-high Mitchell Peak were wakened about 2:00 A.M. by a loud boom and whistling sounds. In the brilliant moonlight they watched a great plume of steam rise from the crater. Another eruption at 3:45 A.M. blew ash three miles into the sky and was followed by three quakes registering 4.0 on the Richter intensity scale. Later observers learned the volcano had blown out a second crater. Three small mudflows, not lava, dribbled a thousand feet down the slope. The east and south slopes turned gray from the ash projected by gases roiling from the magma far below the surface.

Marian T. Place, *Mount St. Helens: A Sleeping Volcano Awakes*

Examples. *Examples* are specific instances or illustrations of a general idea. Soccer and football are examples of team sports played with a ball. Getting grounded is an example of what might happen if you disobey your parents.

In the following paragraph the author gives examples of how animals behave when they're angry.

When animals are angry, they use a different kind of body language. If one animal invades another's territory, the first animal threatens it. Animals may threaten by displaying their teeth or claws. Some try to make their bodies look bigger. Birds fluff up their feathers. Fish stick their back fins straight up and open their gill covers outward. Angry cats arch their backs and make their hair stand on end. These messages say, "I'm a BIG angry animal. Don't come any closer!"

"Animal Body Talk," *National Geographic World*

Unity and Coherence

A paragraph may have a main idea, topic sentence, and supporting sentences. But the reader may still not understand it fully. Unity or coherence may be missing.

Unity

When a paragraph has *unity,* all the sentences relate to the main idea. For example, in a paragraph explaining the origin of baseball, every sentence should give some information about baseball's beginnings. To include a sentence about this year's best team or one about the rules of play will ruin the paragraph's unity. Those sentences aren't about the paragraph's main idea—how baseball began.

As you read the following paragraph, notice how each sentence is directly connected to the main idea: that sailors once believed in mermaids.

> Another monster that was equally dreaded by sailors was the beautiful mermaid. Like the sirens, mermaids were thought to be half woman and half fish. Such creatures were said to carry a mirror in one hand and a comb in the other, and from time to time they would run the comb through their long seagreen hair. Most sailors were convinced that it was very bad luck to see a mermaid. At best, it meant that someone aboard their ship would die soon afterward. At worst, it meant that a terrific storm would arise, the ship would sink, and many of the crew would drown.
>
> William Wise, "Strange and Terrible Monsters of the Deep"

Coherence

In addition to having unity, a paragraph needs to be coherent. When a paragraph has *coherence,* the reader can easily see how one idea relates to the next. One way to create coherence in a paragraph is to use *transitional words and phrases*. These are words or phrases that show how ideas are related. The chart on the following page lists some common transitions. You'll notice that the transitions you use depend, in part, on the kind of paragraph you are writing.

TRANSITIONAL WORDS AND PHRASES		
Comparing Ideas/Classification and Definition		
also	another	similarly
and	moreover	too
Contrasting Ideas/Classification and Definition		
although	in spite of	on the other hand
but	instead	still
however	nevertheless	yet
Showing Cause and Effect/Narration		
as a result	for	so that
because	since	therefore
consequently	so	
Showing Time/Narration		
after	eventually	next
at last	finally	then
at once	first	thereafter
before	meanwhile	when
Showing Place/Description		
above	beyond	into
across	down	next to
around	here	over
before	in	there
behind	inside	under
Showing Importance/Evaluation		
first	mainly	then
last	more important	to begin with

Notice how the underlined transitions in the next paragraph help show how ideas are related.

COMPOSITION

> Doesn't the earth sometimes seem like one big mess? That's <u>because</u> it is. Think about how much trash you make in one day. Where does it go? The garbageman picks it up <u>and</u> it's gone. <u>But</u> where? <u>Sometimes</u> trash is burned, releasing harmful pollutants into the air—<u>not</u> a smart idea. <u>Other times</u> it goes to a dump <u>or</u> a landfill, where it's buried with dirt. <u>Not</u> a great idea <u>either</u>, <u>but</u> it doesn't matter anymore, <u>because</u> we're fast running out of space for landfills—<u>so</u> where to next?
>
> "Earth SOS," *Seventeen*

Ways of Developing Paragraphs

Here is a list showing four different strategies for developing your main idea.

WAYS OF DEVELOPING PARAGRAPHS	
Description	Describing a person, place, or thing
Narration	Telling how a person or situation changes over time
Classification	Showing relationships between items
Evaluation	Deciding on the value or importance of an item

STYLE NOTE

Often, you'll use more than one strategy in a paragraph. You may, for example, describe a person and also narrate a story about the person. This blend of strategies will give your writing variety and interest.

Description

You use *description* to tell what something is like or what it looks like. You use mostly sensory details to tell about what you can see, hear, smell, taste, or touch.

Descriptions are usually organized by *spatial order*—how items are arranged in space. In the following paragraph, the writer uses spatial order to describe part of his family's restaurant.

> In a glass case near the cash register, cardboard boxes overflow with bags of fortune cookies and almond candies that my father gives away free to children. The first dollar bill my parents ever made hangs framed on the wall above the register. Next to that dollar, a picture of my parents taken twenty years ago recalls a time when they were raising four children at once, paying mortgages and putting in the bank every cent that didn't go toward bills.
>
> David Low, *Winterblossom Garden*

Garfield reprinted by permission of UFS, Inc.

Narration

In narration, you tell how a person or how a situation changes over a period of time. You can narrate to tell a story, explain a process, or explain causes and effects. Paragraphs that use narration are often organized in *chronological order.* That is, events are told in the order in which they occur.

NOTE Many narrative paragraphs do not have topic sentences. Because a narrative paragraph is about a series of events, it begins with an action. The other sentences tell about additional actions.

Telling a Story. When you tell a story, you tell what happened. The story may be about either imaginary or real events. Here is a narrative paragraph that tells what happens during a ride in a theme park.

> Transporting his passengers on the Roosevelt Island tramway, the operator suddenly announces that King Kong has escaped and is wreaking havoc on Manhattan. Suddenly a wall of water breaks from mains and floods the streets below. Fires rage. Then Kong appears in all his terror, hanging from the Queensboro Bridge. He swats at a police helicopter and sends it crashing to the ground. Then the six-ton, four-story-tall gorilla turns his attention to you, grabbing the tram as if it were a Tonka toy. Twisting and turning the vehicle, he picks it up, blasts you with his banana-scented breath, and hurls you to the ground. Falling at 12 feet per second with 1.75 g's of acceleration, the tram is saved from certain disaster by a single cable.
>
> A.J.S. Rayl, "Making Fun"

Explaining a Process. Whenever you tell someone how something works or how to do something, you're explaining a process. To help readers follow the steps in the process, you use chronological order once again.

In this paragraph, the writer explains how to pan for gold. Once the gold pan is filled with rock and sand, the panning begins.

> Swirl your pan around and around just below the surface of the water. The water will cause the light sand and gravel to rise to the top. Pour off the sand, pick out the pebbles and repeat the process. When the top dirt is stripped off, you will see black streaks in the bottom of your pan. These are tiny grains of iron magnetite. This is the "pay dirt." Be

careful not to wash it away. Magnetite is heavy, but gold is heavier. Your gold, if it is there, will be under the black sand.

Jean Bartenbach, *Rockhound Trails*

Explaining Cause and Effect. Narration is also used to explain how one event causes another event. To make the cause-and-effect connections clear, events are often narrated in the order in which they happened.

In the following paragraph, the cause is an October storm. The effects of the storm are what happens to the people, the trees, the animals, and the buildings.

Cause

A storm came this year, against which all other storms were to be measured, on a Saturday in October, a balmy afternoon. . . . It built as it came up the valley as did every fall storm, but the steel-gray thunderheads, the first sign of it anyone saw, were higher, much higher, too high. In the stillness before it hit, men looked at each other as though a fast and wiry man had pulled a knife in a bar. They **Effect** felt the trees falling before they heard the wind, and they dropped tools and scrambled to get out. The wind came up suddenly and like a scythe, like piranha after them, like seawater through a breach in a dike. The first **Effect** blow bent trees half to the ground, the second caught them and snapped them like kindling, sending limbs raining down and twenty-foot splinters hurtling through the air like mortar shells to stick quivering in the ground. **Effect** Bawling cattle running the fences, a loose lawnmower bumping across a lawn, a stray dog lunging for a child racing by. The big **Effect** trees went down screaming, ripping open holes in the wind that were filled with the

> broken-china explosion of a house and the
> yawing screech of a pickup rubbed across as-
> phalt, the rivet popping and twang of phone
> and electric wires.
>
> Barry Holstun Lopez, *River Notes*

Classification

When you *classify,* you tell how a specific subject relates
to other subjects that belong to the same group. Country
music, for example, belongs to the group *music,* which includes rock, jazz, blues, rap, folk, gospel, classical, opera,
and other types of music. You classify by defining or by
comparing and contrasting.

When you write a paragraph to classify, you usually
arrange your ideas in *logical order*. Logical order means
that related ideas are grouped together.

Defining. Usually, a *definition* has two parts. First, it
identifies the large group, or general class, that the subject
belongs to. Second, it tells how the subject is different from
all other members that belong to this general class.

Here is a one-sentence definition of tae kwon do. The
general class that the subject, tae kwon do, belongs to is
italicized. Notice how the other details in the sentence tell
how tae kwon do is different from other martial arts.

EXAMPLE   Tae kwon do is an ancient form of *martial art*
from Korea that uses kicks and punches in a hard
style.

Now here's a paragraph that defines tae kwon do. As
you read, think about how the paragraph goes beyond the
one-sentence definition.

> Tae kwon do is a martial art more than 2,000
> years old. An assortment of kicks and punches that
> focus power with deadly effectiveness, it's a so-
> called hard style. Hard style? I ask Master Son.

"Punch, side kick, roundhouse," Son replies. "One kick, fight finished."

Bob Berger, "Road Warrior"

Comparing and Contrasting. When writing about two or more subjects, you may want to compare and contrast them. *Compare* them by explaining how they're alike. *Contrast* them by telling how they're different. In a single paragraph, you'll probably focus on one or the other, not both.

Read this paragraph carefully. See if you can identify the major differences between moths and butterflies as you read.

There are three main differences between butter-flies and moths. Butterflies are out by day while moths usually fly at night, but this is not an infalli-ble guide since some moths fly by day. Second, moths spread their wings sideways at rest whereas butterflies hold them together over their backs, though again there are exceptions. Third, the but-terfly's antennae are long and slender with clubbed ends, whereas a moth's are shorter and feathery.

Gerald Durrell with Lee Durrell,
The Amateur Naturalist

Evaluation

Evaluating is the process of judging something's value, deciding whether something is good or bad. Remember, though, just giving your opinion is not enough. You also have to give reasons, or support, for your opinion.

When you write an evaluation, you'll often give the reasons for your opinion in the ***order of importance***. That is, you'll tell the most important reason first, the second most important reason next, and so on. Or you may decide to reverse the process and tell the least important reason first. Here is the opening paragraph of a review of a recent recording by Tito Puente. Notice the reasons on which the writer bases his evaluation.

> On one recent drizzly day in San Francisco, Tito Puente walked casually into a recording studio to make yet another album of his patented Latin jazz. He also made history. With his latest release, the 68-year-old musician has likely accomplished something none of his peers ever will: his 100th album. Indeed, that landmark is unique in the entire music world. No one else has even come close. And since any recording by "The King of the Mambo" is worth a shelfful by most others—if craftsmanship and style are the criteria—no one ever will. In a day when pop singers fake their way to the top and when for many artists, success is the child of hype, Puente is one of only a handful of musicians who deserve the title "legendary."
>
> Mark Holston, "The One-Man Band of Latin Jazz"

Reason

Reason

Reason

Evaluation

What Makes a Composition?

A composition, like a paragraph, develops a main idea. However, a composition is a longer piece of writing and is made up of a number of paragraphs. These paragraphs give the composition its form or structure: *introduction, body, conclusion.*

You'll use this form in your writing for school to explain a process, to write a persuasive essay, to write about literature, or to write a research report. You'll also use it outside school to write letters, to apply for jobs, and to write business reports.

Peanuts reprinted by permission of UFS, Inc.

The Composition Plan

Writing compositions takes planning. And the more planning you do, the easier your job will be.

The Main Idea Statement

Every composition has a *main idea.* And that's where you begin your planning. For example, after some thought, you've chosen "movies" as the topic of your composition. What point will you make about movies? After brainstorming, you might decide to limit the topic of movies to "what makes a good movie." This would become the main idea of your composition.

NOTE You do not have to use your original main idea. As you study, do research, and think of more details and different ways to discuss your topic, you may decide you want to say something different. Changing your mind is not a problem; change is part of the writing process. Simply rewrite your main idea.

COMPOSITION

Early Plans

An early plan, also called an *informal outline*, is one way of sorting your ideas to make your job of writing easier. You put items into groups and then arrange your groups in order.

Grouping.   After you've listed all the details you can think of on your topic, look them over. Ask yourself: *Which items are the most alike? What do they have in common? Which items don't fit at all?* (You can cross these out.) Follow these steps to group ideas.

- Group items that have something in common with each other.
- Write a heading for each group that shows how the items in it are related.
- Set aside any items that don't seem to fit. You can delete them or fit them in later.

Here's how one writer grouped and labeled items for a composition with the main idea "what makes a good movie."

—STRONG PLOT—
interesting beginning, high interest level
—STRONG CHARACTERS—
real and interesting people, sympathetic to viewers
—SPECIAL FEATURES—
special effects, unusual settings, different time periods, music

Ordering.   You also have to think about how to order, or arrange, your ideas so that they will make sense. What should you tell your readers about first? second? last? How will you arrange your ideas so that they will make sense? Sometimes, the topic itself suggests the order. If you're explaining to readers how to program a VCR, a step-by-step process, you would use *chronological* (time) *order.* For the composition on what makes a good movie (pages 368–370), it made sense to the writer to use *order of importance.* If you were describing an old haunted house, however, you would probably want to use *spatial* (space or location) *order.*

You can use any order that makes sense. With whatever order you use, ask yourself these questions: *Will my readers be able to follow my thoughts easily? Does each group of details make sense from what comes before?*

 REFERENCE NOTE: See page 337 for more information about ordering ideas.

 Sometimes you won't have a clear idea of how a particular arrangement will work until you see a complete rough draft. That's where using a computer comes in handy. With a computer, it's easy to rearrange words, sentences, and even paragraphs to make your composition more effective. You might even want to create two different versions of a composition. Try them out on several readers to see which one gets the better response.

Formal Outlines

A *formal outline* is similar to the early plan except that the outline is more structured. It uses letters and numbers to show the relationships between ideas. A formal outline can help you plan. Often such an outline is written after the composition is complete to provide a summary or a table of contents for the reader.

There are two kinds of formal outlines. A *topic outline* states ideas in words or brief phrases. A *sentence outline* states ideas in complete sentences.

Here is the topic outline that the writer prepared when planning to write the composition on what makes a good movie.

Title: Good Movies: Two Thumbs Up
Main Idea: Good movies share certain qualities that
        make them winners.

I. Plot
  A. Strong beginning
  B. Interesting plot developments

II. Characters
  A. Real and interesting
  B. Sympathetic in some way

III. Special features
  A. Special effects
  B. Interesting or unusual settings
  C. Historical time periods
  D. Music

 REFERENCE NOTE: To learn more about formal outlines, see
pages 384–385.

A COMPOSITION MODEL

Here's a composition on what makes a good movie. After
you read it, look to see how it follows both the early plan
and the formal outline. Also, notice how each paragraph
topic supports the main idea throughout the composition.

Good Movies: Two Thumbs Up

INTRODUCTION   You are slumped in your seat, jumbo-
sized popcorn in your hand. The lights
dim, and you're ready for another escape
into the world of movies. Maybe you'll
find adventure, comedy, romance, or
suspense. But maybe you won't. In fact,
you may enjoy your popcorn more than
you like the movie. What makes the
Main idea   difference? What makes a good movie?

BODY

Main topic:
Plot

Main topic:
Characters

Main topic:
Special features

First of all, a good movie has a strong beginning. It draws you into the action quickly so that you are instantly hooked. <u>Home Alone</u>, for example, begins with this scene: A couple of distracted parents forget to take their eight-year-old son on their trip to Paris. He's home alone trying to protect the house from a couple of burglars. Who could resist this plot?

But a movie has to keep you interested throughout. <u>Home Alone</u> does this with strong plot developments that pit Kevin against the determined burglars. You keep watching to find out who will finally win.

A good movie also has characters who catch your interest or your sympathy. Edward Scissorhands, the main character in the movie of that name, did both. He is interesting because he is so different—a strange-looking, forlorn kid with scissors and knives for hands. But he also seems real because his actions and reactions are believable. When he tries to protect Kim from her bully boyfriend, you understand his actions. And when he runs from the police, you understand that, too. But he also captures your sympathy. He makes you realize what it feels like to be different, not to fit in.

Some characters may not catch your sympathy, but they are still interesting. It's easy to hate the Wicked Witch in <u>The Wizard of Oz</u>. But with her cackling voice, flying monkeys, and evil threats, she makes the movie more fun to watch.

Finally, a really good movie has special features. It has something extra

COMPOSITION

that sets it apart from other movies. One of these extras might be great special effects. For example, in <u>Honey, I Shrunk the Kids</u>, the special effects make you experience what it's like to be the size of an ant. Another special feature might be the setting. In <u>Dances with Wolves</u>, for example, it is easy to imagine living on the frontier or in an Indian village. The beautiful, unusual setting makes a good story even better.

A historical setting, especially one based on actual events, can also make a good movie. <u>Glory</u> tells the true story of the first black company to fight for the Union army. This gives the plot a special edge. You just cannot help thinking that these were once real soldiers facing real bullets.

Finally, music is another special feature that can improve a movie. Think of <u>The Sound of Music</u> without its songs. It wouldn't be nearly as interesting.

CONCLUSION By the time the lights come up in the theater, you know which was better—the popcorn or the movie. If you're lucky, the movie won out. But if you're not, there are always new movies to see. Maybe the next one will get it right—both the popcorn and the movie will be two thumbs up!

The Parts of the Composition

You have a topic, a main idea, and an early plan or outline. Now you need to think about the three parts of a composition: the introduction, the body, and the conclusion.

COMPOSITION

The Introduction

With their introductions, compositions make first impressions on their readers. A lively introduction hooks its readers and makes them eager to read more. A dull introduction runs the risk of boring its readers, who might stop reading.

Capturing the Reader's Interest. In the composition on good movies, the writer could have written the following introduction.

> Some movies are fun to watch. Some aren't.
> But good movies do have things in common.

Does this introduction make a good impression? You'd probably agree that it doesn't. It does do one thing—it tells what the composition is about. But it's so boring that many people might not read any further.

Now, take another look at the introduction in the model on page 368. The writer begins by describing a scene familiar to most moviegoers. The writer then encourages the reader to think: What *does* make a good movie?

Presenting the Main Idea. You'll usually want to include your main idea statement in your introduction. This keeps both you and your readers on track. Do you see how the writer stated the main idea in the last sentence of the introduction on page 368? Even though it's a question, there's no doubt what this composition is about.

Ways to Write Introductions

Writers use a variety of techniques to grab their readers' attention with interesting introductions. Here are three.

1. **Ask a question.** The writer of the composition on good movies ends the introduction by asking a question: *What makes a good movie?* This beginning quickly gets

the reader's attention and involves the reader in the paper. Most people would want to read more.

2. **Tell an anecdote.** An *anecdote* is a short, interesting story. Since most people like a good story, an anecdote is a good way to begin your composition. Notice how the following introduction uses an anecdote from Antonia Novello's childhood to introduce her.

> As a little girl in Puerto Rico, Antonia Novello dreamed of becoming "a pediatrician—a doctor for the little kids in my hometown." Last year, this smart, funny, 46-year-old pediatrician became a doctor for all Americans when she was sworn in at the White House as the nation's first Hispanic and also first female surgeon general.
>
> Carol Krucoff, "Antonia Novello:
A Dream Come True"

3. **State an intriguing or startling fact.** A surprising or unusual fact can get your readers' attention right away. The fact can be eye-opening or it can even shock readers. Either way, readers are curious. They can't wait to read on.

> First, an amazing, astonishing, *totally rad* fact: American teen-agers spent a whopping $49.8 billion in 1985.
>
> David Holmstrom,
"What Makes Johnny Spend?"

The Body

The body of a composition develops the main idea with paragraphs. Each paragraph supports or proves a main point by developing it with supporting ideas.

 REFERENCE NOTE: See pages 358–364 for information on strategies of paragraph development.

Maybe you've read compositions that ramble on and on or seem disjointed. These compositions are missing unity and coherence.

> **NOTE** Like any long form of writing, compositions are made up of paragraphs. And each paragraph can be made up of several sentences or even just one sentence. What's most important is how each paragraph, no matter how long or how short, helps the writer to support the main idea of the whole composition.

Unity. You know you have *unity* in your composition when all your body paragraphs develop a point about the main idea of your introduction. Look at the model composition on pages 368–370. Do you see how each paragraph has its own main idea (topic)? In every case, the paragraph topic relates to or supports the main idea of the whole composition.

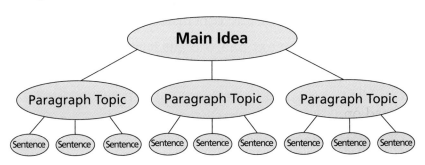

Coherence. The ideas in your paragraphs should be easy to follow. When they are, your paragraphs have *coherence.* Every sentence leads easily to another. Every paragraph leads to the next.

How can you work on coherence? First, arrange your ideas in an order the reader will understand. Then, make it easy for the reader to see how your ideas are connected.

You can make it easy for readers by using transitional words and phrases, such as *next, first, however, in addition to,* and *finally.* They help readers connect the ideas in your composition.

REFERENCE NOTE: See pages 357–358 for more information on and examples of transitional words and phrases.

The Conclusion

When a composition ends suddenly, readers can feel dissatisfied, let down. Your goal when writing the conclusion is to let your readers know that your composition has come to an end. Here are some ways you can do this.

Ways to Write Conclusions

1. **Refer to your introduction.** A favorite technique used by writers is to refer to something in the introduction. This method is the one the writer of "Good Movies: Two Thumbs Up" (page 368) used. The introduction describes a scene at the movie theater. The conclusion comes back to that scene. The last line also ties the title, introduction, and conclusion together.

   > Maybe the next one will get it right—both the popcorn and the movie will be two thumbs up!

   This statement has a finality to it. It lets the reader know that the paper has come to an end.

2. **Restate the main idea.** One of the most direct ways to end a composition is to restate your main idea in different words. In the following example, the writer uses different words to describe the importance of one artist's drawings.

   > However, Käthe Kollwitz did what few other artists have done—and especially artists who portray children. She would not let us forget the children of the poor and miserable, or the very old, or the overworked mothers struggling for their children. *Their* lives are important, too, she told us in her pictures.
   >
   > Elsa Marston, "Pictures of the Poor"

3. Close with a final idea. Leaving the reader with one last thought can pull your composition together. Here, a teenage writer explains some of the devastating effects of Hurricane Hugo and points to some hope in the crisis.

> Yesterday I saw another T-shirt. This one read: HUGO 1 CHARLESTON 0. I thought to myself how wrong that was. The people here have all worked together to rise above defeat. Right now it's HUGO 1, CHARLESTON 1. And gaining.
>
> Jennifer Cohen, "Disaster Hits Home"

Looking at the Whole

Words, sentences, and paragraphs are like players on a team or musicians in a band. All three are important parts of a composition because they help make up the whole. All are team players. Pay close attention to your composition at all three levels—words, sentences, and paragraphs—and you will write a winning composition.

19 THE RESEARCH REPORT

Research reports play an important role in all of our lives. Magazines and news programs often feature reports on products that are dangerous or poorly made. Politicians and people in business make decisions based partly on information that they find in reports.

Research reports can be developed in different ways. But what they all have in common is that they

- give information about a subject
- use print and nonprint sources
- provide lists of sources for the information

 *Prewriting*

Getting Started

Choosing Your Subject

What do you wonder about? What's important to you? What have you read or seen lately that you'd like to know more about? Answering these questions can help you decide on a subject for a report.

Here are some broad subjects. Think of others that interest you.

snakes	Cuba	space labs
hairstyles	animals	holiday customs
robots	games	lasers

Narrowing Your Subject

You can find information on almost any subject in books and magazine articles, on videotapes, and on TV. In fact, you'll find far too much information for a short report. You can narrow your subject by focusing on just one part of it.

NOTE You may need to narrow your subject more than once, depending on the length of your report and how much information is available.

Here's how the subjects you've just read about can be narrowed.

rattlesnakes	Havana	space labs in
men's hairstyles	greyhounds	the year 2000
of the past fifty	the origins of	Cinco de Mayo
years	lacrosse	lasers for
robots for the home		dentistry

Remember that each subject contains many topics. For example, here's a cluster of the subject "holidays."

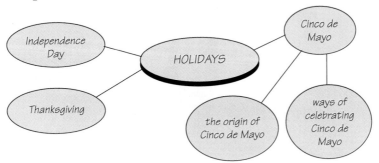

COMPOSITION

Before deciding on a topic, ask yourself these questions:

1. Can I find enough facts about this topic? Where?
2. Is my topic too broad for a short report? (Or is the topic too narrow? If the topic is too narrow, it will be difficult to find enough information.)
3. Do I have time to get the information I need? (If you have to send away for information, how long will it take to get it?)
4. Is the topic interesting enough to hold my attention? (You'll be more willing to put extra time and effort into a topic you like.)

NOTE A well-written report can't be done in just a day or two. Think about the time you have, and make out a schedule that will give you time to do the following six things. Then stick to your schedule.

1. Find information about your topic.
2. Take notes about the information.
3. Organize your information.
4. Write a first draft.
5. Evaluate and revise your first draft.
6. Proofread and publish your report.

Shoe, by Jeff MacNelly, reprinted by permission: Tribune Media Services.

COMPOSITION

Planning Your Report

Thinking About Audience and Purpose

Why are you writing a report? The main *purpose* of a report is to give information. The information consists mostly of facts and the opinions of experts.

Who is your audience? Probably your first *audience* will be your teacher and classmates, but reports might be for different audiences. Ask yourself these questions about your audience:

- What does my audience already know about my topic?
- What does my audience need to know about my topic?
- What new or unusual information will interest my audience? What will surprise them?

Don't bore your readers by telling them what they already know. But don't confuse them by not telling enough, either. If you use a word they may not know, define it. If they need to know how something works, explain it.

Making an Early Plan

Before you begin your research, make an *early plan* for your report by listing the main ideas that you want to cover. An **early plan,** sometimes called an *informal outline,* is a list of headings that will guide your research. Here is a writer's early plan for a report on men's hairstyles.

HERE'S
HOW

Report topic: men's hairstyles of the past fifty years

when hairstyles have changed the most

what these hairstyles were like

people who influenced the hairstyles

what the hairstyles have meant

REFERENCE NOTE: For more information about early plans, see pages 366–367.

Asking Questions

What do you want to know about your topic? What does your audience need to know? Ask yourself questions that will help you find the information needed to fill out your early plan. The questions will help guide your research and keep you focused on your topic.

You can start with the *5W-How?* questions: *Who? What? When? Where? Why? How?* These questions will often make you think of other questions you can ask. For the report on "men's hairstyles of the past fifty years," the writer began research with the following questions:

Who has influenced hairstyles?
What have been some of the most popular hairstyles?
What have different hairstyles meant to men?
When have hairstyles changed the most?
Where do styles change first?
Why do styles change?
How are men wearing their hair now?

 If you don't know much about your topic, you may want to do some general reading first. Then you will be better prepared to make your early plan and ask questions. Encyclopedia articles, magazines, or videotapes can give you a good overview of your topic. You might also talk to people who know about the topic.

Finding Sources

You'll probably need at least three sources of information for your report. Begin your search in the library, where you'll find print sources (encyclopedias, books, magazines, newspapers, booklets, pamphlets) and nonprint sources (videotapes, audiotapes, slides).

Videotapes on many historical and scientific topics are available in libraries and bookstores. Depending on your topic, you can ask about available information at museums, supermarkets, zoos, hospitals or clinics, colleges, or government offices. You can also check radio and TV guides for programs related to your topic.

Interviewing. An interview is a good nonprint source. If you know of an expert on your topic, arrange to talk with him or her. The expert could be a teacher, a parent, a businessperson, an artist, a zookeeper, or even another student. An expert is just someone who knows a great deal about your topic.

Evaluating Sources

When you're researching a topic, it's important to evaluate the sources of information. Not all your sources will be equally useful. Here are some questions that will help you evaluate, or judge, the usefulness of a source.

1. **Is the source nonfiction?** You're looking for facts, so don't use print or nonprint sources that are fiction, such as stories and novels. Also, steer away from television docudramas.
2. **Can you trust your sources?** Don't believe everything you read. Usually, reference books, textbooks, books written by experts, and respected magazines and newspapers are reliable. Newspapers and magazines that tell about sensational and strange happenings aren't. Evaluate TV and radio programs and videotapes in the same way. Use only those that actually present facts about your topic.
3. **Is the information current?** Some topics, such as modern science, technology, and medicine, need the latest available information. However, if your topic is "the origin of hot-air balloons," your information doesn't need to be as up-to-date. You can find the publication date on the copyright page of a book or magazine.

4. Is the information objective? Sometimes information is biased. That is, only one side of a topic is presented, and you don't get a balanced view.

Listing Sources

To keep track of the sources you find, make out *source cards* on index cards or half-sheets of notebook paper. Write the name of each source on a separate card and give it a *source number*. Write the source number in the upper right corner of the card. Source cards save you time when you take notes, and you'll use the information on them at the end of your report.

There are several ways to list sources. The following method is recommended by the Modern Language Association (MLA). You should use whatever form your teacher recommends. No matter what form you use, follow the capitalization, punctuation, and order of information exactly for each item on your source list.

MLA GUIDE FOR LISTING SOURCES
1. Books: author, title, city of publication, publisher, and copyright year. Nunn, Joan. <u>Fashion in Costume, 1200–1980</u>.   New York: Schocken, 1984.
2. Magazines and Newspapers: author, title of article, name of magazine or newspaper, date, and page numbers. If there is no author, begin with the title.

(continued)

COMPOSITION

MLA GUIDE FOR LISTING SOURCES *(continued)*

Orlean, Susan. "The Always-in-Fashion Ponytail." <u>Vogue</u>
Feb. 1990: 160–66.

---

3. **Encyclopedia Articles:** author, title of article, name of encyclopedia, year and edition (ed.). If there is no author, begin
with the title.
Sassoon, Vidal. "Hairdressing." <u>The World Book
Encyclopedia</u>. 1990 ed.

---

4. **Interviews:** expert's name, the words *Personal interview* or
Telephone interview, and date.
Tavares, Cosme. Personal interview. 15 Feb. 1991.

---

5. **Films and Videotapes:** director's or producer's name, title of
film or tape, studio name, year of release.
Sanders, Denis, dir. <u>Elvis: That's the Way It Is</u>. MGM,
1970.

1

Nunn, Joan. <u>*Fashion in Costume, 1200–1980.*</u>
New York: Schocken, 1984.

Taking Notes

Let your early plan and questions about your topic guide
you as you take notes. Scan through your sources for information that relates to your headings and your questions. Don't be afraid to add new, interesting information
you find, but add headings to your early plan that include

these new ideas. These tips can help you take efficient notes:

- Use a separate 4 x 6-inch note card or sheet of paper for each source and for each note.
- Use abbreviations and short phrases. You can also make lists of ideas. You don't need to write complete sentences.
- Use your own words. If you copy someone's exact words, put quotation marks around the words. (Not doing so is called *plagiarism.* It is dishonest.)
- Label each card by writing at the top a key word or phrase that tells what the card is about. These words and phrases can come from your early plan.
- Put the source number at the top of each card.
- At the bottom of each card, write the number of the page where you found the information.
- Take notes from each of your sources.

Look at the following example of a note taken from *Fashion in Costume, 1200–1980* by Joan Nunn.

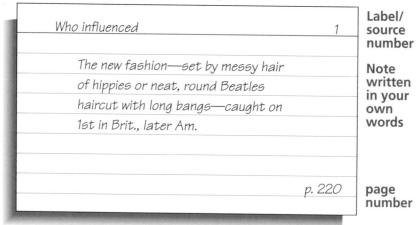

Label/source number

Who influenced   1

The new fashion—set by messy hair
of hippies or neat, round Beatles
haircut with long bangs—caught on
1st in Brit., later Am.

Note written in your own words

p. 220

page number

Organizing and Outlining Your Information

Now that you have most of your information, you need to organize it. You may make some changes as you write and

COMPOSITION

revise, but the outline you make now will be a useful guide. Here are some steps you can take to organize your information.

1. Separate your note cards into stacks with the same or similar labels.
2. Think of a heading to identify each stack. It should be similar to the labels you used on your cards.
3. Decide on the order of your main headings—perhaps order of importance or chronological (time) order.
4. Sort the cards in each stack to make subheadings for your outline.
5. Create an outline from your main headings and sub-headings.

 REFERENCE NOTE: For more information on formal outlines, see pages 367–368.

The following is an example of a formal outline. After you've finished writing and revising, you can create one like this and include it with your paper.

From Crew Cut to Flattop

I. Changes in the forties and fifties
   A. Forties: crew cuts
   B. Fifties: ducktails
     1. Influence of Tony Curtis
     2. Influence of Elvis Presley
II. Changes in the sixties and seventies
   A. Sixties: long hair
     1. Influence of the Beatles
     2. Influence of African ancestry
   B. Seventies: group identification
     1. Shaved heads
     2. Mohawks: now and long ago
III. Changes in the eighties and today
   A. Eighties: outrageous statements
   B. Today: easy care and personal style

Writing a First Draft

Understanding the Parts of a Report

Introduction. The *introduction* of a report is a short beginning paragraph that grabs your reader's attention. It tells in an interesting way what your report is about. In the model report on pages 387–390, the writer uses facts about what people do to their hair, followed by a surprising statement, to catch the reader's interest. The reader can tell what the main idea of the report is from this statement.

Body. The *body* of the report is where the information from your note cards goes. Each of the main headings from your outline can be discussed in one or more paragraphs. Some of your subtopics may also need separate paragraphs. Or, you may combine some subtopics in a single paragraph. Just be sure each paragraph tells enough to make its main idea clear.

Conclusion. The *conclusion* of a report sums up your main points in an interesting way. Your conclusion may be short, but it should give a finished feeling to your paper. Notice that the model report ends with a question, yet it lets readers know that they've reached the end.

Works Cited Page. A *Works Cited page* lists all of the print and nonprint sources you used in your report. If your readers want to know more about your topic, they can refer to this list. Here's how to make your Works Cited page.

1. Make a new page with the heading *Works Cited*.
2. List your sources in alphabetical order by the author's last name. (When there is no author, alphabetize by the first word of the title.)
3. Use the same style you used on your source cards. You

can use the sample *Works Cited* list on page 390 as a model for writing your own list of sources.

Writing Your Report

Except for direct quotations, write your report in your own words. Although your outline helps to guide you, you don't have to follow it exactly. As you're writing, you may decide it would be better to rearrange the order of the ideas. You may even decide to add something new or not to use some of the information. Keep referring to your notes, and go back to your sources if you need more information. You can use the following sample report as a model.

STYLE NOTE   A long report is not necessarily a good report. A short report is not necessarily a bad report. The acceptable length of any piece of writing depends upon two things: (1) what you want your report to do and (2) what your limits are. A five-hundred-page book and a two-paragraph newspaper article on the same topic can both be good writing.

As you write a first draft, try not to worry about length. Writing a good report is the most important thing. You can always go back and cut or add ideas and information to meet the length requirements of your assignment.

A MODEL REPORT

From Crew Cut to Flattop

INTRODUCTION   Since the beginning of history, men
Interest grabber   and women have cut, dyed, braided,

Main idea

curled, and straightened their hair. However, in the past fifty years, men's hairstyles have changed even more than women's. Hair has become one way that men show who they are and what they stand for.

BODY
Changes in
1940s and 1950s

For many years before 1940, most men wore a standard hairstyle. It was parted on the left and tapered at the back. With the outbreak of the Second World War, U.S. Army and Navy men adopted the crew cut. It was a short-all-over style that was easy to keep clean. During the early fifties, the crew cut became the "in" fashion on college campuses. Whether men knew it or not, their crew cuts announced that they were clean cut, athletic, and patriotic.

Influence of
Tony Curtis

Crew-cut wearers laughed at men brave enough to try a new style, the ducktail, but many eventually wore it. The film star Tony Curtis was one of the first to comb and oil his curly hair to a flipped-up point at the back. A ducktail suggested that its wearer was romantic, healthy (so much hair!), and carefree.

Influence of
Elvis Presley

Elvis Presley copied the Tony Curtis look and took it to new heights. Elvis's own hair was mousy brown, but he dyed it blue-black. Then he teased it into a high wave in front and used gel and spray to make it look as lush as possible on top. Elvis attracted attention by combing and stroking his long woolly sideburns onstage.

Changes in
1960s

The true revolution in hairstyles began in the sixties with the Beatles.

COMPOSITION

Influence of the Beatles

Their haircut, the "moptop," was cut in a bowl shape, with bangs over the eyebrows. The moptop looked completely different from other styles because it was so natural and childlike. Many American men quickly copied the Beatles. It was the first time they had let their hair grow long and natural since the 1780s.

Influence of African ancestry

In the late sixties, a hairstyle became a symbol of racial pride and the civil rights movement. To emphasize their African ancestry and distinctive culture, African American men and women let their hair grow out in an "Afro." It was a round, naturally curly hairstyle.

Changes in 1970s

In the seventies, men's hairstyles continued to identify the group they belonged to. Men who wanted to look responsible returned to shorter hairstyles. To show their scorn of

Shaved heads

longhaired "idealists," some men shaved off all their hair.

Mohawks

The seventies saw the rebirth of spiked hair. Some versions of this were called "Mohawks," but they were more like styles worn long ago by the Huron, Osage, and Omaha nations. As a way of daring their enemies to scalp them, some Native Americans would arrange their hair in a row of long spikes. They used bear grease to stiffen the spikes and shaved the rest of their heads to emphasize the frightening effect.

Changes in 1980s

In the eighties and early nineties, trendsetters wanted to look different from everyone else. They thought the more outrageous the better. One unisex style, called the "buzz" or "flattop," had closely cut or shaved sides like a Mohawk. However, the top hair of a flattop was clipped into a geometric shape and stood up straight—like Bart Simpson's hair. Neon colors emphasized the effect.

Styles today

Men's hairstylist Cosme Tavares says that many men today want a haircut that's easy to care for. He says most of his customers usually ask for something **Direct** "short and flat at the sides, showing just **quotation** a little personal style on top, in front, or at the back."

CONCLUSION As you have seen, the way modern **Summary of** men wear their hair can have political, **main ideas** social, and personal meanings. The journey from the crew cut to the flattop has taken fifty years. As the journey continues, what new hairstyles will men wear to show who they are and what they stand for?

Works Cited

Corson, Richard. Fashions in Hair: The First Five Thousand Years. London: Owen, 1971.

Flinker, Susan. Hip Hair. New York: Dell, 1985.

Jones, Dylan. Haircults. London: Thames and Hudson, 1990.

Sanders, Denis, dir. Elvis: That's the Way It Is. MGM, 1970.

Tavares, Cosme. Personal interview. 15 Feb. 1991.

Evaluating and Revising

Evaluating a report means determining its strengths and weaknesses. Revising a report means making changes to improve it. Every piece of writing can benefit from evaluation and revision. After you write the first draft of your report, set it aside. Getting some distance from your work will help you think about it objectively. After a day or two, use the chart on the next page to help you evaluate and revise your writing. Begin by asking yourself the questions in the left-hand column. These questions will help you evaluate your paper. If your answer to any question in the evaluation column is *no*, use the revision technique suggested in the right-hand column to correct the problem.

Here are the changes the writer made in one paragraph while revising "From Crew Cut to Flattop." Look at the changes carefully. Refer to the **Symbols for Revising and Proofreading** chart on page 350 if you don't understand what a particular mark means.

In the eighties and early nineties, trendsetters wanted to look different from everyone else. They thought the
more outrageous
~~funnier~~ the better. Neon colors   **replace/reorder**
emphasized the effect. One unisex style,
called the "buzz" or "flattop," had closely
cut or shaved sides like a Mohawk. ~~It's~~
~~my favorite style.~~ However, the top hair   **cut**
of a flattop was clipped into a geometric
                        --like Bart Simpson's hair. **add**
shape and stood up straight.

EVALUATING AND REVISING REPORTS

EVALUATION GUIDE	REVISION TECHNIQUE
1 Does the report use several different sources?	**Add** sources. Try to find and use at least one nonprint source.
2 Does the report consist of facts and the opinions of experts?	**Add** facts or an expert's opinion. **Cut** your own thoughts and feelings.
3 Is the report in the writer's own words? If someone else's words are used, are they in quotation marks?	**Replace** with your own words, or **add** quotation marks where you've used someone's actual words.
4 Is the information well organized?	**Reorder** sentences or paragraphs in order of importance or chronological order.
5 Is the introduction interesting? Does it tell what the report is about?	**Add** attention-getting details. **Add** a sentence that tells the main idea.
6 Does the conclusion bring the report to a close?	**Add** a sentence that summarizes the main idea.
7 Is the list of sources on a separate sheet at the end of the report? Is the form correct?	**Add** the list of sources, and make sure the sources are presented in the correct form.

Proofreading and Publishing

Proofreading is reading carefully for mistakes in spelling, capitalization, usage, and punctuation and then correcting them. *Publishing* is sharing your report with others. Here are two ideas for publishing.

- Staple your report or put it in a binder. Offer it to the school librarian as a resource on your topic.
- Give an oral report based on your written report to a class that might be interested in your topic.

COMPUTER NOTE　If you use a computer when you write, you're probably already aware of how handy it can be when you need to revise and proofread your papers. But have you thought about how a computer can also help your writing look better? Most word processors and printers allow you to adjust the size and style of printed letters to create an interesting look. A centering feature allows you to center headings on a page. With some software programs, you can create attractive charts, graphs, and tables with very little effort. Use any of these techniques or a combination of them to publish a professional-looking report.

PART SIX

RESOURCES

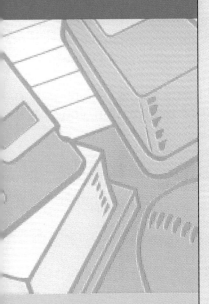

RESOURCES

Getting to Know the Library; Using Dictionaries; Preparing Letters, Forms, and Manuscripts

The Library/Media Center

The best place to look for information is the library or media center. To make the most of a library's resources, you must know what information the library contains and understand how that information is arranged and classified.

The information in a library takes many forms. The resource you use depends on the type of information you need.

BOOKS	
Fiction	Stories (novels and short stories)
Nonfiction	Factual information about real people, events, and things; essays; includes biographies and "how-to" books
Reference books	General information about many subjects

OTHER PRINTED MATERIALS	
Magazines and newspapers	Current events, commentaries, and important discoveries
Pamphlets	Brief summaries of facts about specific subjects
Audiotapes, CDs, records, films, filmstrips, slides, videotapes	Stories (narrated, illustrated, or acted out), music, instructions and educational material, facts and information about many specific subjects
Computers	Information stored electronically, allowing for easy access and frequent updates
Maps, globes, atlases, and almanacs	Geographical information, facts, dates, and statistics

The Arrangement of a Library

Libraries give a number and letter code—a *call number*—to each book. The call number tells you how the book has been classified and where to find it in the library. Most school libraries use the *Dewey decimal system* to classify and arrange nonfiction books by their subjects.

DEWEY CLASSIFICATION OF NONFICTION		
NUMBERS	SUBJECT AREAS	EXAMPLES OF SUBDIVISIONS
000–099	General Works	encyclopedias, handbooks
100–199	Philosophy	psychology, ethics, personality
200–299	Religion	bibles, mythology, theology
300–399	Social Sciences	government, law, economics
400–499	Languages	dictionaries, grammars
500–599	Science	general science, mathematics
600–699	Technology	engineering, business
700–799	The Arts	music, theater, painting, recreation
800–899	Literature	poetry, drama, essays
900–999	History	biography, geography, travel

Biographies are often placed in a separate section of the library. They are arranged in alphabetical order according to the last name of the person the book is about. If there are several books about the same person, the biographies are then arranged according to the last names of the authors.

Dewey Decimal Arrangement of Fiction

In most libraries, books of fiction are located in one specific section. The books are arranged alphabetically by the authors' last names. Books by the same author are arranged alphabetically by the first word of their titles (not counting *A, An,* or *The*). Some libraries group collections of short stories separately from other works of fiction. Many libraries also group certain kinds of fiction, such as mysteries or westerns, into separate sections.

The Card Catalog

You can find the call number of any book in the library by looking in the *card catalog*. The **card catalog** is a cabinet of small drawers containing cards. These cards list books by title, author, and subject. Fiction books have at least two cards—a *title card* and an *author card*. If the book is nonfiction, there is a third card—a *subject card*. Occasionally, you may find "*see*" or "*see also*" cards. These are cross-reference cards. They direct you to another section of the card catalog where more information on a subject may be found. For example, if you were to look in the card catalog for books by author Samuel Clemens, you would most likely find a card that said "See also Mark Twain." You would have to look up *Twain,* Clemens's pen name, to find books by him.

An **on-line catalog** is a computerized version of the card catalog. It contains the same information as title, author, subject, and "see also" cards. Many libraries are switching over from card catalogs to the on-line catalog because the computerized version saves space and is more efficient than the cards.

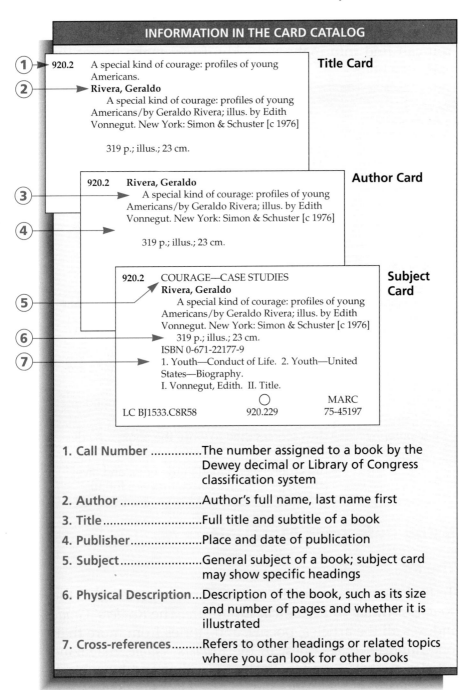

INFORMATION IN THE CARD CATALOG

(1) 920.2   A special kind of courage: profiles of young   **Title Card**
            Americans.
(2)   **Rivera, Geraldo**
            A special kind of courage: profiles of young
            Americans/by Geraldo Rivera; illus. by Edith
            Vonnegut. New York: Simon & Schuster [c 1976]

            319 p.; illus.; 23 cm.

            920.2   **Rivera, Geraldo**   **Author Card**
                A special kind of courage: profiles of young
(3)   Americans/by Geraldo Rivera; illus. by Edith
                Vonnegut. New York: Simon & Schuster [c 1976]

(4)   319 p.; illus.; 23 cm.

            920.2   COURAGE—CASE STUDIES   **Subject**
                Rivera, Geraldo   **Card**
(5)   A special kind of courage: profiles of young
                Americans/by Geraldo Rivera; illus. by Edith
                Vonnegut. New York: Simon & Schuster [c 1976]
(6)   319 p.; illus.; 23 cm.
                ISBN 0-671-22177-9
(7)   1. Youth—Conduct of Life. 2. Youth—United
                States—Biography.
                I. Vonnegut, Edith. II. Title.
                            ◯   MARC
            LC BJ1533.C8R58   920.229   75-45197

RESOURCES

1. **Call Number** ....The number assigned to a book by the
                    Dewey decimal or Library of Congress
                    classification system

2. **Author** ....Author's full name, last name first

3. **Title**.............................Full title and subtitle of a book

4. **Publisher**.....................Place and date of publication

5. **Subject**.........................General subject of a book; subject card
                    may show specific headings

6. **Physical Description**...Description of the book, such as its size
                    and number of pages and whether it is
                    illustrated

7. **Cross-references**.........Refers to other headings or related topics
                    where you can look for other books

Parts of a Book

You can find information quickly if you make use of the parts of a book.

INFORMATION FOUND IN PARTS OF A BOOK	
PART	**INFORMATION**
Jacket	contains descriptions or summaries of the book and biographical information about the author
Title page	gives full title, author, publisher, and place of publication
Copyright page	gives date of first publication and of any revisions
Table of contents	lists titles of chapters or sections of the book and their starting page numbers
List of illustrations	lists pictures, charts, maps, and diagrams that can be found in the book and gives their page numbers
Appendix	provides additional information about subjects found in the book; maps and charts are sometimes found here
Glossary	defines difficult or technical words found in the book
Bibliography	lists sources used to write the book; provides titles that concern related topics
Index	lists topics mentioned in the book and gives the page or pages where they are found

Using Reference Materials

The *Readers' Guide*

To find a magazine article, use a reference book called the **Readers' Guide to Periodical Literature.** The *Readers' Guide* indexes all the articles, poems, and stories from more than one hundred magazines. In the *Readers' Guide*, magazine articles are listed alphabetically by author and by subject. These headings are printed in boldfaced capital letters.

Entries may contain abbreviations. Use the key at the front of the *Readers' Guide* to find the meanings of these abbreviations.

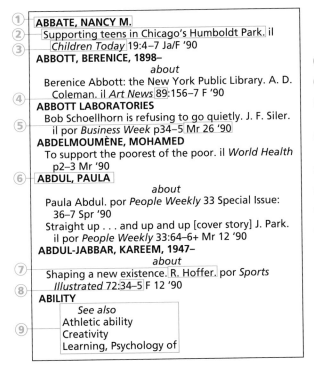

① **ABBATE, NANCY M.**
② Supporting teens in Chicago's Humboldt Park. il
③ *Children Today* 19:4–7 Ja/F '90
ABBOTT, BERENICE, 1898–
about
Berenice Abbott: the New York Public Library. A. D.
④ Coleman. il *Art News* 89:156–7 F '90
ABBOTT LABORATORIES
⑤ Bob Schoellhorn is refusing to go quietly. J. F. Siler.
il por *Business Week* p34–5 Mr 26 '90
ABDELMOUMÈNE, MOHAMED
To support the poorest of the poor. il *World Health*
p2–3 Mr '90
⑥ **ABDUL, PAULA**
about
Paula Abdul. por *People Weekly* 33 Special Issue:
36–7 Spr '90
Straight up . . . and up and up [cover story] J. Park.
il por *People Weekly* 33:64–6+ Mr 12 '90
ABDUL-JABBAR, KAREEM, 1947–
about
⑦ Shaping a new existence. R. Hoffer. por *Sports*
⑧ *Illustrated* 72:34–5 F 12 '90
ABILITY
See also
Athletic ability
⑨ Creativity
Learning, Psychology of

① **Author entry**

② **Title of article**

③ **Name of magazine**

④ **Volume number of magazine**

⑤ **Date of magazine**

⑥ **Subject entry**

⑦ **Author of article**

⑧ **Page Reference**

⑨ **Subject cross-reference**

Special Information Sources

The *vertical file* is a special collection that contains up-to-date materials such as pamphlets, newspaper clippings, government publications, catalogs, and business and educational information.

Microforms are reduced-size photographs of pages from publications. The two most common kinds of microforms are *microfilm* (a roll or reel of film) and *microfiche* (a sheet of film). A special projector enlarges the images to a readable size.

Libraries can also store reference sources (and other information) on a computer in a *database* for easy retrieval.

RESOURCES

RESOURCES

COMMON REFERENCE WORKS	
EXAMPLES	**GENERAL DESCRIPTION**
ENCYCLOPEDIAS *Collier's Encyclopedia* *Compton's Encyclopedia* *The World Book Encyclopedia* *The Encyclopaedia Britannica*	■ multiple volumes ■ articles arranged alphabetically by subject ■ contains general information ■ may have index or annuals
GENERAL BIOGRAPHICAL REFERENCES *Current Biography Yearbook* *Dictionary of American Biography* *The International Who's Who* *Webster's New Biographical Dictionary* *Who's Who in America*	■ information about birth, nationality, and major accomplishments of outstanding people
SPECIAL BIOGRAPHICAL REFERENCES *American Men & Women of Science* *Biographical Dictionary of American Sports* *Mexican American Biographies*	■ information about people noted for accomplishments in various fields or for membership in specific groups
ATLASES *Atlas of World Cultures* *National Geographic Atlas of the World* *Goode's World Atlas*	■ maps and geographical information
ALMANACS *The Information Please Almanac, Atlas and Yearbook* *The World Almanac and Book of Facts*	■ up-to-date information about current events, facts, statistics, and dates
BOOKS OF QUOTATIONS Bartlett's *Familiar Quotations* Flesch's *The New Book of Unusual Quotations* *The Oxford Dictionary of Quotations*	■ famous quotations indexed or grouped by subject

(continued)

COMMON REFERENCE WORKS *(continued)*	
EXAMPLES	**GENERAL DESCRIPTION**
BOOKS OF SYNONYMS *Roget's International Thesaurus Webster's New Dictionary of Synonyms The New Roget's Thesaurus in Dictionary Form*	▪ lists of more vivid or more exact words to express ideas
REFERENCES TO LITERATURE *Granger's Index to Poetry The Oxford Companion to American Literature Short Story Index Subject Index to Poetry Book Review Digest*	▪ information about various works of literature

Newspapers

A daily newspaper has a variety of reading materials in its various sections. The following chart shows contents that you may find in a typical newspaper. The chart also gives you some tips on how to read the different sections.

WHAT'S IN A NEWSPAPER?		
AIMS OF WRITING EXAMPLES	**READER'S PURPOSE**	**READING TECHNIQUE**
to inform news stories sports	to gain knowledge or information	Ask yourself the *5W-How?* questions (see page 334).
to persuade editorials comics reviews ads	to gain knowledge, to make decisions, or to be entertained	Identify points you agree or disagree with. Find facts or reasons the writer uses.
to create or *to express* comics featured columns	to be entertained	Identify ways the writer interests you or gives you a new viewpoint or ideas.

The Dictionary

Types of Dictionaries of the English Language

There are many types of dictionaries. Each type contains different kinds of information. However, all dictionaries contain certain general features. An *abridged* dictionary is a shortened version of an *unabridged* dictionary. The unabridged version attempts to cover the entire English language. The abridged version covers the words that are more commonly or regularly used.

TYPES OF DICTIONARIES		
TYPE AND EXAMPLE	**NUMBER OF WORDS**	**NUMBER OF PAGES**
Unabridged *Webster's Third New International Dictionary*	460,000	2,662
College or Abridged *Merriam-Webster's Collegiate Dictionary:* Tenth Edition	160,000	1,559
School *The Lincoln Writing Dictionary*	35,000	932
Paperback *The Random House Dictionary*	74,000	1,056

Arrangement of a Dictionary

The words listed in a dictionary are called *entries*. Entries are listed in alphabetical order. To help you follow this order, each page of entries has a pair of *guide words* at the top. The first guide word tells you what the first entry on the page is. The second guide word tells you what the last entry on the page is. Each entry usually includes the information shown on pages 405 and 406.

Contents of a Dictionary Entry

large (lärj) *adj.* **larg'er, larg'est** [OFr < L *largus*: see LARD] **1** [Archaic] liberal; generous **2** big; great; specif., *a*) taking up much space; bulky *b*) enclosing much space; spacious *[a large office] c*) of great extent or amount *[a large sum]* **3** big as compared with others of its kind; of more than usual or average size, extent, or amount **4** comprehensive; far-reaching *[to have large views on a subject]* **5** pompous or exaggerated *[large talk]* **6** operating on a big scale *[a large manufacturer]* **7** *Naut.* favorable; specif., quartering: said of a wind **—***adv.* **1** in a large way; so as to be large *[to write large]* **2** *Naut.* with a favoring wind, specif. one on the quarter **—***n.* liberty: now only in the phrase AT LARGE (see phrase below) **—at large 1** free; not confined; not in jail **2** fully; in complete detail **3** in general; taken altogether ☆**4** representing an entire State or other district rather than only one of its subdivisions *[a congressman at large]* **— large'ness** *n.*

SYN.—large, big, and **great** are often interchangeable in meaning of more than usual size, extent, etc. *[a large, big, or great oak]*, but in strict discrimination, **large** is used with reference to dimensions or quantity *[a large studio, amount, etc.]*, **big,** to bulk, weight, or extent *[a big baby, big business]*, and **great,** to size or extent that is impressive, imposing, surprising, etc. *[a great river, success, etc.]* **—ANT. small, little**

From *Webster's New World Dictionary,* Third College Edition. Copyright © 1988 by Webster's New World Dictionaries, a Division of Simon and Schuster, New York. Reprinted by permission of the publisher.

1. **Entry word.** The entry word shows how the word is spelled and how it is divided into syllables. The entry word may also tell whether the word is capitalized and provide alternate spellings.
2. **Pronunciation.** The pronunciation of a word is shown by the use of accent marks, phonetic symbols, or diacritical marks. *Accent marks* show which syllables of a word are said more forcefully. *Phonetic symbols* represent a specific sound. *Diacritical marks* are special symbols placed above the letters to show how they sound. A pronunciation key like the one shown on pages 406 and 407 is provided as a guide to diacritical marks or phonetic symbols. Different dictionaries have different ways to indicate pronunciation.
3. **Part-of-speech labels.** These labels (usually in abbreviated form) show how the entry word should be used in a sentence. Some words may be used as more than one part of speech. In this case, a part-of-speech label is

provided before each set of definitions that apply to a certain part of speech.

4. **Other forms.** These may show spellings of plural forms of nouns, tenses of verbs, or the comparative forms of adjectives and adverbs.

5. **Etymology.** The *etymology* is the origin and history of a word. It tells how the word (or its parts) entered the English language.

6. **Examples.** Phrases or sentences may demonstrate how the defined word is to be used.

7. **Definitions.** If there is more than one meaning for a word, definitions are numbered or lettered.

8. **Special usage labels.** These labels identify the circumstances in which a word has a special meaning or is used in a special way.

9. **Related word forms.** These are alternate forms of the entry word, usually created by adding suffixes or prefixes. Sometimes a common phrase is shown in which the entry word appears.

10. **Synonyms and antonyms.** Sometimes synonyms and antonyms are listed at the end of a word entry. *Synonyms* are words that are similar in meaning. *Antonyms* are words that are opposite in meaning.

Pronunciation Key

Symbol	Key Words	Symbol	Key Words
a	asp, fat, parrot	b	bed, fable, dub, ebb
ā	ape, date, play, break, fail	d	dip, had, dodder
ä	ah, car, father, cot	f	fall, after, off, phone
e	elf, ten, berry	g	get, haggle, dog
ē	even, meet, money, flea, grieve	h	he, ahead, hotel
i	is, hit, mirror	k	kill, tackle, bake, coat, quick
ī	ice, bite, high, sky	l	let, yellow, ball
ō	open, tone, go, boat	m	met, camel, trim, summer

Symbol	Key Words	Symbol	Key Words
ô	all, horn, law, oar	n	not, flannel, ton
o͝o	look, pull, moor, wolf	p	put, apple, tap
o͞o	ooze, tool, crew, rule	r	red, port, dear, purr
yo͞o	use, cute, few	s	sell, castle, pass, nice
yo͝o	cure, globule	t	top, cattle, hat
oi	oil, point, toy	v	vat, hovel, have
ou	out, crowd, plow	w	will, always, swear,
u	up, cut, color, flood		quick
ʉr	urn, fur, deter, irk	y	yet, onion, yard
ə	a in ago	z	zebra, dazzle, haze, rise
	e in agent	ch	chin, catcher, arch,
	i in sanity		nature
	o in comply	sh	she, cushion, dash,
	u in focus		machine
ər	perhaps, murder	th	thin, nothing, truth
		th	then, father, lathe
		zh	azure, leisure, beige
		ŋ	ring, anger, drink

Letters and Forms

Like all other forms of communication, letters have a purpose and an intended audience.

LETTERS		
TYPE	**PURPOSE**	**AUDIENCE**
Personal	to express emotions and ideas	close friends or relatives
Social	to express appreciation or to communicate information about a specific event	close friends or social acquaintances
Business	to inform a business that you need its services or to tell how well or badly a service was performed	a business or organization

Personal Letters

Personal messages are often best expressed in the form of letters. Often a written message is more effective—and more appreciated—than a telephone call or other form of communication. A ***personal letter,*** sometimes called a *friendly letter,* is a good way to send a written message to a friend or a relative. Like a conversation, a friendly letter contains a specific, personal message from you to the person with whom you're communicating. Unlike a conversation, a letter can be enjoyed over and over again. And it can't be interrupted. With a personal letter, you can make a thoughtful, loving gesture to a friend or a family member who lives nearby. Or you can keep in touch with someone who lives far away.

Social Letters

A *social letter* is a courteous announcement or response concerning a particular event. Social letters may include thank-you letters, invitations, or letters of regret.

Thank-you Letters. These are letters that you send to tell someone that you appreciate his or her taking time, trouble, or expense to do something for you. Always respond promptly, and try to say something specific about the kindness that that person has done you. You might mention that you are aware of the person's effort, or you might tell why the person's gift is special to you.

Invitations. In an informal invitation, include specific information about the occasion, the time and place, and any other special details your guest might need to know (such as that everyone is expected to bring a friend, dress casually, or donate food).

Letters of Regret. A letter of regret is written to inform someone that you will not be able to accept an invitation. You should always respond in writing to invitations that include the letters *R.S.V.P.* (in French, an abbreviation meaning "please reply"). Be sure to respond quickly so that your host knows how many people to prepare for.

5455 Blackstone Street
Chicago, IL 60615
March 20, 1994

Dear Felicia,

    I was so happy to receive your invitation to your birthday slumber party next Friday evening. I really would like to be there. Unfortunately, my parents have already made plans for the whole family for that night.
    Thank you very much for inviting me. I hope you have a happy birthday and a lot of fun at your party.

Your friend,

Bianca

Bianca

RESOURCES

Business Letters

The Parts and Style of a Business Letter

The six parts of a business letter are
(1) the heading
(2) the inside address
(3) the salutation
(4) the body
(5) the closing
(6) the signature

Block Style

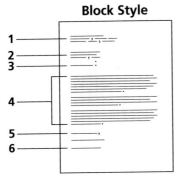

Modified Block Style

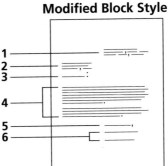

The six parts of a business letter are usually arranged on the page in one of two styles, shown on page 409. In the **block form** of a business letter, every part of the letter begins at the left margin, and paragraphs are not indented. In the **modified block form,** the heading, the closing, and your signature are placed to the right of the center of the page. However, the other parts of the letter begin at the left margin, and paragraphs are indented.

The Heading. The heading usually has three lines:

- your street address
- your city, state, and ZIP Code
- the date the letter was written

The Inside Address. The inside address gives the name and address of the person or company to whom you are writing.

- If you're directing your letter to someone by name, use a courtesy title (such as *Mr., Ms.,* or *Mrs.*) or a professional title (such as *Dr.* or *Professor*) in front of the person's name. After the person's name, include the person's business title (such as *Principal* or *Service Manager*).
- If you don't have a person's name, use a business title or position title (such as *Editor in Chief* or *President*).

The Salutation. The salutation is your greeting.

- If you are writing to a specific person, begin with *Dear,* followed by a courtesy title or a professional title, the person's name, and a colon (such as *Dear Dr. Alañiz:*).
- If you don't have the name of a specific person, use a general salutation (such as *Dear Sir or Madam:* or *Ladies and Gentlemen:*). Or you can use a department or position title (such as *Activity Director* or *Committee Leader*), with or without the word *Dear.*

The Body. The body is the main part of your letter. This part is where you state your message. If your letter contains more than one paragraph, leave a blank line between paragraphs.

The Closing. You should end your letter politely. To close a business letter, use a standard phrase such as *Sincerely, Yours truly,* or *Respectfully yours.*

The Signature. Sign your name in dark blue or black ink below the closing. Type or print your name neatly just below your signature.

HOW TO WRITE EFFECTIVE BUSINESS LETTERS

- *Use a polite, respectful, professional tone.* A courteous letter is much more effective than a rude one. Your reader is more likely to pay attention and respond well to a letter that is politely worded.
- *Use standard English.* Avoid slang, contractions, and abbreviations. Informal language that might be acceptable in a telephone conversation or personal letter is not usually acceptable for a business letter.
- *Get to the point.* State the reason for your letter clearly and promptly. Be polite, but don't ramble.
- *Include all necessary information.* Be sure your reader can understand why you wrote and what you are asking.

RESOURCES

Types of Business Letters

The Request or Order Letter

In a request letter, you are asking for something. You might write to ask for information about a product or a service or to request sample materials. Or you may ask for someone's time or services. In an order letter, you ask for something specific such as a free brochure advertised in a magazine. You might also write an order letter to purchase, by mail, a product for which you don't have a printed order form. In your letter, it is important to be clear about exactly what you want.

Here is the body of a sample request letter. The writer is asking a state tourism board to send travel information.

> My family is planning a two-week vacation in Wyoming in July. We'd like to visit Jackson Lake, Yellowstone National Park, and Grand Teton National Park. Please send me any information—free brochures, pamphlets, or maps—that might help us on the trip. We would be interested in any information about attractions, such as museums or natural rock or cavern formations, that lie on our route.
>
> We'll be driving down from Bozeman in a large camper, so we would also appreciate a list of campsites and fees.

When you are writing a request or order letter, remember the following points.

1. Clearly state your request.
2. If you are requesting information, enclose a self-addressed, stamped envelope.
3. Make your request well in advance of the time you need the materials or the product.
4. If you want to order something, include all important information. Give the size, color, brand name, or any other specific information about the product. If there are costs involved, such as sales tax or shipping costs, add the amount correctly.

The Complaint or Adjustment Letter

If an error has been made or if you have a specific complaint about a product or service, you may write a complaint or adjustment letter.

Here is a sample adjustment letter.

387 Needle Road
Bozeman, Montana 59715
May 25, 1994

Vargas Pool Supply
600 West Main, Suite 100
Jackson, Wyoming 83001

Dear Sir or Madam:

On April 30, I ordered a pair of green, heavy-duty swim fins with adjustable straps. In your spring catalog, these fins are item number 820. This morning, however, I received a big, yellow, inflatable sea serpent, which I am returning to you. Please exchange the sea serpent for the swim fins.

Thank you for your help.

Sincerely yours,

Paula Kotran

Paula Kotran

When you are writing a complaint or adjustment letter, remember the following points.

1. Register your complaint as soon as possible.
2. Be sure to mention specifics. Necessary details might include the following ones:
   - why you are unhappy with the product or service
   - how you were affected (lost time or money)
   - what solution you believe will correct the problem
3. Keep the tone of your letter calm and courteous.

The Appreciation or Commendation Letter

You write an appreciation or commendation letter to express appreciation, gratitude, or praise for a person, group, or organization. State exactly why you are pleased.

Here is a sample appreciation letter.

210 Valley View Place
Minneapolis, MN 55419
March 10, 1994

Sgt. Latrice Jeffreys
Second Precinct Police Station
850 Second Avenue South
Minneapolis, MN 55402

Dear Sgt. Jeffreys:

    Thank you very much for coming to speak to our school about safety. We are aware of this issue and how much it can affect our lives. It's good to know that there are so many things we can do to keep ourselves from becoming victims of crime.

    I hope you will continue to speak to students about this very important subject. We should all know what our part is in fighting crime.

Sincerely yours,

Ben Johansen

Ben Johansen

The Appearance of a Business Letter

- Use unlined 8½" x 11" paper.
- Type your letter if possible (single-spaced, leaving an extra line between paragraphs). Otherwise, neatly write the letter by hand, using black or blue ink. Avoid smudges, erasures, and crossed-out words. Check for typing errors and misspellings.
- Center your letter on the paper with equal margins on the sides and at the top and the bottom.
- Use only one side of the paper. If your letter won't fit on one page, leave a one-inch margin at the bottom of the first page and carry over at least two lines onto the second page.

Addressing an Envelope

On your envelope, put your own address in the top left-hand corner. Place the name and address of the person to whom you are writing in the center of the envelope. Make sure all addresses are correct, and include ZIP Codes. On the envelope for a business letter, the name and the address to which the letter is being sent should exactly match the inside address of the letter. Use standard two-letter postal abbreviations for states, such as *IA* for *Iowa*.

 REFERENCE NOTE: For a complete list of state abbreviations, see pages 419–420.

Tama Wuliton
2703 Bryant Road
Dana Point, CA 92629

Clasprite Paper-Clip Company
1605 S. Noland Rd., Building 6
Bonita, CA 91902

Completing Printed Forms

Printed forms differ. However, if you follow a few standard guidelines, you should be able to fill out most forms accurately and completely.

HOW TO FILL OUT FORMS

1. Look over the entire form before you begin.
2. Take note of any special instructions, such as "Please print clearly" or "Use a pencil."
3. Read each item carefully.
4. Supply all the information requested. You may want to indicate that some information requested does not apply to you. In this case, you might use a dash or the symbol *N.A.*, which means "not applicable."
5. When you're finished, proofread your form to make sure you didn't leave any blanks. Also, check for errors, and correct them neatly.

Manuscript Style

A *manuscript* is any typed or handwritten composition. Learning standard manuscript style can help you to give your compositions a professional look. A paper that is neat and free of errors and smudges will always be appreciated by readers. In this section, you will also learn to use abbreviations and numbers correctly and to avoid using sexist language.

Materials and Arrangement

Use the following guidelines as you make a final copy of your paper.

Handwritten Papers

- Use regular 8½" x 11" lined paper. Do not use ragged-edged paper torn from a spiral-bound notebook.
- Use blue or black ink.
- Write legibly: Dot your *i*'s; cross your *t*'s; and distinguish your *o*'s, *a*'s, and *e*'s.
- Use only one side of a sheet of paper.
- Do not skip lines unless your teacher tells you to do so.

Typewritten Papers

- Use regular 8½" x 11" typing paper. Avoid very thin (onionskin) paper and erasable paper.
- Use a fresh black ribbon.
- Double-space between lines.

Word-Processed Papers

- Use letter-sized sheets or continuous-feed paper that separates cleanly along the edges.
- Make sure that the printer you use can produce clear, dark, letter-quality type.
- Check with your teacher to be sure that the typeface you plan to use is acceptable.
- Double-space between lines.

General Guidelines

Set up your pages to make them clear and readable. Whether you are preparing a handwritten, typed, or word-processed paper, use the following format.

- Leave one-inch margins at the top, sides, and bottom of each page.
- Indent the first line of each paragraph five spaces from the left margin.
- Number all pages (except the first page) in the upper right-hand corner, one-half inch from the top.
- Follow your teacher's instructions for placement of your name, the date, your class, and the title of your paper.
- Make corrections neatly. You may make a few corrections with correction tape, but they should be barely noticeable. To insert a word or a short phrase, use a caret mark (∧) and add the word(s) immediately above it.

Word-processing software and printers can help you format your paper in some or all of these ways:

- producing *italic* and **bold** type
- centering heads
- numbering pages
- adding footnotes

Abbreviations

An *abbreviation* is a shortened form of a word or phrase. Only a few abbreviations are appropriate in the text of a formal paper. Many other abbreviations are used to save space in tables, notes, and bibliographies.

Titles

Certain abbreviations are acceptable when used with a person's name. If they do not accompany a name, spell out the words instead of using the abbreviations.

EXAMPLES **Mr.** Arroyo   **Dr.** Doris Yen
          Mrs. Smith   **Sen.** Daniel Inouye
          Gen. John Galvin   Charles Grant, **Jr.**

Have you met the **doctor**?
What is your opinion of the tax increase,
    Senator?

NOTE Abbreviate given names only if the person is most commonly known that way.

EXAMPLES W. Somerset Maugham   D. H. Lawrence
          J.R.R. Tolkien

Notice that there is a space between two such initials, but not between three or more.

Time

The abbreviations *A.M.*, *P.M.*, *A.D.*, and *B.C.* are acceptable when they are used with numbers.

EXAMPLES **The meeting is called for 3:30 P.M.**
          Augustus Caesar lived from 63 B.C. to A.D. 14.
          [Notice that the abbreviation *A.D.* precedes the number, but *B.C.* follows it.]

Agencies and Organizations

After spelling out the first use, abbreviate the names of agencies and organizations commonly known by their initials.

EXAMPLE **The NATO (North Atlantic Treaty Organization) meeting is scheduled for next month. Spain and Portugal are both members of NATO.**

States

In text, spell out the names of states whether the names stand alone or follow any other geographical term. In tables, notes, and bibliographies, use the first of the two forms shown in the following table. Use the second form only in addresses that include the ZIP Code.

ABBREVIATIONS FOR STATES AND TERRITORIES

STATE OR TERRITORY	TRADITIONAL	POSTAL SERVICE
Alabama	Ala.	AL
Alaska	Alaska	AK
Arizona	Ariz.	AZ
Arkansas	Ark.	AR
California	Calif.	CA
Colorado	Colo.	CO
Connecticut	Conn.	CT
Delaware	Del.	DE
District of Columbia	D.C.	DC
Florida	Fla.	FL
Georgia	Ga.	GA
Guam	Guam	GU
Hawaii	Hawaii	HI
Idaho	Idaho	ID
Illinois	Ill.	IL
Indiana	Ind.	IN
Iowa	Iowa	IA
Kansas	Kans.	KS
Kentucky	Ky.	KY
Louisiana	La.	LA
Maine	Maine	ME
Maryland	Md.	MD
Massachusetts	Mass.	MA
Michigan	Mich.	MI
Minnesota	Minn.	MN
Mississippi	Miss.	MS
Missouri	Mo.	MO
Montana	Mont.	MT
Nebraska	Nebr.	NB
Nevada	Nev.	NV
New Hampshire	N.H.	NH
New Jersey	N.J.	NJ
New Mexico	N.Mex.	NM
New York	N.Y.	NY
North Carolina	N.C.	NC
North Dakota	N.Dak.	ND
Ohio	Ohio	OH
Oklahoma	Okla.	OK
Oregon	Oreg.	OR
Pennsylvania	Pa.	PA
Puerto Rico	P.R.	PR

RESOURCES

(continued)

STATE OR TERRITORY	TRADITIONAL	POSTAL SERVICE
Rhode Island	R.I.	RI
South Carolina	S.C.	SC
South Dakota	S.Dak.	SD
Tennessee	Tenn.	TN
Texas	Tex.	TX
Utah	Utah	UT
Vermont	Vt.	VT
Virgin Islands	V.I.	VI
Virginia	Va.	VA
Washington	Wash.	WA
West Virginia	W.Va.	WV
Wisconsin	Wis.	WI
Wyoming	Wyo.	WY

ABBREVIATIONS FOR STATES AND TERRITORIES *(continued)*

REFERENCE NOTE: For information about punctuating abbreviations, see pages 258–260.

Numbers

Spell out a number that states how many if it can be expressed in one or two words. Otherwise, use numerals.

EXAMPLES   **twelve** jurors   **twenty-three** days
                five thousand fans   **345** freshmen
                three quarters of a cup $^{15}/_{16}$ inch
                986 hours   **10,233** pounds
                21.5 seconds   a **million** dollars

Spell out numbers that express order, such as *second* and *fifth*. If a number represents the day of the month, use a numeral only.

EXAMPLES   I was the **first** [*not* 1st] customer at the bank this morning.
                Flag Day is **June 14.**

REFERENCE NOTE: For more information on spelling numbers, see pages 319–320.

Nonsexist Language

Nonsexist language is language that applies to people in general, both male and female. For example, you might use the nonsexist term *synthetic* or *manufactured* instead of the gender-specific term *manmade.* Similarly, you might use the term *humankind* or *humanity* instead of *mankind.*

In the past, many skills and occupations excluded either men or women. Expressions like *laundress, tailor,* and *policeman* show these restrictions. Now that most jobs are held by both men and women, language is adjusting to reflect this change. When you are referring to humanity as a whole, use nonsexist expressions rather than gender-specific ones. Below are some examples.

GENDER-SPECIFIC	NONSEXIST
businessman	executive, businessperson
chairman	chairperson, chair
fireman	firefighter
foreman	supervisor
housewife	homemaker
salesman	sales representative, salesperson

Sometimes the antecedent of a pronoun may be either masculine or feminine. In such a case, use both masculine and feminine pronouns to refer to it.

EXAMPLE   Any **student** who wishes to go on the field trip must bring **his or her** permission slip.

You can often avoid the awkward *his or her* construction by substituting an article (*a, an,* or *the*) for the construction or by rephrasing the sentence.

EXAMPLES   Any **student** who wishes to go on the field trip must bring **a** permission slip.
Any **students** who wish to go on the field trip must bring **their** permission slips.

 REFERENCE NOTE: For more information on using pronouns and antecedents correctly, see pages 87–93.

DIAGRAMING SENTENCES

A *sentence diagram* is a picture of how the parts of a sentence fit together.

Subjects and Verbs (pages 181–184)

To diagram a sentence, first find the subject and the verb. Write the subject and the verb on a *horizontal* line (that is, a line drawn from left to right). Then, separate the subject and verb with a *vertical* line (that is, a line drawn from top to bottom).

EXAMPLES The reporter dashed to the fire.

reporter	dashed

Have you been studying?

you	Have been studying

Notice that a diagram shows the capitalization but not the punctuation of a sentence.

Understood Subjects (page 211)

To diagram an imperative sentence, place the understood subject *you* in parentheses on the horizontal line.

EXAMPLE   Listen to the beautiful music.

(you)	Listen

Compound Subjects (page 185)

EXAMPLE   **Vines** and **weeds** grew over the old well.

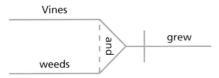

Compound Verbs (pages 185–186)

EXAMPLE   We **ran** to the corner and barely **caught** the bus.

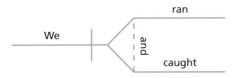

Compound Subjects and Verbs (pages 185–186)

EXAMPLE   **Ken** and **LaDonna dived** into the water and
swam across the pool.

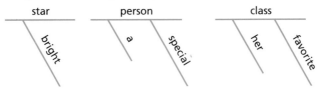

Adjectives and Adverbs (pages 53–56 and 62–64)

Both adjectives and adverbs are written on slanted lines
below the words they modify. Note that possessive pronouns are diagramed in the same way adjectives are.

Adjectives (pages 53–56)

EXAMPLES   **bright** star   **a special** person   **her favorite** class

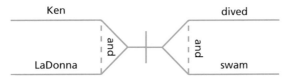

Two or more adjectives joined by a connecting word are diagramed this way:

EXAMPLE   a **lovely** and **quiet** place

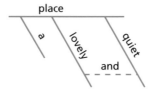

Adverbs (pages 62–64)

EXAMPLES   studies **hard**   does **not** exercise **daily**

Sometimes an adverb modifies an adjective or another adverb. In such cases, the adverb is placed on a line connected to the word it modifies.

EXAMPLES   **extremely** strong wind   tried **rather** hard

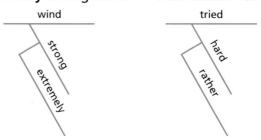

Objects (pages 193–196)

Direct Objects (pages 193–194)

A direct object is diagramed on the horizontal line with the subject and the verb. A vertical line separates the direct object from the verb. Notice that this vertical line does not cross the horizontal line.

EXAMPLE   The rain cleaned the **street.**

Compound Direct Objects (page 194)

EXAMPLE   We sold **lemonade** and **oranges.**

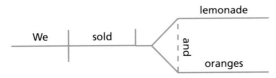

Indirect Objects (pages 195–196)

To diagram an indirect object, write it on a short horizontal line below the verb. Connect the indirect object to the verb by a slanted line.

EXAMPLE   The artist showed **me** his painting.

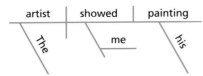

Compound Indirect Objects (page 196)

EXAMPLE   The company gave **Corey** and **Kareem** summer jobs.

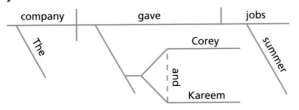

Subject Complements (pages 196–199)

A subject complement is placed on the horizontal line with the simple subject and the verb. The subject complement comes after the verb. A line slanting toward the subject separates the subject complement and the verb. This slanted line shows that the complement refers to the subject.

Predicate Nominatives (page 197)

EXAMPLE   William Least Heat-Moon is an **author.**

Compound Predicate Nominatives (page 197)

EXAMPLE   The contestants are **Joan** and **Dean.**

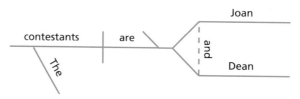

Predicate Adjectives (page 198)

EXAMPLE   The river looked **deep.**

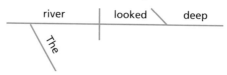

Compound Predicate Adjectives (page 198)

EXAMPLE   This Chinese soup tastes **hot** and **spicy.**

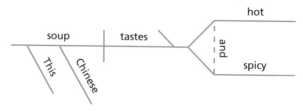

Phrases (pages 147–159)

Prepositional Phrases (pages 148–151)

A prepositional phrase is diagramed below the word it modifies. Write the preposition that introduces the phrase on a line slanting down from the modified word. Then write the object of the preposition on a horizontal line extending from the slanting line.

Adjective Phrases (pages 149–150)

EXAMPLES paintings **by famous artists**

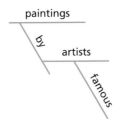

cloth **from Costa Rica and Guatemala**

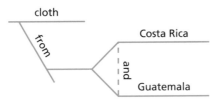

Adverb Phrases (pages 150–151)

EXAMPLES walked **along the road**

went with Hollis and Dave

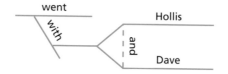

The following example shows the diagram of a prepositional phrase that modifies the object of another prepositional phrase.

EXAMPLE   **camped on the side of a mountain**

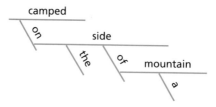

Verbals and Verbal Phrases (pages 152–157)

Participles and Participial Phrases (pages 152–154)
Participles are diagramed as other adjectives are.

EXAMPLE   José comforted the **crying** baby.

Participial phrases are diagramed as follows:

EXAMPLE   **Shaking the manager's hand,** Teresa accepted her new job.

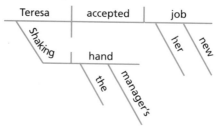

Notice that the participle has a direct object (*hand*), which is diagramed in the same way that the direct object of a main verb is. (*The* and *manager's* modify *hand*.)

Gerunds and Gerund Phrases (pages 154–155)

EXAMPLES   I enjoy **skating.** [gerund used as direct object]

Being slightly ill is no excuse for **missing two days of baseball practice.** [Gerund phrases used as subject and as object of preposition. The first gerund has a subject complement (*ill*). The second gerund has a direct object (*days*).]

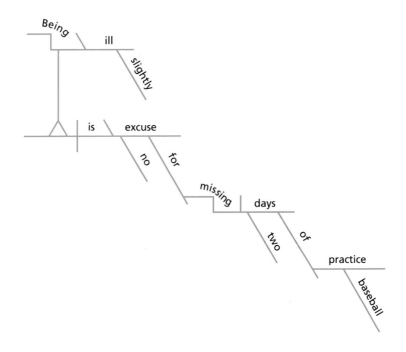

Infinitives and Infinitive Phrases (pages 156–157)

EXAMPLES **To write** is her ambition. [infinitive used as noun/subject]

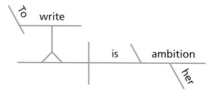

Marge was hoping to go with us. [infinitive phrase used as noun/direct object]

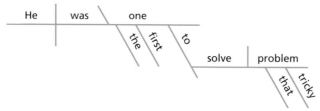

He was the first one to solve that tricky problem. [infinitive phrase used as adjective]

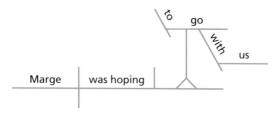

She called to invite us over. [infinitive phrase used as adverb]

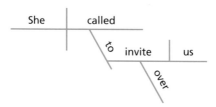

Appositives and Appositive Phrases (page 158)

To diagram an appositive, write it in parentheses after the word it explains.

EXAMPLES Our cousin **Iola** is a chemical engineer.

Bill Cosby, **the popular TV star,** is also the author
of a best-selling book.

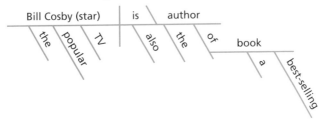

Subordinate Clauses (pages 165–173)

Adjective Clauses (pages 166–169)

Diagram an adjective clause by connecting it with a broken line to the word it modifies. Draw the broken line between the relative pronoun and the word that it relates to.
[Note: The words *who, whom, whose, which,* and *that* are relative pronouns.]

EXAMPLE The grades **that I got last term** pleased my
parents.

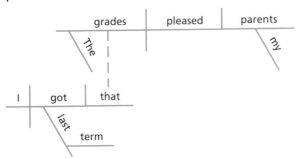

Adverb Clauses (pages 169–172)

Diagram an adverb clause by using a broken line to connect the adverb clause to the word it modifies. Place the subordinating conjunction that introduces the adverb clause on the broken line.

EXAMPLE **When I got home from school,** I ate an apple.

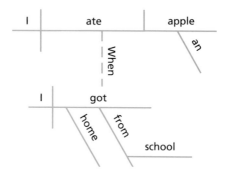

Noun Clauses (pages 172–173)

Diagram a noun clause by connecting it to the independent clause with a solid line.

EXAMPLE **Olivia knew what she wanted.** [The noun clause is the direct object of the independent clause. The word *what* is the direct object in the noun clause.]

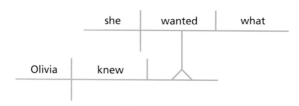

Sometimes the introductory word of the noun clause does not have a specific function in the noun clause. Such a sentence is diagramed in this way:

EXAMPLE   The problem is **that they lost the map.** [The noun clause is a predicate nominative identifying *problem*. The word *that* has no function in the noun clause except as an introductory word.]

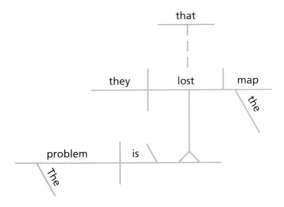

Sentences Classified According to Structure (pages 203–210)

Simple Sentences (page 203)

EXAMPLE   Tracy is building a birdhouse in industrial arts class. [one independent clause]

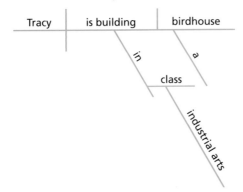

Compound Sentences (pages 204–205)

The second independent clause in a compound sentence is diagramed below the first. A coordinating conjunction joins the two clauses.

EXAMPLE   Darnell threw a good pass, but Clay did not catch it. [two independent clauses]

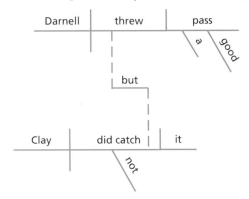

Complex Sentences (pages 206–207)

EXAMPLE   Before they left the museum, Lester and Tess visited the exhibit of masks from Nigeria and the Ivory Coast. [one subordinate clause and one independent clause]

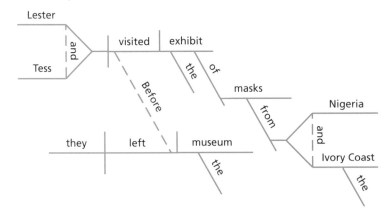

 REFERENCE NOTE: See pages 431–433 for more information on diagraming the three different kinds of subordinate clauses.

Compound-Complex Sentences (pages 208–209)

EXAMPLE   Hamako, whose mother is a musician, studies piano, but her cousin Akio prefers to play tennis. [two independent clauses and one subordinate clause]

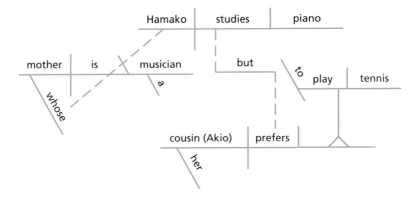

✓ Quick Check Answer Key

Chapter 1
Parts of Speech

p. 48 QUICK CHECK 1

1. day—common; crowds— common; people—common; Lincoln Memorial—proper, compound; Washington, D.C.—proper, compound
2. monument—common; Henry Bacon—proper, compound; Memorial Day—proper, compound
3. Lincoln Memorial—proper, compound; hall—common; statue—common; Abraham Lincoln—proper, compound
4. figure—common; blocks— common; marble—common; armchair—common, compound; meditation— common
5. wall—common; passage— common; address—common; Lincoln—proper; Gettysburg Address—proper, compound; wall—common

p. 53 QUICK CHECK 2

1. herself—reflexive
2. That—demonstrative
3. I—personal; it—personal
4. us—personal; that—relative; she—personal
5. Who—interrogative; me— personal; whose—relative; this—demonstrative

p. 57 QUICK CHECK 3

Adjective —Type	Word Modified
1. My—common	sister
little—common	sister
afraid—common	sister

[Note: My is included for those teachers who prefer to call possessive personal pronouns adjectives.]

2. some—common	ice water

[Note: Ice water is a compound noun.]

3. This—demonstrative	parakeet
enough—common	seed
4. German shepherd—proper	puppy
lively—common	rascal
5. Each—common	club
Cinco de Mayo—proper	parade

p. 61 QUICK CHECK 4

1. linking verb
2. action verb—transitive
3. linking verb
4. helping verb
5. action verb—transitive

p. 64 QUICK CHECK 5

1. Today—studied
2. very—far; far—went
3. How—did win; easily—did win
4. never—occur; long—past
5. quite—funny

p. 67 *QUICK CHECK* 6
1. during—year
2. for—breakfast
3. in spite of—difficulty
4. with—Tomás
5. in front of—castle; by—
   drawbridge

p. 69 *QUICK CHECK* 7
1. Oh—interjection
2. yet—conjunction
3. Both . . . and—conjunction;
   and—conjunction
4. for—conjunction
5. Whoops—interjection

p. 70 *QUICK CHECK* 8
1. a. preposition
   b. conjunction
2. a. noun
   b. verb
3. a. pronoun
   b. adjective
4. a. preposition
   b. adverb
5. a. pronoun or adjective
   b. interjection

Chapter 2
Agreement

p. 79 *QUICK CHECK* 1
1. is   4. encourages
2. have   5. believe
3. reflects

p. 81 *QUICK CHECK* 2
1. chorus—chirps
2. Several—are
3. either—Does
4. Most—look
5. price—is

p. 83 *QUICK CHECK* 3
1. wash   4. indicate
2. contain   5. catch
3. reads

p. 86 *QUICK CHECK* 4
1. Joneses—were
2. present—is
3. You—don't
4. hitter—comes
5. jury—is

p. 87 *QUICK CHECK* 5
1. is   4. Have
2. is   5. is
3. is

p. 91 *QUICK CHECK* 6
1. their—Iowa, Kansas, Nebraska
2. their—Two
3. it—Each
4. them—Lisa, Rick; their—Lisa,
   Rick
5. he—Larry, Carlos

p. 93 *QUICK CHECK* 7
1. their   4. it
2. it   5. it
3. it

Chapter 3
Using Verbs

p. 100 *QUICK CHECK* 1
1. crossed   4. bounded
2. visited   5. used
3. repaired

p. 103 *QUICK CHECK* 2
1. thought   4. told
2. spent   5. built
3. caught

p. 105 *QUICK CHECK* 3

1. rang   4. driven
2. threw   5. chosen
3. swam

p. 105 *QUICK CHECK* 4

1. let   4. set
2. burst   5. spread
3. cost

p. 109 *QUICK CHECK* 5

(Note: Paragraph should be rewritten either with all verbs in the present tense, as indicated by the first italicized verb in each set below, or with all verbs in past tense, as indicated by the italicized verbs in parentheses below.)

1. Across the water, I *see* (or *saw*) the ripples.
2. "I have to catch some fish," I *say* (or *said*) to myself.
3. I *throw* (or *threw*) my lure near where I *see* (or *saw*) the ripples and *reel* (or *reeled)* in the line.
4. The fish *don't* (or *didn't*) seem interested.
5. I *see* (or *saw*) more ripples and *throw* (or *threw*) the line in the water again.
6. "I have a strike!" I *shout* (or *shouted*) to the trees around me.
7. As I *reel* (or *reeled*) in the line, a beautiful trout *jumps* (or *jumped*) out of the water and *spits* (or *spit* or *spat*) out the hook.
8. Feeling down, I *go* (or *went*) back to the house.
9. Grandpa *is* (or *was*) sitting at the kitchen table with a bowl of hot oatmeal for me.

10. I *say* (or *said*), "Oh well, maybe tomorrow we'll have fresh trout for breakfast."

p. 112 *QUICK CHECK* 6

1. raise   4. rises
2. sat   5. laid; lying
3. set

Chapter 4
Using Pronouns

p. 119 *QUICK CHECK* 1

1. they   4. he
2. she   5. she
3. he; she

p. 121 *QUICK CHECK* 2

1. her   4. them
2. me   5. me
3. us; him

p. 124 *QUICK CHECK* 3

1. whom   4. Whom
2. Who   5. who
3. whom

p. 126 *QUICK CHECK* 4

1. We   4. themselves
2. me   5. we
3. us

Chapter 5
Using Modifiers

p. 133 *QUICK CHECK* 1

1. slower (less slow); slowest (least slow)
2. more (less) cautiously; most (least) cautiously
3. earlier (less early); earliest (least early)
4. more (less) thankful; most (least) thankful

5. more (less) possible; most (least) possible
6. shorter (less short); shortest (least short)
7. easier (less easy); easiest (least easy)
8. more (less) confident; most (least) confident
9. more (less) seriously; most (least) seriously
10. more (less) loyal; most (least) loyal

p. 134 *QUICK CHECK 2*

1. more; most
2. more (less) easily; most (least) easily
3. more; most
4. tastier (less tasty); tastiest (least tasty)
5. more (less) enthusiastic; most (least) enthusiastic
6. more (less) generous; most (least) generous
7. hotter (less hot); hottest (least hot)
8. better; best
9. better; best
10. worse; worst

p. 136 *QUICK CHECK 3*

1. than anyone else that is on the team
2. The largest ancient cliff dwellings
3. the more playful one
4. than any other city
5. likes homemade sauerkraut better than canned sauerkraut

p. 137 *QUICK CHECK 4*

(Answers will vary.)
1. We hardly have time to relax.

2. Josie hasn't ever been to Tennessee.
3. He never had a problem with public speaking.
4. The athletes hardly have a break between events.
5. The authorities don't allow cars on Michigan's popular Mackinac Island.

p. 141 *QUICK CHECK 5*

(Answers may vary.)
1. While the singing group performed, guards protected them from being swarmed.
2. Attempting to raise money for the homeless, the group sang many songs.
3. Hoping to please the fans, the group performed brand-new songs.
4. Few fans could tell how nervous the singers were the first time they played their new songs.
5. When the audience cheered heartily, the singers' fears were relieved.

Chapter 6
Phrases

p. 151 *QUICK CHECK 1*

1. for both his sunny smile and his athletic skill—adverb phrase—was known
   during his career—adverb phrase—was known
2. For twenty-five years—adverb phrase—played
   on one—adverb phrase—played
   of the most popular teams—adjective phrase —one

in basketball's history—
adjective phrase—teams
3. with the Harlem
Globetrotters—adjective
phrase—star
in 1961—adverb phrase—
beginning
4. in 1927—adverb phrase—was
started
for its humorous performances
—adverb phrase—famous
5. of skill and humor—adjective
phrase—combination
to Globetrotter fans—adverb
phrase—appeals
throughout the world—
adjective phrase—fans

p. 154 *QUICK CHECK 2*

1. Noted for her beauty—Venus
2. knowing her charms—Jupiter
3. known to the Greeks as Ares—
Mars
4. Terrified by Ares' power—
Greeks
5. destroyed by him—land, people

p. 155 *QUICK CHECK 3*

1. the howling of wolves—
predicate nominative
2. the slow rocking of the boat—
direct object
3. boycotting grapes—object of a
preposition
4. The frantic darting of the
fish—subject
5. settling disputes fairly—object
of a preposition

p. 157 *QUICK CHECK 4*

1. to take care of my bicycle—
noun
2. to lubricate the chain—adverb

3. to fill the inner tube—adjective
4. none
5. to give me tips about taking
care of my bicycle—adjective

p. 158 *QUICK CHECK 5*

1. tacos, tamales, and fajitas—
some
2. tuna salad on rye bread—
sandwich
3. one of my heroes—Barbara
Jordan
4. Bianca—friend
5. "I've Been Working on the
Railroad"—song

Chapter 7
Clauses

p. 164 *QUICK CHECK 1*

1. sister—subject; read—verb
2. she—subject; told—verb
3. I—subject; made—verb
4. comic strip—subject;
was created—verb
5. *Jump Start*—subject;
features—verb

p. 166 *QUICK CHECK 2*

1. independent clause
2. subordinate clause
3. subordinate clause
4. independent clause
5. subordinate clause

p. 169 *QUICK CHECK 3*

1. which appears after a star has
collapsed; which—black hole
2. whose work had most
improved; whose—student
3. who for years has been poet
laureate of Illinois; who—
Gwendolyn Brooks

4. that have influenced many; that—ideas
5. whom you can trust; whom—person

p. 172 *QUICK CHECK 4*

1. (Although) they lived in different regions of North America
2. (since) there were no toy stores
3. (Before) they started playing
4. (After) snow had fallen
5. (because) the cones were so easy to find

p. 173 *QUICK CHECK 5*

1. what happened to the rest of my tuna sandwich—direct object
2. that it doesn't have a carefully developed plot—predicate nominative
3. whatever spots had dried—indirect object
4. what we should do as our service project—object of a preposition
5. That Coretta Scott King spoke for peace—subject

Chapter 8
Sentences

p. 180 *QUICK CHECK 1*

(*Revisions of sentence fragments will vary.*)

1. sentence fragment—Catching the baseball with both hands, Renee got the third out.
2. sentence—In the back of the storeroom stands a stack of boxes.
3. sentence fragment—We found a long, narrow passage with a hidden trapdoor at the end.
4. sentence—The gymnasium is open.
5. sentence—Are you careful about shutting off unnecessary lights?

p. 183 *QUICK CHECK 2*

1. complete subject—People throughout Latin America; simple subject—People
2. complete subject—The all-American sport of baseball; simple subject—sport
3. complete subject—fans in countries such as Cuba, Panama, and Venezuela; simple subject—fans
4. complete subject—the Caribbean Baseball Leagues; simple subject—Caribbean Baseball Leagues
5. complete subject—the teams in Latin America; simple subject—teams

p. 184 *QUICK CHECK 3*

1. complete predicate—was an English government worker; verb—was
2. complete predicate—Between 1660 and 1669, . . . kept a diary; verb—kept
3. complete predicate—Presented in the diary is; verb—is presented
4. complete predicate—For example, in entries during 1666, . . . gave a detailed account of the Great Fire of London; verb—gave

5. complete predicate—might be described in the diary; verb—might be described

p. 186 *QUICK CHECK* 4

1. subject—Aaron Neville, brothers
2. verb—formed, started
3. verb—had performed, (had) toured
4. subject—sounds, rhythms
5. subject—*Yellow Moon, Brother's Keeper*

Chapter 9
Complements

p. 193 *QUICK CHECK* 1

1. people—subject; watched—verb; plays—complement
2. Richard (Burbage), Cuthbert Burbage—subject; built—verb; Globe—complement
3. Globe—subject; enclosed—verb; courtyard—complement
4. Some—subject; watched—verb; play—complement
5. playgoers—subject; did have—verb; seats—complement

p. 194 *QUICK CHECK* 2

1. buffalo
2. performance
3. refugees
4. New York City
5. discount; times

p. 196 *QUICK CHECK* 3

1. slides—direct object; audience—indirect object
2. lie—direct object; you, me—indirect object
3. paintings—direct object

4. books, magazines—direct object; her—indirect object
5. passports—direct object

p. 198 *QUICK CHECK* 4

1. one
2. classics
3. sellers
4. novel
5. winner

p. 199 *QUICK CHECK* 5

1. colorful, inviting
2. powerful
3. crowded, full
4. spicy, delicious
5. large

Chapter 10
Kinds of Sentences

p. 204 *QUICK CHECK* 1

1. people—subject; have invented, (have) used—verb
2. warriors—subject; needed—verb
3. soldiers—subject; wore—verb
4. Greeks—subject; had made—verb
5. knights, foot soldiers—subject; dressed—verb

p. 205 *QUICK CHECK* 2

1. director—subject; visited—verb; we—subject; listened—verb; and
2. workers—subject; are—verb; they—subject; make—verb; yet
3. character—subject; prepared—verb; dagger—subject; was—verb; but
4. Audiences—subject; can be—verb; they—subject; sit—verb; for

5. spectator—subject; became—
verb; he—subject; leaped,
tackled—verb; ;

p. 207 *QUICK CHECK* 3

    S   V
1. China is a largely agricultural
country—independent;
    S   V
that has a population of more
than one billion people—
subordinate
        S
2. A group of popular singers
      V
recorded a song—independent;
    S   V
who donated their time—
        S   V
subordinate; that made people
aware of the problems in
Ethiopia—subordinate
3. The nineteenth-century
        S   V
Hawaiian ruler was Queen
Liliuokalani—independent;
    S   V
who wrote the famous farewell
song *"Aloha Oe"* ("Farewell to
Thee")—subordinate
        S   V
4. While the stage crew was
building the sets—subordinate;
     S   V
the performers continued their
rehearsal—independent;
    S   V
which went on into the night—
subordinate
        S V
5. Although she had had polio as
        S
a child—subordinate; Wilma
     V
Rudolph became a top
American Olympic athlete—
independent

p. 209 *QUICK CHECK* 4

1. Before we conducted the
experiment—subordinate; we
asked for permission to use the
science lab—independent; the
principal insisted on teacher
supervision of our work—
independent
2. Inside the old trunk up in the
attic we found some dusty
photo albums—independent;
which is filled with boxes and
toys—subordinate; one of
them contained pictures from
the early 1900s—independent
3. We told them—independent;
that their plan wouldn't
work—subordinate; they
wouldn't listen to us—
independent
4. Every expedition had vanished
without a trace—independent;
that had attempted to explore
that region—subordinate; the
young adventurer was
determined to map the
uncharted jungle—
independent; because he
couldn't resist the challenge—
subordinate
5. The smoke billowed through
the dry forest—independent;
which grew steadily thicker
and darker—subordinate; the
animals ran ahead of it—
independent; as the fire spread
quickly—subordinate

p. 212 *QUICK CHECK* 5

1. imperative   4. exclamatory
2. declarative   5. imperative
3. interrogative

Chapter 11
Writing Effective Sentences

p. 222 *QUICK CHECK* 1

1. fragment   4. run-on
2. run-on   5. run-on
3. fragment

(Revisions may vary.)

Godzilla is a movie about a huge reptile. Godzilla looks like a dinosaur, but he breathes fire like a dragon. When an atomic bomb wakes him up, Godzilla can melt steel with his atomic breath. He is big enough to knock down huge buildings. In the film, he destroys the city of Tokyo, but he is defeated at the end.

p. 229 *QUICK CHECK* 2

(Revisions may vary.)

The Arctic is a cold region around the North Pole. Although the Arctic seems barren, berries and vegetables actually do manage to grow in a few places. The area also has rich mineral deposits. Mines in Alaska and Canada produce gold and copper, while mines in arctic Russia produce tin. Discovering many natural resources in the area, early explorers revealed that the Arctic is far from worthless.

p. 232 *QUICK CHECK* 3

1. wordy
2. stringy
3. wordy
4. wordy
5. stringy

(Revisions may vary.)

On Halloween night in 1938, an amazing event took place. Many families were gathered around their radios listening to music when they heard that Martians had invaded Earth. Actually, the news report was a radio version of H. G. Wells's novel *The War of the Worlds*. But Orson Welles, the producer of this famous hoax, made the show very realistic. Thousands of Americans were frightened. Many people jumped in cars to escape from the aliens, and some people even reported seeing the Martians and spaceships.

Chapter 12
Capital Letters

p. 241 *QUICK CHECK* 1

1. I; I   4. O
2. oh   5. C
3. Oh

p. 247 *QUICK CHECK* 2

1. decisions of the United States Supreme Court
2. the Apaches of the Southwest
3. power produced at Boulder Dam
4. the Tomb of the Unknown Soldier
5. 512 West Twenty-fourth Street
6. pictures of Saturn sent by *Voyager 2*
7. Maui, one of the islands that make up Hawaii
8. the Great Lakes

9. Monday, April 29
10. the Stone Age

p. 248 *QUICK CHECK* 3

1. a lesson in Spanish
2. this valuable Elizabethan manuscript
3. a program on Japanese customs
4. problems in Geometry I
5. studying German, chemistry, and Government II

p. 251 *QUICK CHECK* 4

1. Grandmother
2. *American Heritage Dictionary; Webster's New World Dictionary*
3. Commissioner of Education Smathers's
4. C
5. Dr.; *Field and Stream*

Chapter 13
Punctuation

p. 260 *QUICK CHECK* 1

1. Have you ever heard of Little Tokyo?
2. It's a neighborhood in Los Angeles, Calif., bordered by First St., Third St., Alameda St., and Los Angeles St.
3. Our friends from Los Angeles, Mr. and Mrs. Albert B. Cook, Sr., and their son, Al, Jr., introduced us to the area.
4. They met our 11:30 A.M. flight from Atlanta, Ga., and took us to lunch at a restaurant in the Japanese Plaza Village.
5. What a great day we had exploring Japanese culture!

p. 263 *QUICK CHECK* 2

1. Someday I would like to visit Thailand, Nepal, China, and Japan.
2. Charlayne Hunter-Gault's skillful, probing interviews have made her a respected broadcast journalist.
3. The California condor, the ocelot, the brown pelican, and the red wolf are only some of the endangered mammals in North America.
4. This book describes the harsh, isolated lives of pioneer women in Kansas.
5. We now know what we will write about, where we will find sources, and how we will organize our reports.

p. 265 *QUICK CHECK* 3

1. architects, yet
2. structure, and
3. tree, and
4. C
5. workers, for

p. 268 *QUICK CHECK* 4

1. My favorite performer is Gloria Estefan, who is the lead singer with the Miami Sound Machine.
2. Harper Lee, well-known author of *To Kill a Mockingbird*, is from Alabama.
3. Have you signed up for a baseball team yet, Aaron?
4. C
5. *Cilantro*, by the way, is the Spanish name for the herb coriander.

p. 270 *QUICK CHECK 5*
1. 1991,   4. collectors,
2. 1978,   5. albums,
3. Why,

p. 271 *QUICK CHECK 6*
1. 11687 Montana Avenue, Los Angeles, CA 90049
2. Dresser Road at North First Street in Lynchburg, Virginia
3. from December 1, 1991, to March 15, 1992
4. Dear Joanne,
5. Yours truly,

p. 274 *QUICK CHECK 7*
1. Scientists have explored almost all areas of the earth; they are now exploring the floors of the oceans.
2. Some scientists predict the development of undersea cities; however, other scientists question this prediction.
3. St. Augustine, Florida, was the first European settlement in the United States; the Spanish founded it in 1565.
4. In 1991 Mike Powell set a world record for the long jump; his leap of 29 feet, $4\frac{1}{2}$ inches beat Bob Beamon's 1968 record by 2 inches.
5. Some reptiles like a dry climate; (*or* climate,) others prefer a wet climate.

p. 276 *QUICK CHECK 8*
1. During the field trip our teacher pointed out the following trees: sugarberry, papaw, silver bell, and mountain laurel.
2. The first lunch period begins at 11:00 A.M.
3. This is my motto: Laugh and the world laughs with you.
4. In Ruth 1:16, Ruth pledges her loyalty to Naomi, her mother-in-law.
5. The artist showed me how to make a pale peach color: Simply mix white, yellow, and a little red.

Chapter 14
Punctuation

p. 284 *QUICK CHECK 1*
1. o, thorough, through
2. Guernica
3. Washington Post
4. My Left Foot
5. 4

p. 288 *QUICK CHECK 2*
[1] "Gordon, do you ever think about pencils?" Annie asked.
[2] "I'm always wondering where I lost mine," Gordon replied.
[3] "Well," said Annie, "let me tell you some of the things I learned about pencils."
[4] "Sure," Gordon said, "I love trivia."
[5] "People have used some form of pencils for a long time," Annie began. [6] "The ancient Greeks and Romans used lead pencils. [7] However, pencils as we know them weren't developed until the 1500's, when people started using graphite."
[8] "What's graphite?" asked Gordon.

[9] "Graphite is a soft form of carbon," Annie explained, "that leaves a mark when it's drawn over most surfaces."

[10] "Thanks for the information, Annie," Gordon said. "Now, do you have a pencil I can borrow?"

p. 290 *QUICK CHECK* 3

1. "Has anyone read the story 'To Build a Fire'?" asked the teacher.
2. "I have," said Eileen. "It's a terrific story, and it was written by Jack London."
3. Do you know the poem "To Make a Prairie"?
4. Our chorus will sing "When You Wish upon a Star" at the recital.
5. In the chapter of our social studies book called "Workers' Rights," the author discusses Cesar Chavez's efforts to help migrant workers.

Chapter 15
Punctuation

p. 296 *QUICK CHECK* 1

1. everybody's favorite
2. women's careers
3. friend's comments
4. three days' homework
5. its muffler
6. Joneses' cabin
7. men's shoes
8. C
9. cities' mayors
10. oxen's yokes

p. 298 *QUICK CHECK* 2

1. A's; B's
2. isn't; &'s
3. 80's; 90's
4. it's; we're; they'll
5. Who's

p. 301 *QUICK CHECK* 3

1. two-thirds
2. C
3. thirty-five
4. Forty-second
5. twenty-two

p. 302 *QUICK CHECK* 4

1. The old fort (it was used during the Civil War) has been rebuilt and is open to the public.
2. Yellowstone National Park (established in 1872) covers territory in Wyoming, Idaho, and Montana.
3. The writer Langston Hughes (1902–1967) is best known for his poetry.
4. Alligators use their feet and tails to dig water holes (also called "gator holes") in marshy fields.
5. On the Sabbath we eat braided bread called challah (pronounced "khä´lə").

p. 303 *QUICK CHECK* 5

1. A beautiful grand piano—it was once played by Chopin—was on display in the museum.
2. "I'd like the red—no, give me the blue—cycling shorts," said Josh.
3. Frederic Remington—he was an artist, historian, and lover of

the western frontier—painted the West as it really was.

4. In 1993, Ruth Bader Ginsburg—she's the second woman associate justice—was nominated to the U.S. Supreme Court.

5. Cheryl wondered aloud, "Where—oh, my poor Muffy—could that hamster be?"

Chapter 16
Spelling and Vocabulary

p. 312 *QUICK CHECK 1*

1. conceited	6. neither
2. eight	7. friend
3. piece	8. mischief
4. shriek	9. reign
5. freight	10. sheik

p. 312 *QUICK CHECK 2*

1. succeeded
2. superseded
3. exceeded
4. concede
5. preceded

p. 313 *QUICK CHECK 3*

1. immigrate
2. resettle
3. uncertain
4. illegal
5. semicircle

p. 316 *QUICK CHECK 4*

1. dryness
2. jogger
3. carried
4. advantageous
5. trimming
6. luckily
7. displayed

8. traceable
9. referral
10. naturally

p. 319 *QUICK CHECK 5*

1. cargos *or* cargoes
2. diaries
3. Gómezes
4. sit-ups
5. children
6. car pools
7. hooves
8. Japanese
9. *M*'s
10. 1900's

p. 322 *QUICK CHECK 6*

1. c *or* g	4. f
2. e	5. h
3. a	

p. 323 *QUICK CHECK 7*

1. antonyms	4. synonyms
2. synonyms	5. synonyms
3. antonyms	

Index

INDEX

449

INDEX

Acknowledgments

For permission to reprint copyrighted material, grateful acknowledgment is made to the following sources:

Américas Magazine: From "The One-Man Band of Latin Jazz" by Mark Holston from *Américas*, vol. 42, no. 6, 1990. Copyright © 1990 by Américas Magazine. Reprinted from *Américas*, a bimonthly magazine published by the General Secretariat of the Organization of American States in English and Spanish.

Rudolfo A. Anaya: From *Bless Me, Ultima* by Rudolfo A. Anaya. Copyright © 1972 by Rudolfo A. Anaya.

Andrews and McMeel: From "River Notes" from *River Notes: The Dance of Herons* by Barry Holstun Lopez. Copyright © 1979 by Barry Holstun Lopez. All rights reserved.

Atheneum Publishers, an imprint of Macmillan Publishing Company: From *Rockhound Trails*, written and illustrated by Jean Bartenbach. Copyright © 1977 by Jean Bartenbach.

Gwendolyn Brooks: From "The Sonnet-Ballad" from *Blacks* by Gwendolyn Brooks. Copyright © 1987 by Gwendolyn Brooks.

Curtis Brown Ltd.: From "Strange and Terrible Monsters of the Deep" by William Wise from *Boy's Life*, February 1978. Copyright © 1978 by Boy Scouts of America.

Children's Better Health Institute, Benjamin Franklin Literary & Medical Society, Inc., Indianapolis, IN: From "Kachinas: Sacred Drama of the Hopis" by Lonnie Dyer from *Young World*, 1976. Copyright © 1976 by The Saturday Evening Post Company.

The Christian Science Publishing Society: From "What Makes Johnny Spend?" by David Holmstrom from *The Christian Science Monitor*, August 29, 1986. Copyright © 1986 by The Christian Science Monitor.

Jennifer Cohen/Seventeen: From "Disaster Hits Home" by Jennifer Cohen from *Seventeen*, March 1990, p. 98. Copyright © 1990 by Jennifer Cohen.

Farrar, Straus & Giroux, Inc.: From *A Wind in the Door* by Madeleine L'Engle. Copyright © 1973 by Crosswicks Ltd.

Highlights for Children, Inc., Columbus, OH: From "Pictures of the Poor" by Elsa Marston from *Highlights for Children*, September 1990. Copyright © 1990 by Highlights for Children, Inc.

Barbara Jordan: From "Keynote Address to the Democratic National Convention (1976)" by Barbara Jordan.

Alfred A. Knopf, Inc.: From *The Amateur Naturalist* by Gerald Durrell with Lee Durrell. Copyright © 1982 by Dorling Kindersley Limited, London. Text copyright © 1982 by Gerald Durrell. From "Along the Colorado" from *The Secret Worlds of Colin Fletcher* by Colin Fletcher. Copyright © 1989 by Colin Fletcher. From "Dreams" from *The Dream Keeper and Other Poems* by Langston Hughes. Copyright 1932 by Alfred A.

Knopf, Inc. and renewed 1960 by Langston Hughes. From "Harlem" from *Selected Poems of Langston Hughes*. Copyright © 1926, 1948 by Alfred A. Knopf, Inc.; renewed 1954 by Langston Hughes.

Ray Lincoln Literary Agency, Elkins Park House, Suite 107-B, Elkins Park, PA: From "The Big Bang" from *Mount St. Helens: A Sleeping Volcano Awakes* by Marian T. Place. Copyright © 1981 by Marian T. Place.

David Low: From "Winterblossom Garden" by David Low from *Ploughshares*, vol. 8, no. 4, 1982. Copyright © 1982 by David Low.

National Geographic Society: From "Animal Body Talk" from *National Geographic World*, no. 175, March 1990. Copyright © 1990 by National Geographic Society.

OMNI: From "Road Warrior" by Bob Berger from *OMNI*, March 1990. Copyright © 1990 by Omni Publications International, Ltd. From "Making Fun" by A. J. S. Rayl from *OMNI*, November 1990. Copyright © 1992 by Omni Publications International, Ltd.

The Saturday Evening Post: From "Antonia Novello: A Dream Come True" by Carol Krucoff from *The Saturday Evening Post*, vol. 263, no. 4, May/June 1991. Copyright © 1991 by The Saturday Evening Post.

Seventeen Magazine: From "Earth SOS" from *Seventeen*, April 1991. Copyright © 1991 by Seventeen Magazine.

The University of Texas: From the introduction to "The Gold Fish Monster" by Pearl Crayton from *The Texas Quarterly*, Summer 1967, vol. 10, no. 2.

Webster's New World Publishers, a Division of Simon & Schuster, New York: Entry "large" from *Webster's New World Dictionary of American English*, Third College Edition. Copyright © 1989 by Webster's New World Publishers.

H.W. Wilson Company: Entries from "Abbate, Nancy M." through "Ability" from *Readers' Guide to Periodical Literature*, May 1990. Copyright © 1990 by H.W. Wilson Company.

The following excerpts also appear in *Holt Middle School Handbook.*

From "Salomon's Story" from *Tortuga* by Rudolfo A. Anaya. Copyright © 1988 by Rudolfo A. Anaya. Published by The University of New Mexico Press.

From "The Revolution," October 8, 1868, by Susan B. Anthony.

Quote by James Baldwin from *The Writer's Chapbook*, edited from *The Paris Review* interviews by George Plimpton. Copyright © 1989 by The Paris Review, Inc. Published by Viking Penguin, a division of Penguin Books USA Inc.

From "Sonnets from the Portuguese #43" by Elizabeth Barrett Browning.

From *On the Art of War* by Ulysses S. Grant.

From a speech by Patrick Henry in the Virginia Convention of 1775.

From "A Birthday" by Christina Rossetti.

From "Song of the Sky Loom" by Tewa Indians.

From *I Have a Dream* by Booker T. Washington.

From "A Time of Beginnings" from *No Chinese Stranger* by Jade Snow Wong.

ILLUSTRATION CREDITS

Tom Gianni—187, 221, 378
Linda Kelen—23, 194, 317
Martin Kornick—98, 133, 258, 338
Rich Lo—56, 78, 149, 298, 308

Executive Editor: Mescal Evler

Managing Editor: Robert R. Hoyt

Project Editor: Amy Strong

Editorial Staff: Laura Britton, Max Farr, Karen Forrester, Connie Giles, Guy Holland, Eileen Joyce, Christy McBride, Kathleen Magor, Michael Neibergall, Amy Simpson, Elizabeth Smith, Atietie Tonwe

Editorial Support Staff: Carla Beer, Margaret Guerrero, Stella Galvan, Ruth Hooker, Pat Stover

Editorial Permissions: Catherine Paré, Janet Harrington

Design, Photo Research, and Production: Pun Nio, *Senior Art Director;* Diane Motz, *Senior Designer;* Beth Prevelige, *Production Manager;* Joan Eberhardt, *Production Assistant;* Debra Saleny, *Photo Research Manager;* Angi Cartwright, *Photo Coordinator;* Carol Martin, *Electronic Publishing Manager;* Debra Schorn, *Electronic Publishing Senior Coordinator;* Monica Shomos, *Electronic Publishing Staff;* Preface, *PE Design and Production*